City Form and Everyday Life
Toronto's Gentrification and Critical Social Practice

One feature of contemporary urban life has been the widespread transformation, by middle-class resettlement, of older inner-city neighbourhoods formerly occupied by working-class and underclass communities. Often termed 'gentrification,' this process has been a focus of intense debate in urban study and in the social sciences.

This case study explores processes of change in Toronto's inner neighbourhoods in recent decades, integrating an understanding of political economy with an appreciation of the culture of everyday urban life. The author locates Toronto's gentrification in a context of both global and local patterns of contemporary city-building, focusing on the workings of the property industry and of the local state, the rise and decline of modernist planning, and the transition to postindustrial urbanism.

Drawing on a series of in-depth interviews among a segment of Toronto's inner-city, middle-class population, Caulfield argues that the seeds of gentrification have included patterns of critical social practice and that the 'gentrified' landscape is highly paradoxical, embodying both the emerging dominance of a deindustrialized urban economy and an immanent critique of contemporary city-building.

Jon Caulfield is a professor in the Division of Social Science at York University. He is the author of *The Tiny Perfect Mayor: David Crombie and Toronto's Reform Aldermen*.

City Form and Everyday Life

Toronto's Gentrification and Critical Social Practice

JON CAULFIELD

UNIVERSITY OF TORONTO PRESS
Toronto Buffalo London

© University of Toronto Press Incorporated 1994
Toronto Buffalo London
Printed in Canada

ISBN 0-8020-2997-3 (cloth)
ISBN 0-8020-7448-0 (paper)

Printed on acid-free paper

Canadian Cataloguing in Publication Data

Caulfield, Jon
    City form and everyday life : Toronto's
    gentrification and critical social practice

    Includes bibliographical references.
    ISBN 0-8020-2997-3 (bound) ISBN 0-8020-7448-0 (pbk.)

    1. Gentrification – Ontario – Toronto.
    2. Neighborhood – Ontario – Toronto.   3. Urban
    renewal – Ontario – Toronto.   4. Sociology, Urban –
    Ontario – Toronto.   5. Toronto (Ont.) – History.
    I. Title.

    HT178.C22T65 1994   307.76'4'09713541

                                                    C93-094866-1

This book has been published with the help of a grant from the
Social Science Federation of Canada, using funds provided by the
Social Sciences and Humanities Research Council of Canada.

Contents

Maps and Illustrations

MAPS

ILLUSTRATIONS

Acknowledgments

Greg Nielsen's teaching and counsel were essential in conceiving and doing this project. The fieldwork was made possible by the assistance and patience of sixty-three anonymous respondents. The text benefited from comments on earlier drafts by Terry Fowler, Michael Goldrick, John Jackson, Gottfried Paasche, Tony Turritin, three anonymous readers at University of Toronto Press, and – in respect to chapter 5 – Guy Metraux and two anonymous readers at the *Canadian Review of Sociology and Anthropology*. (An earlier version of sections of chapter 5 appeared in *CRSA* 26:4 [1989], and material drawn from part 3 appeared in *City and Society* 6:1 [1992]; as well, parts of chapter 1 appeared in the *Social Science Journal* of the Division of Social Science at York University, 1990, edited by Bill Swanson.) Preparation of the manuscript was aided by the advice and encouragement of Virgil Duff at University of Toronto Press and the excellent copy-editing of Ken Lewis. The illustrations on pages 19, 100, 120, and 121 appear courtesy (respectively) of the National Archives, Ottawa, the Buffalo Bisons Baseball Club, the Yaneff Gallery, Toronto, and the Rodman Hall Arts Centre, St Catharines, Ontario. The maps on pages 70 and 72 appear courtesy of the City of Toronto Planning and Development Department; the remaining photographs are the author's. Last but by no means least, Ellen Murray offered perspective, forbearance, and assistance in initiating the snowballs.

Introduction

This book is a case-study of urban change in Toronto. It focuses on the recent widespread pattern of middle-class residential settlement of older inner-city neighbourhoods formerly occupied mainly by working-class and underclass communities. This process is sometimes termed 'gentrification,' but this word probably obscures as much as it clarifies about the social forces at work. Hence, while the term does appear in several chapters that follow, it is often bracketed by quotation marks meant to indicate a problematic usage borrowed from another discourse. The reasons why it is problematic are discussed in due course.

The book has three objectives. The first arises from the almost utter silence of 'gentrifiers' themselves in the substantial scholarly literature on the topic that has appeared in the last couple of decades, an *oeuvre* consisting mostly of demographic/statistical studies and impressionistic theoretical treatments. The book seeks to break this silence by giving voice, in part 3, to a group of middle-class in-movers to inner-city neighbourhoods. This group was relatively small in number and, as will be seen, was drawn from only one segment of downtown's middle-class population; it in no sense represents 'gentrification' in general. But within the framework of this limitation, the book's approach differs methodologically from much work in the field insofar as it culminates in an account of the attitudes of a series of downtown middle-class residents, about their neighbourhoods and neighbours, their housing choices, and their everyday lives, told largely in their own words.

Direct contact with 'gentrifiers' is delayed, however, until the stage on which their activities occurred has been set. This gives rise to the book's second objective, the work of part 1: to locate Toronto's middle-class inner-city resettlement in its historical context. In a more global framework, this has involved a comprehensive process of urban restructuring evident in many societal settings of which 'gentrification' has been only one component – the emergence of what is sometimes termed the 'postindustrial city' (a second problematic usage, also discussed in due course). More locally, the origins of the process were closely interwoven with a collision in Toronto's civic politics between pro-growth boosterism oriented to modernist urban form and two oppositional groupings that contested this agenda of city-building. Hence, the book approaches recent middle-class resettlement of the inner city in two contexts, both as a local manifestation of wider patterns of urban change and as the outcome of specific local processes of social action and conflict.

The latter perspective suggests the book's third objective: to widen space for a critical sociology of urban forms that stresses the salience of willed human action in specific social contexts in constituting the circumstances of everyday life. In this regard, the book directly echoes an earlier voice that arose in urban study, that of Walter Firey, whose 1945 paper 'Sentiment and Symbolism as Ecological Variables' tersely established the basis for an understanding of urban place rooted in local social meanings and social practices. The focus of Firey's critique was 'economic ecology,' a term with which he connoted the naturalization of the paradigm of neoclassical economics within the urban study of his era and against which he argued that 'certain locational processes seem to defy a strictly economic analysis' (1945: 140). The book parallels Firey but is generally directed toward a different antagonist, the neo-Marxian structuralist model of urban study.

The neo-Marxian school, which burst onto the scene in the mid-1970s with publication of David Harvey's *Social Justice and the City*, shook the foundations of urban study and opened its horizons to essential new paths of inquiry. The field in Canada – formerly dominated by spatial functionalism and atheoretical positivism – was invigorated by writers whose approach was grounded in the view that the construction of urban form was not 'a random, haphazard process propelled by a constellation of private decisions ... mediated by government intervention' but 'a particular spatial expression of

[the] production, reproduction, circulation and organization of ... capital' (Goldrick 1978: 30). The book seeks in no way to diminish their work. But while the contribution of the structuralist problematic has been seminal, it has often shared the same tendency toward economistic reasoning that characterized the neoclassical approach. This preoccupation has truncated the horizons of critical urban study – the questions that might be asked, how they might be approached – in a manner closely paralleling the pattern of thinking from which Firey demurred. One 'ideological straightjacket' has been replaced by another (Gottdiener 1985: 281). Moreover, it is an approach that often tends to view city-building almost solely in structural terms, as an epiphenomenon of larger societal or global forces in which city-dwellers are reduced to 'mere bearers of processes determined independently of them' (Rose 1984: 56). The book dissents from this metatext, preferring a less monologic approach.

To be sure, the book is firmly committed to the crucial role of political economy in critical urban study and, in this vein, has occasion to make some fairly ill-humoured observations about the influence of capital on the construction of urban space. But the book is also committed to an understanding of urbanism that does not privilege capital as the sole font of city form and, hence, also has occasion to take issue with the structuralist paradigm represented by writers like Harvey and, in specific respect to 'gentrification,' Neil Smith. This critique of economistic reasoning is rooted in an understanding of the relationship between capital and the culture of everyday life that is briefly discussed in part 1 and developed at more length in connection with 'gentrification' in part 2. The ideas developed in part 2 are not conclusions arising from the fieldwork but, in the orthodox tradition of social science inquiry, are a set of theoretical considerations that informed the fieldwork and are useful to review in approaching the fieldwork.

In viewing city-dwellers as effective actors whose behaviours may help constitute the circumstances of their everyday lives ('social agents,' in the language of current theory), the book is particularly concerned with what are sometimes termed *critical* social practices: efforts by human beings to resist institutionalized patterns of dominance and suppressed possibility and create new conditions for their social activities (termed by Quebec sociologist Marcel Rioux 'emancipatory practices' [1984]). In focusing on this theme – the core interest of critical social science* – the book does draw on neo-Marxian thought (with its misgivings noted). As well, however, it draws on such other sources of critical thought in Canadian social science and urban study as Edward Relph's neo-humanist approach (1976, 1981, 1987), the feminist perspective of Damaris Rose (1984, 1989), and an understanding of social movements framed by Warren Magnusson and Rob Walker (1988). In the latter respect, the book argues that middle-class settlement of older inner-city neighbourhoods has, in part, constituted an urban social movement consistent with a definition of these formations framed by Manuel Castells (1983). This discussion is linked, particularly in chapter 4, to some reflections about the meaning of 'postmodernism' for contemporary urban form and urban politics.

In general terms, the book's argument is that among the seeds of middle-class resettlement of older inner-city neighbourhoods in Toronto were patterns of critical social practice oriented toward specific social possibilities perceived by some city-dwellers to be embodied in these residual urban forms (use values found here) and to be diminished or erased by recent dominant patterns of city-building – in particular, by modernist and suburban forms constructed under the aegis of property capital and the technocratic local state. To be sure, downtown middle-class resettlement in Toronto has also occurred in a framework partly established by wider structural forces and is a pattern of residential activity that has been rapidly absorbed and refracted by the commodity market. Hence, the 'gentrified' landscape is a highly paradoxical urban form, on the one hand representing the emerging dominance of a deindustrialized urban economy (and irrelevance of working-class city-dwellers to this process) and the logic of property capital but, on the other hand, having fossilized within it an immanent critique of key facets of contemporary city-building. Consistent with this paradox, the book views the production of urban space as, at least in part, a dialogical process of critical rejoinder to forces of dominance and hegemonic appropriation of these critical practices. In addition to 'gentrification,' modernist and suburban forms are also interpreted in this context.

Finally, a last perspective that informs the book – consistent with the insight of Canadian geographer David Ley (1984: 201) – is that, while current processes of middle-class inner-city resettlement do

---

* An excellent recent Canadian discussion of the critical perspective in social science is made by Hansen and Muszynski (1990).

emerge in the context of specific features of contemporary urbanism, they also seem to represent a deeper historical fact: an apparent enduring affinity of the bourgeois for the heart of the city that, in some social settings, has been only briefly disrupted by the turmoil of industrial urbanism.

To reiterate, then, part 1 ('Context') sets the stage for exploring middle-class settlement of Toronto's older downtown neighbourhoods by examining the main forces that shaped urban form in the decades immediately preceding and congruent with the emergence of 'gentrification.' Part 2 ('Theory') explores theoretical issues germane to 'gentrification' that helped shape the fieldwork and suggests a framework for understanding 'gentrification' distinct from neoclassical and structuralist approaches. Part 3 ('Fieldwork') reports on fieldwork carried out among a specific subgroup of middle-class inner-city resettlers in Toronto, at a specific moment in time, with an eye toward issues of critical social practice.

Chapter 1 begins in the streets of the city with a survey of four downtown landscapes, an exercise undertaken in the spirit of Allan Jacobs's trenchant adage that 'you can tell a lot about a city by looking' (1985: 1).

Part One

_____

CONTEXT

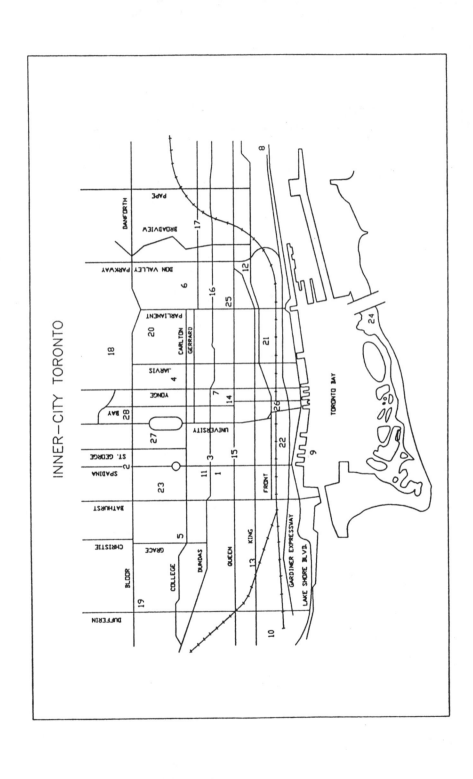

INNER–CITY TORONTO

1 Alexandra Park
2 The Annex
3 Chinatown (Southeast Spadina)
4 Church Street neighbourhood
5 Clinton Street at College
6 Donvale
7 Eaton Centre
8 Gardiner Expressway termination
9 Harbourfront
10 Jameson Avenue (Parkdale)
11 Kensington
12 King–Parliament
13 Massey–Ferguson site
14 Old City Hall

15 Queen Street West
16 Regent Park
17 Riverdale
18 Rosedale
19 Rusholme Road
20 St Jamestown
21 St Lawrence
22 Skydome
23 Sussex–Ulster
24 Toronto Island neighbourhood
25 Trefann Court
26 Union Station
27 University of Toronto
28 Yorkville

1

Contrasts, Ironies, and Urban Form
The Remaking of the Historical City

Four Inner-City Neighbourhoods*

Rusholme Road

Gladstone Avenue is in an inner-city planning district named Bloor-Dufferin centred around a subway station in west-end Toronto. Near the top of Gladstone are a pair of marginal storefront uses that have spilled around the corner from the Bloor Street commercial strip: an East Indian travel agency with a big picture of the Taj Mahal in the window, and a community agency with a sign over the door that says 'Working Women Community Centre' in English, Italian, and Portuguese; a bulletin board beside the door announces English-as-a-second-language classes and daycare services for single mothers.

South of the storefronts, the commotion of Bloor is left quickly behind. Gladstone is lined on both sides by large brick houses, about seventy or eighty years old, on narrow lots. The small front yards, shaded by big maples, have tidy lawns and well-kept flower-gardens. The houses themselves are in good shape; their trim is mostly freshly painted, a lot of the eavestroughs are new, and the roofs, porches, and windows are in good repair. Although several of the people coming and going appear to be middle-class, there are only a handful of flashy renovations on the street – the kind associated with the

---

* Observations reported in this chapter were made in autumn 1989.

showy whitepainting common in many other inner-city neighbour-hoods; only a couple of houses here have been sandblasted. Still, according to the listings in a real estate weekly available in a newsbox back at the corner, houses in this area run upwards of $250,000, so there probably are not too many women on the street who use the community centre, not unless they have been living here a long time, since before property prices escalated. At the bottom of the street is a large park where a bunch of children are playing and other people are just sitting – some on the grass, some on benches along the paths, and, at a picnic table, two old Italian men in workmen's clothes involved in an intense card game.

The next street east, Havelock Street, is a lot like Gladstone. The block south of Bloor is lined by big brick houses in good condition, although not so many of them are as carefully kept up as they are on Gladstone. The front yards are not as meticulously tended, and the exterior decoration and landscaping of several of the houses suggests they are still working-class homes. Other houses, though, are clearly owned by middle-class people who have probably arrived in the neighbourhood over the last five or ten years as property prices ballooned. Havelock seems to be a family street; a lot of children are around.

After Havelock is Rusholme Road, and on the west side of Rusholme are more solid old houses like those on Gladstone and Havelock. The east side of Rusholme, though, is a quite different kind of city landscape. Three apartment towers rise here, one sixteen stories, the others twenty stories, massive slabs of white brick striped up-and-down by columns of windows and side-to-side by tiers of small balconies. They are plain-looking buildings, not too well kept up, clearly not luxury condos or housing for up-and-coming yuppies. Here and there, the buildings' monochromatic façades are broken by tiny patches of colour – a few flowers in a flowerbox on a balcony rail, a wind sock, or some other small adornment.

At the buildings' base is a large tract of greenspace, a lawn landscaped with small bushy trees. Unlike the park, though, no one is using this space as anything more than a short-cut to the next street; paths are worn in the grass. Part of the reason no one is here may be that there are no benches or picnic tables or anything else to attract people's use; there are not even any children playing, though there do seem to be some children living in the buildings. On one side of the greenspace, beside one of the high-rises, are seven dumpsters, some with garbage piled in them, and near them the air smells of

Rusholme Road, west side. On the west side of Rusholme are more solid old houses like those on Gladstone and Havelock.

garbage. On the front door of one of the buildings is a decal that says 'Belmont, where the living is easy.' Among the people coming in and out of the buildings are a lot of East and West Indians; the travel agency and community centre probably find some clients here.

Belmont is the name of the construction company that built the high-rises; the development is actually named Dover Square. It was put up in 1964 at a time when the neighbourhood's residents were mainly working-class and immigrant households. To make way for the apartments, Belmont first had to purchase and demolish fifty old houses in good condition (Andras 1971), houses just like the ones across the street and on Havelock and Gladstone that lately have been selling for $250,000 and $350,000. The planning wisdom that encouraged this kind of clearance was expressed in city hall's policy of designating a number of districts in the vicinity of subway stops for high-density redevelopment with little or no consideration for what was already there. Gladstone and Havelock, even closer to the subway than Rusholme, were also zoned for high-rises despite the city planning staff's acknowledgment that they were streets of good-quality housing making up part of a good-quality neighbourhood (CTPB 1972a: 45–53); and a few years after Dover Square was built,

Rusholme Road, east side. The east side of Rusholme is a quite different kind of city landscape. Three apartment towers rise here, one sixteen stories, the others twenty stories, massive slabs of white brick.

a company named Lionstar Investments began to buy options on the houses on Gladstone and Havelock. Lionstar planned a $50-million development that would have razed 151 houses to clear way for a six-tower apartment complex. The company meant first to develop the westerly block between Gladstone and Havelock, and then turn its attention to the block between Havelock and Rusholme (Andras 1971).

Residents in the area had mixed feelings about the project. Some homeowners were happy to sell out to a developer and move, so long as the price was right. Others, though, did not want to see their homes and neighbourhood wrecked; they included some other home-owners and also a large number of tenants, many of whom lived in houses owned by absentee landlords attracted to speculate in the area by its high-density zoning (McDonnell 1972). A specific sticking point arose in respect to homeowners on the Havelock-Rusholme block who did not like the two-phase plan. They did not want to live next door to the chaos of demolition and construction for several months while risking the prospect that their own properties, then trapped between two high-rise projects (Lionstar phase-one and Dover Square), might lose some of their value, and they wanted to be bought out at the same time Lionstar was assembling its first-phase properties. City council, though, did not share their concerns, nor those of tenants and homeowners who objected outright to the development. It approved Lionstar's plan after being assured by a local alderman from the Bloor-Dufferin area that opposition to the project was simply the work of a few 'activists ... trying to ferment things' (Sewell 1971, McDonnell 1972).

In the end, no high-rises were built; Lionstar's reach had exceeded its grasp. Rumours the company was not the small player it appeared to be but was fronting for a major development corporation turned out to be wrong (Samuel 1971). Its principals were out of their depth, unable even to finance partial assembly of the first-phase properties. And so in spite of the failure of Lionstar's opponents to persuade city hall to alter its plan for the area, Gladstone and Havelock remain today streets of old houses, still zoned for high-rise apartments but effectively protected from redevelopment by their property values.

There is an irony here. During the Lionstar controversy, when the local people fighting the project were doing their 'fermenting,' one of their arguments was that the high-rises would obliterate a lot of lower-cost housing and replace it with more expensive housing. At the time, a five-bedroom house in the area rented for around $250

monthly, a couple of small rooms with a kitchen for about $20 weekly
– rents affordable for working-class people, senior citizens, students,
or anyone else who did not have a lot of money. Comparably sized
apartments in the proposed high-rises would have cost more than
twice as much (Andras 1971). Nearly twenty years later, the same
houses rent for around $2,000 a month, the same small flats for about
$150 a week. Current rents in Dover Square are not especially cheap
but (partly thanks to rent control) are more affordable than space in
most of the houses. Today, a majority of the working-class people
and new immigrants still left in the neighbourhood are concentrated
in the Rushholme high-rises.

Dundas Street

Half a kilometre from the office towers and fancy hotels of the downtown core, the air at the north end of Kensington Avenue is scented
with smells of fish lying in open tubs of ice and cheese wafting out
the open doors of cheese shops. Recorded music also drifts from some
of the shops; a loud Portuguese pop song collides with blaring reggae.
Between the press of people and the rows of bins outside the green-
grocers – heaped with eggplants, pineapples, green peppers, ginger-
root, tomatoes – the sidewalks are jammed, and at several points
passers-by have to step around small trucks parked by the curb of
the narrow street to make any headway.

Halfway down the block, the food stores end, and the sidewalks
are less busy. Here are some new- and used-clothing shops patronized
mainly by the avant-garde crowd, places that originated as the kind
of marginal commercial uses pushed around the city like flotsam in
the currents of the real estate trade and that appended themselves to
the southern edge of the market. Some of the clothing shops are in
small stores built decades ago onto the fronts of old houses when
Jewish merchants first created the market; others just occupy the main
floors of houses. The houses are the narrow, steeply roofed Victorian
kind common all over downtown, like cookies stamped from a cookie-
cutter; they are about ninety or one hundred years old, with postage-
stamp front yards.

Most of the clothing shops – places with names like 'Jagg' and
'Noise' and 'Courage, My Love' – have racks of garments out front.
A couple of them are playing music too, loud rock. The houses that
have not been converted to commercial use still have people living
in them, apparently mainly working-class Chinese immigrants. In-

terspersed among the shops and houses are cafes with tables out front where bohemian-looking young people are sitting, sipping coffee and talking. Near the bottom of Kensington, close to Dundas Street, are a couple of small dim sum restaurants.

There is a streetcar line on Dundas, and a trolley rattles past. Along the north side of the street is the west edge of Chinatown, and among the stores are a Chinese hardware store, Chinese dry cleaner, and Chinese hairdresser. There are also a few Vietnamese jewelry stores; a lot of Vietnamese have been moving into Chinatown lately. The sidewalk is not as busy as it was on Kensington, but there is still heavy pedestrian traffic. On the south side of the street, though, there are fewer people – not surprisingly; there are no storefronts here. What is here is a six-foot grillwork iron fence. On the other side of the fence is a concrete walkway shaded by some young trees. Beside the walkway is an oblong parking lot, and behind that is a long row of utilitarian-looking red-brick row-housing of fairly recent vintage, the kind of buildings that unmistakably say 'public housing.'

The fence opens at a couple of places for paths into the walkway and for an entrance to the parking lot. The parking lot is an important clue to the design of the project (whose name is Alexandra Park): it was built according to the Radburn principle, separating the pedestrian life of the housing from contact with cars (Relph 1987: 65–7). The path through the fence leads to a passage between the row-housing into the project's interior, and here the Radburn principle becomes apparent. Unlike a traditional city place like Kensington, where the buildings are oriented to the street, Alexandra Park turns inward. Lines of plain row-housing, each house with a tiny yard, are arranged along a network of walkways that also lead to some low-rise and high-rise apartments. It is a style of design reminiscent of some of the traditional elements of suburban development: simplification, segmentation, withdrawal (SPCMT 1979: 49–52). Land-use here has been rigorously segregated; there is not even a convenience store in the project.

In a way, it works. Late on a warm early-autumn afternoon there is a kind of pleasant, slow-moving tranquility inside Alexandra Park. The noises echoing along the brickwork are mostly sounds of domesticity – a screen door slapping shut, some kids playing, a dog barking. Beyond the project the city hums – Kensington, Chinatown, the downtown core only a few blocks away – but its din is muffled; it seems more distant. In other inner-city neighbourhoods, the well-to-do have created their own protected enclaves. It is nearly impos-

Dundas Street, north side. Along the north side of Dundas is the west edge of Chinatown. Among the stores are a Chinese hardware store, Chinese dry cleaner, and Chinese hairdresser. There are also a few Vietnamese jewelry stores; a lot of Vietnamese have been moving into Chinatown lately.

sible, for instance, to drive through Rosedale, where the very rich live, without a map; outsiders are effectively deterred by a seemingly random pattern of quiet, tree-lined residential streets that seem to lead nowhere (and often do). Here in Alexandra Park, meanwhile, several hundred public-assistance households have their sheltered neighbourhood. The trouble, though, is that public-assistance households are just about the only people who live here; the project is an impermeable ghetto with the underclass on the inside, behind their fence and cut off from the city. As much as anything, Alexandra Park's physical form is a kind of camouflage; the usual social problems of a large public-housing project are all present here but turned inward, beneath a veneer of humane design, and not so readily visible.*

---

* Since these observations were made, Alexandra Park's exterior walls have been

Dundas Street, south side. On the south side of Dundas there are fewer people–not surprisingly; there are no storefronts here. What is here is a grillwork iron fence. Unlike a traditional city place where buildings are oriented to the street, Alexandra Park turns inward.

There used to be a very different kind of neighbourhood in Alexandra Park – a gridwork of narrow streets lined by old houses with commercial and other kinds of uses mixed in – but it was expropriated and demolished by city hall in the mid-1960s. The city's planners had labelled the neighbourhood a blighted slum that required wholesale clearance and 'renewal.' As they did in the Gladstone-Havelock neighbourhood, many local residents resisted redevelopment here; in his book about public-housing politics of the era, Graham Fraser reported that at a number of meetings in the area during the project's planning 'city officials had to sneak out the back doors ... to avoid being beaten up by furious immigrant homeowners who were going to have their houses taken away' (1972: 67–8).

Not everyone at city hall was convinced redevelopment of Alex-

---

partly demolished. Besides the grillwork fences, some were made of concrete, and they had been offering cover for drug traffickers to do their deals protected from effective police surveillance. Project residents brought pressure on the housing authority to tear them down (Appleby 1990).

andra Park was a good idea. Toronto's metropolitan tier of government – a federation made up of the city and its surrounding suburbs
– opposed clearance too, arguing that while the area was overcrowded
and did need more maintenance, its houses were mostly structurally
sound and that building infill housing on the neighbourhood's vacant
land was probably a better way to allocate public funds (Fraser 1972:
66). But after several years of fighting this two-front battle against
the project's opponents, the city finally got its way; 334 houses were
acquired and wrecked. Some of the worst fears of the expropriated
homeowners were realized when the city paid them substantially less
for their properties than they would likely have been worth on the
open market (Fraser 1972: 107–8).

The Kensington neighbourhood, too, had been labelled a slum and
slated for expropriation and demolition. Its street market was to have
been replaced as the local commercial centre by an enclosed shopping
mall nearby. For decades the area had been an immigrant-receptor
area where newcomers to Canada – Irish, Jews, Hungarians, Portuguese – had settled, gone into business, and raised families, and in
the 1960s it continued to serve this role. But the city's government
was uninterested in Kensington's heritage or urban function; many
of its planners and politicians saw only what seemed to them a pocket
of blight impeding their vision of urban progress. Unlike Alexandra
Park, however, opposition to 'renewal' in Kensington was successful.
An organization of local residents and businessmen named KARA –
Kensington Area Residents' Association – managed to prevent the
neighbourhood's destruction and were able to force the city to include
them in its planning for the area, a process that resulted in proposals
that 'conserved, strengthened and improved' the existing fabric rather
than erasing it (CTPB 1978: 16, Lorimer 1970: 54). Today, Kensington
remains a vital city district.

One element of this vitality is that things change. Every year a
couple of the market's old buildings are torn down and replaced, and
others are renovated, sometimes for new uses. In part, these changes
represent 'renewal' of the neighbourhood from within, a function of
what Jane Jacobs calls 'gradual money' accruing to a vigorous local
economy (1961: 143–317); and in part they reflect shifting demography. The Jews, who dominated Kensington into the 1960s, are nearly
all gone, and lately the Portuguese have been leaving; Chinese, bohemians, West Indians, as well as a few well-to-do urban professionals have been arriving in the wake of the departed shopkeepers
and residents. In Alexandra Park, in contrast, a neighbourhood that

was altered by 'cataclysmic money' (Jacobs 1961: 293), nothing much will ever change. The project is what it is, frozen in time, an immutable hybrid landscape of well-meaning social planning and less well-meaning municipal boosterism.

Again, there is an irony here. Alexandra Park, with its tidy new housing and innovative design, is an almost unknown Toronto neighbourhood. Hardly anyone who does not live there ever goes there, and very few people who do not work or live in adjacent areas are even aware of its existence. Kensington, meanwhile, has become a kind of icon, fetishized by artists and writers, touted by the tourist bureau to out-of-town conventioneers ('A genuine European-style market!'), and patronized on Saturday mornings by well-to-do shoppers from nearby middle-class neighbourhoods who enjoy the area's cachet of traditional urbanity. Kensington's success, though, is its undoing. Like those in the Gladstone-Havelock area, houses here have become too expensive for immigrants or working-class people. Already there are some sandblasted 'townhomes' on the fringe of the district, and fashionable renovations are becoming more common. As the houses change, the commercial area will change too; a first sign of this process is a gourmet-coffee franchise that recently opened in the heart of the market. Kensington's future is likely to be as a sort of museum of working-class urban history occupied by affluent urbanites. In Alexandra Park, low-income people at least have some security from the threat of displacement.

Bay Street

Bay Street at Queen Street, in the heart of downtown, is jammed on a weekday afternoon. Office-workers, shoppers, and sightseers wait several deep on the sidewalks for streetlights to change. The traffic lanes are crowded with cars, cabs, buses, delivery vans; bicycle couriers scurry among them.

On the northeast corner, behind a small lawn, is a massive Romanesque building of red Ontario sandstone and ornamental masonry, Toronto's Old City Hall. On the one hand, it is regarded as a distinguished work of architecture, grouped by Eric Arthur as one of the two 'most important buildings' constructed in Toronto in the latter decades of the nineteenth century (1974: 117). Like many other remarkable public edifices, on the other hand, it was an unambiguous ideological statement, 'a symbol of Toronto's civic pride and confidence in the 1890s' (Dendy 1978: 130); this message is accented by a large stained-glass window dominating the lobby that portrays the 'union of commerce and industry.' Grand architecture and municipal boosterism have always been compatible bedmates. Faithful to the tradition of civic monument-building, Old City Hall ran somewhat over budget; targeted at $300,000, it cost $2.5 million (Arthur 1974: 205).

This double-edged social meaning is what makes Old City Hall interesting today – not just that it is a striking work of design and construction but that it is a palpable icon of a historical epoch, Toronto's *fin de siècle* boom years of economic growth and social change. Were a novelist to write a time-travel story in which a current-day Torontonian is transported ninety years into the city's past, it might well begin with the hero's passage through the doors of this building – particularly inasmuch as it is one of the few venerable buildings left in a downtown landscape that is otherwise almost relentlessly contemporary. To Old City Hall's east are the Eaton Centre shopping mall and its book-end office towers. West are Viljo Revell's New City Hall and a slablike high-rise hotel. South are the shiny new steel, glass, and concrete skyscrapers of the Bay Street financial canyon. Old City Hall is not quite alone. Simpson's old department store, the Osgoode Hall courthouse, and a handful of other old buildings are still nearby. But core-area buildings that antedate the city's recent period of boom and growth have been a vanishing breed.

Perhaps predictably, Old City Hall nearly did not survive the 1960s. The original scheme that later became Eaton Centre was for a superblock slated to gobble up everything from Bay to Yonge streets. The city's politicians and planners, ensconced in their neo-expressionist conversation piece across the street, seemed unconcerned about the old building's preservation, and only concerted pressure by a citizens' group named Friends of Old City Hall assured that their namesake did not become an entry in Dendy's *Lost Toronto* (McHugh 1985: 106, Dendy 1978). Redevelopment of the superblock, as it eventually occurred, angled beside and behind Old City Hall, and today the building remains, used mainly as a provincial courthouse.

Within a block of Old City Hall is a case of a building that suffered a different fate. Today, kitty-corner across the Bay-Queen intersection, is a thirty-two-storey office tower that was built in 1970 and is usually known as 390 Bay, a name as picturesque as the structure it denotes: an upwardly elongated box with strong vertical lines that emphasize its height. The building directly abuts the sidewalk at its base, a placement meaning that it is impossible to see it from any nearby

Old City Hall and 390 Bay Street. Within a block of Old City Hall is a case of a building that suffered a different fate. Today, kitty-corner across the Bay-Queen intersection, is a thirty-two-storey office tower built in 1970, usually known as 390 Bay. The building that used to be here, demolished to make way for 390 Bay, was named the Temple Building.

location without looking straight up; 390 Bay was meant to be viewed from a block or two away, across the expanse of the new city hall's public square. Seen from this distance, just one of the dense cluster of oblong towers that make up the core's skyline, it has the kind of utilitarian majesty common to most office buildings of its era constructed across the downtowns of North America – the buildings about which John Updike wrote, 'Thinking the other afternoon that we ought to welcome the future to our city, we strolled over to say hello to the massive, glinting architectural newcomers ... and discovered that once "Hello" was pronounced, the conversation threatened to end' (Relph 1987: 194).

Three-ninety Bay does not have a front entrance; people come and go through a couple of revolving doors. Nor does it have a main lobby; a small foyer and narrow passage lead past a bank-branch to the elevator bays. In each respect, lack of a portal and lack of an entrance-hall, it is distinguishable from most memorable works of urban architecture, old or new. Dendy, kindly, calls it 'boring' (1978: 102), but it is more than boring; it represents a kind of serene hypermodernism, the marriage of unornamented functionalism with efficient property management that squeezes from a structure the utter maximum of income-yielding space – a decisive example of what Edward Relph has called the 'corporatisation' of urban landscape (1987: 166–89).

The building that used to be here, demolished to make way for 390 Bay, was named the Temple Building. Completed in the same year as Old City Hall, 1899, it rose to a lofty height of ten stories, making it the tallest building in the British Empire, a distinction it retained for five years (CTA 1987: 14). It was the last major Toronto office building framed with cast iron, the first major Canadian office building wholly designed by a Canadian architectural firm, and the first major office building in the Bay Street corridor, presaging the emergence of Toronto's modern financial district (Arthur 1974: 217–18, Dendy 1978: 102, Dendy and Kilbourn 1986: 214). To be sure, the building's owners (the International Order of Foresters) viewed it as an investment, not an heirloom; and, in appearance, it was not a uniquely striking example of urban design.

Still, it was a handsome and perfectly good old building and a vital piece of the city's history. But in the heady days of Toronto civic government of the 1960s, in a kind of caricature of Le Corbusier (Fishman 1982: 209), history was viewed as simply an impediment to 'progress.' Typical of the mood, a leading alderman of the period

The Temple Building. Completed in the same year as Old City Hall, 1899, the Temple Building rose to a lofty height of ten stories, making it the tallest building in the British Empire, a distinction it retained for five years. It was the last major Toronto office building framed with cast iron, the first major Canadian office building wholly designed by a Canadian architectural firm, and the first major office building in the Bay Street corridor, presaging the emergence of Toronto's modern financial district. (Photograph from the F.W. Micklethwaite Collection, National Archives, Ottawa, PA 28964.)

was chagrined during a city council debate by the argument that architectural historians believed a particular old bank should be preserved. He pointed out that the city had already saved one old bank at another location, and this seemed quite sufficient to him (Kilbourn 1972: 110, Caulfield 1974: 6). In this milieu – a period when city council rejected not a single major developer's proposal for the commercial core – the Temple Building was doomed to destruction.

Had the Temple Building survived a few more years – had the builders of 390 Bay, like Lionstar, had trouble with their finances, or had a group like KARA or Friends of Old City Hall delayed its demolition – it would likely remain today. Just as the once-condemned houses of Gladstone and Havelock now command top prices and the formerly blighted slum of Kensington runs the risk of becoming a desirable location, many of the handful of old office buildings still remaining in Toronto have been refurbished as prestige addresses. Fashions shift. Today, history sells. But the Temple Building was trapped on the wrong side of this change. Just as its construction marked it in several ways as a unique Toronto building, its demolition distinguished it in another: it was the last major building of its era to fall to the wrecker's ball (Dendy and Kilbourn 1986: 219).

Clinton Street

Within a block of Clinton Street on the College Street commercial strip, a kilometre and a half from the core, are the Golden Princess Chinese movie theatre, Morris Silverberg's textile shop, a Vietnamese cafe named Saigon, and the Portuguese Cultural Centre. At the northeast corner of College and Clinton is an Italian expresso bar, the Cafe Diplomatico (the other corners are occupied by a fruit market, a small haberdasher's, and a convenience store). In clement weather, the Diplomatico is mainly a sidewalk cafe – round patio tables under yellow umbrellas behind a low white grillwork fence. Across Clinton is another sidewalk cafe, and just down the street past College is a sidewalk restaurant popular among the fashionable-food set; its menu includes squid-in-ink-sauce. Beyond the cafes and the restaurant, the houses on Clinton Street are a potpourri. Some are just old houses in old condition, others are stylishly whitepainted, others are mediterraneanized. 'Mediterraneanized' denotes a style of incumbent upgrading popular among the city's Italian and Portuguese homeowners that features angel-brick façades, porches with grillwork rails or brick arches, and aluminum fascia and window-trim; middle-class upgraders prefer restored brick façades, either no porch or a wooden one that replicates the original design, and refurbished fascia and trim.

A curious feature of the College-Clinton district are the red, green, and white streetsigns put up a few years ago that identify the area as 'Little Italy.' At one time Italian households did predominate in the surrounding neighbourhood; the Diplomatico, some pizza shops, and the studios of Johnny Lombardi's CHIN Radio are evidence of their former presence. But that was a while ago. When Italy won soccer's World Cup in 1982, and tens of thousands of the 300,000 Torontonians of Italian heritage spontaneously thronged from all over the city to a streetcorner to celebrate, it was in an entirely different neighbourhood, three kilometres away, at Dufferin–St Clair. City hall and the city's Italians are apparently not of one mind about where 'Little Italy' is.

This sort of signage to denote parts of town, without necessarily paying much attention to the accuracy or appropriateness of the names, is something city hall has been doing lately, now that old neighbourhoods are *au courant*. The impetus comes from local shopkeepers, who request and pay the bill for special streetsigns; the city then installs them. Sometimes the names do fit. The signmakers have the ideograms that identify Chinatown correctly located. But the streetsigns along the commercial strip in a whitepainted area east of downtown (named Donvale) say 'Old Cabbagetown.' The neighbourhood that was old Cabbagetown, immediately south of Donvale, was razed for public housing in the 1950s; there is no old Cabbagetown any more. An area west of the core, where for several years the rag trades have been systematically decimated by deindustrialization and by speculators who have been plucking up old loft buildings in anticipation of up-market redevelopment, has signs that say 'Fashion District.' Along Bloor in the Gladstone-Havelock area the street signs say 'Bloorcourt Village,' a name no one seems to use or ever to have used except some of the local merchants in their advertising flyers; the residents' group calls itself the Dufferin Grove Association.

What comes to mind here is Jean Baudrillard's notion of 'simulation' – 'to feign to have what one hasn't.' 'Simulation' is a kind of distortion of 'representation' ('the reflection of a basic reality') that 'masks and perverts a basic reality' or 'masks the absence of a basic reality' or 'bears no relation to any reality whatever' (1983: 5, 11). Calling one part of town by the name of an adjacent neighbourhood that was wilfully obliterated thirty years ago does suggest, if not outright mendacity, a kind of perversion of meaning – misrepresentation that at least has been useful to real estate firms who find the name 'Cabbagetown,' with its connotation of ye olde Toronto, a highly marketable commodity. Ironically, 'Cabbagetown' originated as a term of derogation, a disdainful reference to vegetables planted by Irish immigrants in the small front-yard gardens of their workers' cottages (Fraser 1972: 31). Now it has become a symbol of affluent urbanity. A kind of Disneyesque thinking is at work here (Disneyland is a favourite metaphor of Baudrillard [1983: 23–6]): the city as theme park, with each part of town given its own folksy moniker – *Gemeinschaft* by municipal statute, as urban landscape becomes a pastiche of images.

The College-Clinton district does not really need an official image. Sit with a coffee at a table at the Diplomatico, and Toronto passes by – Portuguese mothers walking tots in strollers, young career-women on bikes riding home from downtown, two Sikh businessmen in suits and saffron turbans animatedly talking shop at a streetlight, a couple of kids in punk garb carrying music-instrument cases. You can run into people you know here; a sociologist making field-notes discovers a student he taught at a suburban university five years ago sitting two tables away. (A van pulls to the curb, and a Japanese fashion photographer and tall blond model in a *haute couture* outfit hop out to do a quick shoot against the backdrop of the expresso bar. Simulation is an endemic fact of modern city life.)

What might be here is an expressway interchange: ramps, traffic, noise, the smell of rubber and exhausts. In the 1960s, this was city hall's plan for the College-Clinton intersection – in this case, not the plan of the city's local tier of government but of the city/suburban metropolitan federation among whose main jobs has been putting in place the infrastructure of roads and subways, watermains and trunk sewers, required to sustain overall metropolitan growth. Anxious to facilitate commuting to the downtown from the northwest suburbs, the metropolitan government meant to build a twenty-kilometre, six-lane, limited-access highway through the city's west end to connect with the lakeshore expressway (CATF 1974: 90). The proposition that roadways are an efficacious mode of suburban-core movement is arguable (Nowlan and Nowlan 1970: 12–38); it is a view that was officially disarmed in Toronto by an exhaustive mid-1970s intergovernmental report whose sixty-fourth and summary volume concluded that by the criteria of land-use effects, dollar-cost, social equity, and environmental impact, public transit was a much preferable form of intra-urban transport (MTTPR 1975). But, a decade earlier, the assumption that expressways would be the basis of Toronto's commuter system had been axiomatic among Metro's planners.

Like Alexandra Park, the motif of the plan was a kind of suburbanization of the city. Traditional urban fabric, built before the hegemony of the car, is hostile to efficient motoring; *ergo*, refashion the city to mimic the suburbs, a landscape made in the auto's image. The planned route for the highway's southerly section was between Clinton and the street just to its west, Christie Street (named Grace Street south of Bloor); College was to be the site of an interchange. The road, which became known in Metro's planning documents as the Christie/Clinton Expressway, was described as 'an essential link' in Toronto's 'inner expressway loop.' Although it would have gutted a series of neighbourhoods, destroyed hundreds of houses, and wiped out scores of small businesses, Metro's transportation planners were sanguine: 'preliminary studies indicate that such an expressway could be constructed with minimum damage to residential and community amenities' (MTPB 1964: 51). Whether such studies were ever done is moot. If so, they seem impossible now to unearth; and the subsequent recommendation of a private consulting firm, that Metro initiate a socio-economic impact analysis of the route, suggests they were not (RVA 1968: 99). Instead, the operative principle in planning the expressway appears to have been the injunction of the metropolitan federation's first chairman, a visionary growth-enthusiast named Frederick Gardiner, who decreed that the interests of Toronto's continuing development required plowing 'a few hallways through living rooms' (Colton 1980: 164), a homey euphemism for wrecking neighbourhoods for roads.

The expressway was not built. By the early 1970s, stalled by successful citizen opposition first to the Crosstown Expressway that would have slashed through picturesque Rosedale Ravine, then to another west-end expressway – the Spadina – that threatened a second string of neighbourhoods, Metro's inner-city expressway-building program foundered. Its demise is fittingly commemorated today in Toronto's east end where the city's lakeshore highway, aptly named the Gardiner, simply stops in mid-air. Its extension to the suburbs – a road named the Scarborough Expressway, a fourth tentacle in Metro's inner-city highway plan – still remains only a gleam in the traffic-planners' eyes.

Sitting at the Diplomatico now, and looking at the stores and houses and streetlife at Clinton and College, it is hard to imagine a cloverleaf here instead of a neighbourhood and hard to understand the vision

College Street at Clinton Street. Within a block of Clinton Street on the College Street commercial strip are the Golden Princess Chinese movie theatre, Morris Silverberg's textile shop, a Vietnamese cafe named Saigon, and the Portuguese Cultural Centre. What might be here is an expressway interchange. Anxious to facilitate commuting to the downtown from the northwest suburbs, the metropolitan government meant to build a twenty-kilometre, six-lane, limited-access highway through the city's west end.

of the politicians and planners who sought to construct it. But theirs was another era – only a few short years ago according to the calendar, but an aeon ago according to how city hall seems to feel about inner-city neighbourhoods. Then, they were detritus that obstructed progress; now they are images given official designations ('Old Cabbage-town,' 'Little Italy,' 'Bloorcourt Village'), treated like artefacts at a gallery exhibit.

The Assault on the Historical City

As these accounts suggest, the incidents described were not unique. Not very long ago, the old physical fabric of inner-city Toronto was under concerted attack on several fronts to make way for high-rise

The end of the Gardiner. By the early 1970s, stalled by citizen opposition, Metro's inner-city expressway-building program foundered. Its demise is commemorated today in Toronto's east end where the city's lakeshore highway, aptly named the Gardiner, simply stops in mid-air. Its extension to the suburbs – a road named the Scarborough Expressway – still remains only a gleam in the traffic-planners' eyes.

developments like Dover Square, public-housing projects like Alexandra Park, upward and outward expansion of the commercial core in the shape of buildings like 390 Bay, and the construction of expressways like the Christie-Clinton. From the late 1940s until the early 1970s, across downtown and its surrounding neighbourhoods, development of these forms eradicated large swathes of the old city and threatened many more. The imperatives that guide Toronto's inner-city planning today – protecting old neighbourhoods and old buildings, restricting major new developments mainly to the heart of the core and to former industrial sites, promoting mixed-use developments, integrating public housing with market housing, and seeking to de-emphasize cars as a mode of movement in and out of downtown – are relatively recent innovations.

Two striking features of this reversal of city-building styles in Toronto are, first, that it was largely unanticipated and, second, the rapidity with which it occurred. In another field, Thomas Kuhn has written that these are precisely the characteristics of major shifts in human knowledge – that changes in the paradigms, or world-views, of scientific disciplines are typically not gradual and orderly but turbulent and abrupt (1970). A good metaphor is an earthquake, the sudden outcome of increasingly implacable tension in the subterranean folds of an apparently stable landscape. Thus, Kuhn borrows a word from politics, 'revolution,' to emphasize the 'parallelism' he finds between intellectual and political 'developmental episodes' (1970: 92). Toronto's recent patterns of city-building suggest that the same word may sometimes be used to denote shifts in cultural landscape. What occurred in Toronto was not an incremental evolution of styles but an upheaval in collective and official perceptions of urban form and function – a revolution in the 'urban meanings' of city places for people (Relph 1976: 47, Castells 1983: 303).

The erasure of entire neighbourhoods to make way for redevelopment, typified in Alexandra Park and nearly repeated in Kensington and in the Gladstone-Havelock neighbourhood, is also illustrated by two areas east of the core, a private-sector high-rise development named St Jamestown and a public-housing project named Regent Park. Building the eighteen apartment towers of St Jamestown, where twelve thousand tenants now make up the densest concentration of population in urban Canada, required removal, with city hall's endorsement, of a stable working-class community occupying several square blocks of large old houses mainly in good condition (Moorhouse 1973). At the time it was built, St Jamestown was successfully marketed as a fashionable residential locale for young downtown white-collar workers, but its glamour was short-lived. It was not well-constructed, has been haphazardly maintained, and today its deteriorating high-rises are, like Dover Square, mainly occupied by a polyglot population of recent Third World immigrants, dominantly employed in lower-status service-sector jobs, who find the area relatively affordable in the milieu of Toronto's high-priced inner-city property market (Allaby 1987).

The development of Regent Park in the 1950s and 1960s, where another twelve thousand tenants now live in Canada's oldest and biggest public-housing project, required the demolition of Cabbagetown, a low-income quarter of old houses and cottages that bore deep scars of slumlording and of the devastating effects of the Depression on working-class Canada. Cabbagetown was a damaged city neighbourhood, though by no means beyond rehabilitation, but its repair was never on city hall's agenda; it suffered nearly total clearance.

St Jamestown. At the time it was built, St Jamestown was successfully marketed as a fashionable residential locale for young downtown white-collar workers, but its glamour was short-lived.

Like Old City Hall, Regent Park is a double-edged urban form. Its row-houses and low- and high-rise apartments reflect the sincere (if paternalistic and, in retrospect, naïve) belief of social reformers at the time it was built that the state could constructively affect the lives of low-income people by dramatically altering their housing conditions (Shein 1987).* But while the impulse to build Regent Park may have been partly benign, its design is monolithic, its implementation was autocratic and often brutal, and its construction seems to have been motivated as much by city hall's concern to enhance Toronto as a locale for property investment – by clearing 'slums' – as by any be-nevolent interest in the housing needs of the city's less affluent (Fraser 1972: 51–62, Goldrick 1978: 32, Magnusson 1983: 114). Only a short

---

* The prevailing attitude of the period is captured in a National Film Board short, *Farewell Oak Street*, in which an unhappy family living in a delapidated old Cab-bagetown house becomes a happy family after moving to a new Regent Park apartment.

Regent Park. The development of Regent Park reflected the sincere belief of social reformers at the time it was built that the state could constructively affect the lives of low-income people by dramatically altering their housing conditions.

time after its completion, Regent Park came to be regarded as a 'social disaster,' especially disliked by its own residents (Fraser 1972: 61) – a pattern common to many large-scale public-housing projects built in the same era in North American cities (of which the most notorious was Pruit-Igoe in St Louis, demolished as unlivable in 1972 less than twenty years after construction of its award-winning design [Relph 1987: 149, 212; Krupat 1985: 173–6]). Today, surrounded by fashionably renovated neighbourhoods, Regent Park resembles nothing so much as a kind of soft concentration camp for a segment of the city's surplus labour force.

St Jamestown and Regent Park have two common features. First, like Alexandra Park, and in spite of their densities, both represent a kind of suburbanization of the city. Although neither is as inwardly designed as Alexandra Park, land-use in each is rigidly segregated, and the streets that criss-crossed the old districts were eliminated with redevelopment, so that each area has an insular character, cut off from the city around it. Second, had St Jamestown and Regent Park not been built, many of the turn-of-the-century houses and worker-cottages wrecked for their construction would by now have been renovated as housing for well-to-do urbanites (and their former residents dislocated).

This is precisely what happened in Donvale, a district of handsome old houses along tree-lined streets just north of Regent Park that was also threatened in the 1960s. City hall planned to expropriate, demolish, and redevelop a large pocket of 'blight' that its planners had identified within the area (Lorimer and Phillips 1971: 190); the remainder of the district was vulnerable to high-rise development. Like the shopkeepers and homeowners of Kensington, though, Donvale's residents managed to thwart the gutting of their neighbourhood and secure its protection from redevelopment (Lorimer 1970: 53–4). But saving the area's physical fabric was the death-knell for its social fabric. A part of town that only a couple of years earlier had seemed an appropriate locale for studying the lives of low-income and working people (Lorimer and Phillips 1971) had already, by the time of its battle with city hall, experienced its first up-market in-movement; many of the new middle-class residents were highly active participants in the fight against the city's 'renewal' plans. During the 1970s, with preservation of the Donvale's old landscape officially encoded in the city's plan, its remaining working-class population was displaced by middle-class resettlers nearly as thoroughly as St Jamestown's former residents had been by the high-rise builders of the

1960s. But at the time when city hall designated the neighbourhood for redevelopment, widespread whitepainting of inner-city neighbourhoods was not foreseen.

Chinatown, immediately west of the core, another district nearly erased for redevelopment, had a somewhat different experience; as in Kensington, an entrenched immigrant community effectively deterred rapid middle-class resettlement. The area, named Southeast Spadina in the city's planning documents, was only starting to become Toronto's main Chinatown when it was zoned for clearance: more than twenty square blocks, occupied by 681 houses whose residents made up a stable moderate- and low-income community. At the time, the district's population was diverse; as well as many Chinese, its low-priced housing was home to the remainder of a once-dominant Jewish community, many migrants from Maritime Canada who had come to the city seeking work during the Depression and Second World War, and a number of households of students, bohemians, young artists, and Vietnam-era American war-resisters drawn to the area by the proximity of the Ontario College of Art, the University of Toronto, and a service-centre for draft-dodgers. City hall had designated the district for high-density commercial use and high-rise apartments (CTPB 1972b). Again, local residents fought back and won a series of victories – stopping construction of a massive hydro facility and new downtown police station in the midst of the neighbourhood; forcing a developer to scale down a large high-rise project on the edge of the area for which demolitions had already wiped out a large block of houses; and, ultimately, securing protection of the district's old form (Sellgren 1971; Smith 1972a, 1972b, Caulfield 1974: 42).

These fights were won, though, as city hall's approach to the inner city was already changing course; in fact, the residents' staunchest ally in their effort to protect their homes was the city's own planning department, which vigorously defended the neighbourhood's old fabric and used the occasion of its initial report on Southeast Spadina to issue a damning indictment of Toronto's inner-city planning policies over the previous two decades (CTPB 1972b: 15–35, Caulfield 1972a). Five or ten years earlier, Southeast Spadina would likely have gone the way of Cabbagetown; but unlike Cabbagetown, Southeast Spadina was not yet demolished by the time the city's inner-city planning policies began to shift direction. Meanwhile, Chinatown, already being squeezed from its former centre of gravity on the west side of the core by commercial and institutional redevelopment, was spreading into the neighbourhood, a process rapidly accelerated by

A whitepainted house in Donvale. Saving the area's physical fabric was the death-knell for its social fabric. Its working-class population was displaced by middle-class resettlers nearly as thoroughly as St Jamestown's former residents had been by the high-rise builders.

Houses in Southeast Spadina. More than twenty square blocks, occupied by 681 houses whose residents made up a stable moderate- and low-income community, were zoned for clearance.

increasing Chinese immigration to the city (Thompson 1979: 309–11). By the 1980s, a majority of the area's residents were Chinese working people, and the retail strip in its midst was an intense node of Chinese shops. While some modest whitepainting was scattered across the area, Southeast Spadina had experienced a pattern of change very different than Donvale.

Two neighbourhoods unluckier than Southeast Spadina were the lower part of a west-end district named Parkdale, where 170 houses along a network of small streets were demolished in 1954 to create a corridor beside the lakeshore for the Gardiner Expressway, and the residential section of the King-Parliament district, east of the core, where 170 more houses were destroyed in the early 1960s to clear space for ramps to connect the downtown street system with an expressway to the northeast suburbs (CTPB 1976: 13, 1974: 10). These demolitions were minor, however, compared to the volume of houses and neighbourhoods to be wrecked had Metro's inner-city expressway plans not been shelved. Along the route of the east-end Scarborough Expressway alone, more than twelve hundred houses were slated for expropriation and razing (Stieren 1973); the Spadina, Crosstown, and Christie-Clinton expressways would have wiped out thousands more.

The Spadina Expressway was an interesting case, in part because it became a dominant symbol in the popular movement that soon arose against Toronto's municipal planning policies of the 1950s and 1960s and in part because it illustrated that not only working-class neighbourhoods were menaced by city hall's style of business. The expressway would have bisected a large, mainly middle-class inner-city district just north of downtown named the Annex; the area was also under pressure from high-rise developers – a number of apartment towers had already been built. The Annex survived the 1960s largely intact only because its residents dug in their heels and battled city hall for every inch of threatened turf (Burton and Morley 1979).*

A less fortunate middle-class area was on Jameson Avenue in the Parkdale district, transformed in the late 1950s from a 'quiet street of single-family homes' to a dense canyon of thirty apartment buildings (CTPB 1976: 14). Another was in a west-end neighbourhood north of the city's largest part, High Park, where several square blocks of

---

* Among them was urban theorist Jane Jacobs, who settled in the Annex after moving to Toronto from New York City and played an active role in the fight against the Spadina. Jacobs's critique of modern city-building figures importantly in this book.

Gardiner Expressway, Jameson on-ramp. In South Parkdale, 170 houses along a network of small streets were demolished to create a corridor beside the lakeshore for the Gardiner Expressway.

old houses were wiped out for high-rise construction. As it was at Bloor-Dufferin, the city's logic for consigning the High Park area to clearance was the proximity of a subway stop; two stations are nearby. This is quite reasonable logic in theory; locating population concentrations close to transit facilities makes abstract sense. The difficulty for the city's politicians became that the area's residents refused to regard their neighbourhood as an abstraction and, in 1971, turned a developer's plan to build more high-rises – by demolishing one hundred houses along two streets named Gothic and Quebec avenues and constructing four thirty-storey towers – into another popular issue in the movement against the old regime (Caulfield 1972b, 1974: 35–41; Sewell et al. 1971: 91–106). (There are no subway stations anywhere near Jameson Avenue; presumably, the transportation logic of the remarkably high densities the city allowed there was an access ramp to the Gardiner at the foot of the street.)

Another case of a residential district that illustrates Toronto's planning approach of the 1950s and 1960s is the Toronto Island neighbourhood. Located close to the core, only a ten-minute ferry ride from the heart of downtown, the Island community is less an inner-city neighbourhood than an idiosyncratic version of the tradition suburban utopia (Fishman 1985): a residential district of considerable natural environmental attraction situated apart from, but affording easy

The Annex, Spadina Expressway route. The Spadina Expressway became a dominant symbol in the popular movement that soon arose against Toronto's municipal planning policies of the 1950s and 1960s. The expressway would have bisected a large, mainly middle-class district just north of downtown named the Annex.

access to, the city. Cars are prohibited from the Island, and so the Radburn principle exists *de facto*. From the turn of the century until the 1940s, the Island community was mainly a summer-cottaging district mixed among stretches of waterside parkland. During and after the Second World War, when demand for housing in Toronto substantially exceeded supply, many Island homeowners winterized their properties and began living there year-round; and by the late 1940s, the community was permanent home to nearly three thousand residents (Gibson 1984: 218, Swadron 1981: 77). In the 1950s, the city-suburban metropolitan federation that then controlled the Island announced plans to terminate the residential community in order to develop the area as a regional metropolitan park.

In the decade that followed, more than two thousand year-round Island residents were evicted from their homes. Hundreds of houses and cottages were razed or removed to make way for picnic grounds,

Parkdale, Jameson Avenue. A less fortunate middle-class area than the Annex was along Jameson Avenue in Parkdale, transformed in the late 1950s from a quiet street of single-family homes to a dense canyon of thirty apartment buildings.

acres of picturesque lawn, and a large kiddie amusement area. By the late 1960s, only about 250 households remained in two small enclaves at the Island's eastern end, destined for imminent demolition to build a pitch-and-putt golf course. Then, at around the same time that communities in neighbourhoods like Kensington, Donvale, and the Annex began to battle back against the municipal bulldozer, the remaining Island residents elected to fight. A Byzantine conflict ensued, played out over the course of nearly two decades at city hall, in several courtrooms (up to the Supreme Court of Canada), and at the Ontario provincial legislature. The Islanders were supported in their struggle by the City of Toronto, whose planning philosophy had now shifted toward sustaining old neighbourhoods and whose planners issued a report strongly favourable to the Islanders' cause (CTPB 1973); Metro,

Houses on Toronto Island. The Toronto Island community is less an inner-city neighbourhood than an idiosyncratic version of the traditional suburban utopia: a residential district of considerable natural environmental attraction situated apart from, but affording easy access to, the city. By the late 1960s, only about 250 houses remained in two small enclaves at the Island's eastern end, destined for imminent demolition to build a pitch-and-putt golf course.

however, was adamant to the end in seeking the neighbourhood's destruction. Eventually, the Islanders won, Metro's wreckers were stayed, and the remaining fragment of Island community survives – though in the long run only the area's physical fabric may survive. As Gladstone-Havelock and Donvale illustrate, protection of an attractive residential locale may displace a neighbourhood's existing population as surely as clearance. The working-class/middle-class/bohemian hodgepodge that made up the Island community during its fight for survival may become the victim of its own success. Paradoxically, among the Islanders' most forceful arguments in defence of their community was, as it was in the case of Gladstone-Havelock, that the local state should not be sanctioning the wrecking of a substantial number of affordable housing units at a time when Toronto's

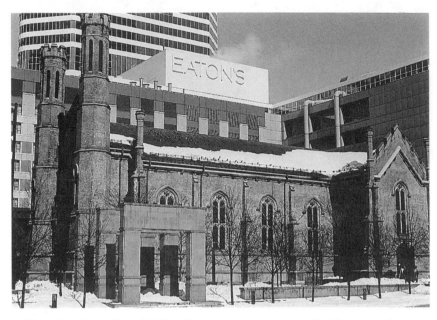

Church of the Holy Trinity. Redevelopment systematically savaged scores of old buildings and threatened others. These included the century-old Gothic-revival Church of the Holy Trinity, slated for erasure by the original Eaton Centre Plan.

housing costs were quickly moving beyond the means of most moderate-income households.*

What is interesting about the Island in the context of examining styles of city-building in Toronto is Metro's approach to the community. Again, the planning logic makes sense in the abstract; waterfront parkland is clearly desirable in a dense urban area bordering a Great Lake. But there is a recurrent pattern here: a rationalist attitude that conceived urban space as a kind of efficient machine to be composed of large blocks of specialized use and that doomed to the dustbin old neighbourhoods obstructing this vision. Deemed irrelevant in the larger project of assembling the machine were the functions and meanings of these places for people who traditionally lived in and used them.

---

* Most recent plans for maintaining the Island community may, however, help to protect its social mix by incorporating it as profit-controlled housing and adding a number of new social-housing units to the neighbourhood.

Union Station. Also slated to be wrecked was the city's monumental neo-classical rail terminal, in order to make way for office towers that were part of a proposed redevelopment of the railyards at the southern edge of the core.

Some of the most conspicuous violence done the city's old fabric during the 1950s and 1960s was in the central business district itself. In part, this involved residential displacement; between 1951 and 1971, the expansion of core commercial and institutional functions into downtown residential pockets eliminated the homes of thirteen thousand people, housing that was mostly moderate-cost (CTPB 1972b: 22). And, in part, it meant destruction of much of the fabric of the city's old business district, where redevelopment systematically savaged scores of sound old buildings that often, like the Temple Building, were structures of particular architectural or historical merit. These included the old Board of Trade Building at 2 Front Street East, which 'stood like a medieval tower adorning the entrance to Young Street' (Dendy 1978: 67, Arthur 1974: 214–16), the General Post Office at Adelaide and Toronto streets, whose 'facade ... was matched by few buildings in the city' (Dendy 1978: 86–7, Arthur 1974: 126–7), and the Bank of Toronto at Bay and King streets, about which Arthur wrote, '... the second half of the 19th Century produced no finer bank building' (Dendy 1978: 98–9, Arthur 1974: 173). Other old buildings, too, were threatened with demolition. Besides Old City Hall, two notable cases included the century-old Gothic-revival Church of the Holy Trinity, also slated for erasure by the original Eaton Centre plan, and the city's monumental neoclassical rail terminal, Union Station, to be wrecked to make way for office towers as part of a proposed redevelopment of the railyards at the southern edge of the core (McHugh 1985: 68, 103–4, Bebout 1972: 97–8). But as they had for Old City Hall, friends of the two old buildings rallied to their defence and, amid Toronto's changing planning climate of the early 1970s, preserved them from destruction.

Conclusion

Widespread middle-class resettlement of older downtown neigh-bourhoods – the process of 'gentrification' that is the main focus of this book – first emerged in the context of the patterns of city-building described in this Chapter. Chapter 2 now takes a closer look at two key forces that helped shape these patterns, urban modernism and civic boosterism. First, however, the chapter seeks to establish an overall framework for the discussion that follows by identifying the general perspective toward urban landscapes that informs the book as a whole.

2

Capital, Modernism, Boosterism
Forces in Toronto's Postwar City-Building

Culture, Capital, and Urban Form

An Understanding of City Form

In accounting for patterns of city-building in a case like Toronto in the 1950s and 1960s, it is important to distinguish between, on the one hand, the *fact* of urban growth or transition – the increasing scale of a metropolitan region or, within the region, changing patterns of urban function – and, on the other, specific landscape *forms* these processes were given.

Growth was a central fact of Toronto life during the 1950s and 1960s. The city itself – the urban area's inner municipality – was not the main locus of growth; its population (about 700,000) and workforce (about 470,000) remained constant during these decades. But this overall statistical stability masked a marked pattern of shifting function. The demolition of houses and construction of apartments, for example, meant that fewer homeowning families and an increasing number of smaller tenant households lived in the city; employment, meanwhile, gravitated away from industrial, warehousing, and wholesaling work toward white-collar, retail, and service jobs (CATF 1974: 266–7, 281–2, 293, 319).

These changes occurred in a context of explosive metropolitan growth in which the urban region's population more than doubled, from about 1.25 million to nearly 3 million. (In the subsequent decades of the 1970s and 1980s, in contrast, the region's population rose by only about .6 million.) Thus, in the same years that downtown neighbourhoods were under attack from high-rise development, office tower construction, public-housing projects, and expressway proposals, vast tracts of land at the city's outskirts were rapidly urbanizing. Farm fields became subdivisions, shopping and industrial malls replaced pastures and woodlots, and highways sliced through once-drowsy ravines as apartment towers rose beside them.*

Overall, this metropolitan growth may be traced to two main factors: Toronto's emergence, superseding Montreal, as Canada's dominant urban centre, and policies at three levels of government designed to spur Toronto's expansion.

A battery of forces dating to the nineteenth century helped account for the emerging pre-eminence of Toronto among Canadian cities. Among the most important were the entrepreneurism of Toronto's banks, the development of the northern Ontario resource industry for which Toronto served as head-office, and the shift in the centre of gravity of sources of foreign investment in Canada from Europe to the United States, for which Toronto also served as head-office (CATF 1974: 33–4, Nader 1975: 214–23, Kerr 1973: 71–2). Measured by such indicators as the value of commercial cheques cashed and of stock-shares traded, Toronto established its economic hegemony in the 1930s (Nader 1975: 217). In subsequent decades, its dominance has steadily grown, and in the emerging world economy of the late twentieth century, Toronto is the primary Canadian centre for corporate administration, international financial activity, and related commercial services.**

Public policy supportive of Toronto's growth involved each of the three levels of the Canadian state: a federal government that viewed city-building as a vital Keynesian vehicle for national economic recovery in the wake of a depression and war, that was especially committed to the development of Toronto as Canada's headquarters for domestic and foreign capital, and that supported these policies through its economic and immigration programs (particularly with major allocations of resources to support private- and public-sector housing construction); a provincial government that was committed to strengthening Ontario's urban-industrial economic base and pro-

---

* These changes are strikingly illustrated in an early-1970s collection of aerial photographs published by a local real estate firm (Kirkup c. 1972).

**The effects of deindustrialization and corporatization on Toronto's urban form are explored in chapter 3.

vided massive funding for the public works required to accomplish this task (and, in Toronto, created the city-suburban metropolitan federation tailored to oversee infrastructural development); and municipal authorities that identified rapid, continuing growth as the principal grounding for local prosperity and fashioned zoning and planning instruments to promote this objective (Magnusson 1983, Goldrick 1978, Colton 1980: 52–73, CATF 1974: 227–8).

But, taken together, these different factors – the simple fact of growth and the historically situated economic and political forces that underlie it – do not go very far toward explaining the particular forms given this growth. Something else is needed in the equation. Take the example of the suburban subdivision, a common form of Toronto development in the postwar years. Knowing that municipalities surrounding Toronto experienced dramatic population increase in the 1950s and 1960s, and that this growth was associated with Toronto's emergent metropolitan dominance and with government policies meant to stimulate urban expansion, does not help very much in accounting for the specific form of the subdivision itself – the low-density enclave of segregated residential use set apart from the city. To be sure, there are connections between the character of Toronto's growth and particular kinds of suburban landscapes that were developed. For example, many suburban subdivisions near Toronto are exclusive districts of 'executive homes' that reflect the nature of Toronto's head-office economy and market-demand among a sector of the city's corporate elite for this housing form. As well, there are links between specific features of state policy and particular landscapes; for example, the three levels of government involved in promoting Toronto's growth each favoured the subdivision as the centrepiece of suburban development.

But these observations still do not explain the occurrence of the subdivision form in the first place – the idea of the subdivision and persistence of this idea. No real sense can be made of the former phenomenon, the idea of the subdivision, without looking two or three centuries back into urban history to examine conditions of daily activity in early industrial cities, the evolution of middle-class family life and gender relations, and the origin of the suburban 'bourgeois utopia'; the idea of the suburb emerged at a particular historical moment in the culture of everyday urban life (Fishman 1987: 3–72, Walker 1981: 396–7, MacKenzie and Rose 1983: 160–7). And no real sense can be made of the latter phenomenon, the subdivision's persistence, without exploring the circumstances in which this idea became an enduring and widespread reality: the economy of urban development that sustained production of this form.

To restate the argument in more general terms, while economic and political forces generating growth or functional transition in a city are the necessary conditions for the *fact* of urban change, they do not constitute the sufficient conditions for the appearance of particular urban *forms* – whether current-day suburban subdivisions, the nineteenth-century Parisian arcades explored by Walter Benjamin, the Gothic cathedrals of medieval cities, or any other city landscape feature. These sufficient conditions include the emergence of the ideas of specific landscape forms in situated contexts of everyday life and the socio-economic infrastructure through which these forms are actually produced.* This argument raises a problematic issue of paradigm that needs to be clarified before turning back to the case of inner-city Toronto in the 1950s and 1960s: the general relationship between these two elements in a case such as Toronto.

The Tradition of Walter Firey

A writer who helped establish a tradition in urban study consistent with the view sketched above, stressing the importance of the culture of everyday life in the process of city-building, and treating culture as a critical determinant of urban landscape, is sociologist Walter Firey. Firey wrote at a particular moment in the development of urban study, when human ecology was a dominant paradigm. He was troubled by the reductionist determinism of forms of 'economic ecology' that conceived of urban space as simply an 'impeditive and cost-imposing' abstract field (1945: 140), and he judged inadequate accounts of the interaction of social practice and urban form that were based on 'premises that the only possible relationship locational activities may bear to space is an economic one.' He argued that this way of thinking overlooked essential cultural factors that he demonstrated were also at play in the city's spatial construction. Firey termed these factors 'sentiment and symbolism.'

Other writers, too, have worked in this tradition – for example, historian Lewis Mumford and geographer Yi-Fu Tuan. Like Firey,

---

* The writer is indebted to Greg Nielsen for essential features of this understanding of urban form, which derives from a model of discursive practice made up of the components of (1) norms, codes, and horizons of expectation and (2) institutional, interactional, and material infrastructures.

each had a quite specific concern, but they shared with him a common outlook. Mumford argued that accounts of the origins of cities have been too often centred on material and technological factors, overlooking vital cultural and ceremonial functions of urban places as locales of ritual and festival, and he sought a more holistic appreciation of early cities that coupled concern for practical and economic forces with a consideration for social and philosophic influences that he also believed guided human activity (1961: 5–10). Tuan was concerned with 'the affective bond between people and ... the material environment,' a bond he termed 'topophilia,' and he argued that the 'persistent' human search for 'the ideal environment' is expressed in varying ways within the frameworks of different cultures and social structures (1974: 4, 93, 248).

While Firey, Mumford, and Tuan each wrote in a particular framework of interest, their ideas are rooted in and illustrate the underlying principle that human *desires* expressed in cultural contexts exert an essential influence on urban spatial arrangements and forms. To return to the example of suburbs, it is partly in the context of everyday culture that the origins of the subdivision must be viewed: the desire of the early industrial middle class 'to "banish the facts of production" from the landscape, ... pollution, noise, crime, the threat and misery of the working class,' and to create a 'separate [spatial] sphere' for an emergent form of domestic life rooted in new notions about the nature of the family for which 'traditional urban form and domestic architecture' were perceived ill-suited (Walker 1981: 396, MacKenzie and Rose 1983: 163, Fishman 1987: 34).

This way of thinking, treating cultural forces as partly distinct from economic matters in the process of urban development, is inconsistent with the classical economic determinism or 'spatial Darwinism' (Gottdiener 1985: 266) that Firey and Mumford were concerned to resist – an approach expressing itself in such precepts as a supposed inexorable gravitation of urban space toward highest-and-best economic use. As well, it is inconsistent with Marxian economic structuralism that focuses on a theorized totalizing role of capital in processes of urban development. Because this book generally shares with the Marxian viewpoint a critical perspective toward capital – a force whose dynamics the book argues have been pivotal in city-building in contemporary Toronto – but also takes an approach quite distinct from the Marxian model, it is important to examine the differences between these outlooks and to clarify the approach taken here.

To turn again to the example of the suburban subdivision, David

Harvey writes in a structuralist vein that 'a strong argument can be made that suburbanization is the creation of the capitalist mode of production' (1985: 122). His reasoning is that suburbs are highly compatible with specific imperatives of capital because they stimulate a demand for products, thus promoting the circulation of money, and encourage 'possessive individualism,' thus buttressing capital's ideological project. He finds this affinity sufficiently strong to conclude that, therefore, the suburb is capital's creature. The perspective underlying this kind of approach is an economic determinism that views society as a system wholly reducible to the dynamic and momentum of the economic realm and that seeks to account for all social relations – cultural and political as well as economic – in this framework. Hence, Harvey regards a cultural preference for suburban life as a kind of ideological illusion traceable to the subterranean workings of capital, 'a created myth arising out of ... the logic of capitalist accumulation' (1985: 122).

In the case of suburban form, however, there is a serious problem with this analysis. For, while it is certainly true that suburbs may be highly consistent with the agenda of capital, it is not clear that this is necessarily so. It is not difficult to conceive of suburban places that might be antagonistic to capital – in fact, an example is directly at hand. As has already been noted, Toronto's Island community is a kind of quintessential suburban form. While highly atypical in some ways – unlike most contemporary Toronto suburbs, the Island is very close to downtown, was not recently built by a private-sector development firm, and is not auto-based – it is thoroughly suburban in its central features: a lower-density, segregated-use arrangement of single-family houses convenient to the city and situated in an environmentally picturesque setting. The Island community embodies the principles of Perry's 'neighbourhood unit' – a main basis of Toronto's postwar suburban design – even to the extent that it has its own school and communal greenspace and is free of car traffic (Relph 1987: 62–5, Hodge 1986: 65, SPCMT 1979: 45–7). It is a community that, like the ideal suburban neighbourhood, is simplified, segmented, and withdrawn (SPCMT 1979: 49–52). But during the long years of its fight for survival with city hall, it was a neighbourhood many of whose members were highly hostile to the sort of consumerism and possessive individualism that, for Harvey, characterize suburban places

(Gibson 1984: 236–95).* For all its idiosyncrasy, the Island community suggests that there is nothing inherent in suburban form intrinsically consistent with the logic of capital accumulation. Rather, the suburban subdivision must be viewed as a cultural form that has often been successfully appropriated by capital, not simply its malleable 'creation' or a form that it invariably and in all cases penetrates.

Capital and Everyday Life

This last conclusion is central to grasping the relationship of the culture of everyday life with the workings of an economy of urban development dominated by capital and, thus, to making sense of the persistent occurrence of specific landscape forms in a city like Toronto. A first step in understanding this relationship is an appreciation of capital.

Capital is an economic system that seeks to configure all human needs, desires, and productive activities and resources (including space and time) within an abstract matrix of numeric equivalence, namely money. Capital seeks a rationalized commodification of human use values in the form of economic exchange values, and its central dynamic is motivation among members of the social system to acquire this specie of numeric equivalence because it is needed to fulfil everyday needs and desires they usually have no other means of realizing. In this context, capital is often hostile to the emergence of alternate methods for meeting human needs; in order to sustain its maximum momentum, it seeks to absorb and maintain productive activity within its own aegis unless it is not to its advantage to do so. (In Toronto, for example, property capital has been generally resistant to state programs that assist development of private-sector mixed-income non-profit housing cooperatives. The creation of low-income housing, however, is left to the state.) And within the framework of capital – the key point in the argument here – the economic system itself has no meaning or primary function apart from the continuous circulation of money. The system's sole purpose is facilitation of the pursuit of individual needs and desires through personal ownership of the specie of exchange. This is the genesis of the ethos within capital that

---

* They remain so. As a footnote in chapter 1 observed, the Island community may sustain its demographic mix by implementing profit-controls on its housing stock, a strategy emerging directly from the work of many Islanders.

Harvey terms 'possessive individualism'; among capital's ideological projects is reifying and naturalizing the autonomy of the individual.

In other words, capital is a form with no ideational content but its own perpetuation. The specific nature of the personal goals and desires of the system's members – the use values that give meaning to their pursuit of the specie of exchange – are irrelevant so long as they present no serious threat to capital's overall dominance. Capital's project is simply to promote ideas and desires consistent with its own central tendencies. Thus, it seeks to encourage individuals to find satisfaction in possession of innovative consumer conveniences or to express status by deployment of the latest styles. These strategies accelerate the circulation of money, are expedited by capital's constant production of new products and fashions, and underscore capital's chronic appetite for novel commodities.

In this connection – the generation of new commodities – it is crucial to stress that 'use value' is a problematic concept that cannot simply be naturalized as a universal relationship between user and object 'whose transparency ... defies history' (Baudrillard 1981: 130). In at least three ways, use value is socially situated. The first of these arises in the context of societies generally, whose mechanics of development may 'set in motion [a dynamic] that refines and multiplies needs, producing more complex modes of civilization' (Levin 1981: 17); that is, horizons of use value may be widened through processes of change in the fabric of everyday life. The second arises in the context of economies dominated by capital, where, as has already been noted, the system's logic enjoins production of new perceived 'needs' – new use values – in order to provide a constantly expanding sphere of vehicles for capital's circulation. The third, again in the context of economies dominated by capital, is the entire construct of 'use value' itself when the term is used to connote 'needs' and 'desires' of discrete individuals. Within capital, observes Baudrillard, 'the individual is an ideological structure' and 'what produces the commodity system in its general form is the concept of need itself, as constitutive of the very structure of the individual ... who ... autonomizes himself and rationalizes his desire, his relation to others and to objects, in terms of needs, utility, satisfaction and use value' (1981: 133, 136). According to this view, the whole apparatus of exchange value is partly based in the logic of the individual pragmatically pursuing use values. It is, of course, possible to decouple the concept of the individual from the logic of capital – to argue that, while the mechanics of capital may require the cult of the individual, the idea of the individual does not necessarily imply an economy rooted in capital. But Baudrillard's central thought, that in each instance the notion 'use value' cannot be naturalized and requires critical rather than ahistorical treatment, is essential in grasping the relations between capital and the culture of everyday life.

According to its proponents, capital is a mode that encourages rational competition and, in doing so, promotes and rewards political, cultural, and scientific innovation and development. Entrepreneurs who successfully identify and provide for the fulfilment of individuals' felt needs and desires will themselves benefit through their own increased possession of the specie of exchange, and their motivation to do so will create 'progress.' But as viewed by its critics, capital has most often functioned as a system of dominance: dominance of person over person, based on relative money-wealth; of social group over social group, based on control of capital – the actual equipment of economic production – versus control only of one's own labour; and of capital over ecological and biological nature, which are rationalized into abstract grids of investment opportunity. Its proponents and critics would both agree, however, that little useful can be said about city life and city-building in urban places like Toronto, whose development is mainly driven by capital, that does not take capital into account.

To return to the issue of the relationship of capital with culture, the approach taken in this book differs sharply from the structuralist perspective illustrated by Harvey's view of suburbs in which, to reiterate, 'the preference for suburban living' is interpreted as 'a created myth arising out of ... the logic of capitalist accumulation' (1985: 122). This kind of analysis envisions capital as a totality in which desires expressed in the course of the culture of everyday life are epiphenomena contingent on a determining economic base. Instead, in the argument here, capital is viewed as an 'unfinished historical project' (Gottdiener 1985: 144), a system in a continuous mode of retrenchment and reinstitution whose genius is not an ability to generate from whole cloth a coherent social totality of thesis and antithesis but is rather an apparent capacity to saturate social life in nearly all its forms – forms that often originate autonomous of, or resistant to, capital's dominance (Williams 1977: 121–7, 1980: 31–49). In fact, in this perspective, capital *requires* the emergence of autonomous ideas susceptible to its appropriation – ideas that are not simply epiphenomenal – precisely because capital itself is incapable of ideas apart from those directly relating to its own functioning and regeneration; it is an economic system whose sole 'logic is the strictly rational and utilitarian one of profit maximization' (Crow 1983: 252). Because it has no other substance, it depends for the sake of its survival, in order to generate a constant supply of new commodities, on extracting the material it works from the social life in which it is situated.

It is this relentlessly parasitic quality of capital – a system that does not inexorably and necessarily absorb all cultural forms but that is sufficiently dominant in modern life that it sometimes appears to do so – that gives rise to the notion of 'spectacle': 'the moment when the commodity has attained the total occupation of social life' (Debord 1983: 42). While Guy Debord originally coined the term 'spectacle' as an epithet to hurl at what he argued was the thorough infestation of current-day society by commodity fetish, it also has a less polemic application, representing an evocative 'effort to theorize the implications for capitalist society of the progressive shift within production towards the provision of consumer goods and services, and the accompanying "colonization of everyday life," ... the invasion and restructuring of whole areas of free time, private life, leisure, and personal expression' (Clark 1984: 9, Bonnett 1989: 131–46). One perspective toward the suburban subdivision is to view it as a form initially rooted in the effort of the early industrial middle class to *escape* the logic of capital: to elude capital's penetration of traditional urban form and urban life in the shapes of the factory and the burgeoning working class (from whom the middle class was now alienated by the wage-relation) and to retrench its everyday culture in the wake of capital's penetration and corporatization of the economic sphere that earlier had often been closely bound up with urban middle-class family life (Fishman 1987: 28–30). But almost from its inception, suburban development has been a vehicle for capital investment. Property 'far beyond the previous range of metropolitan expansion could [now] be transformed immediately from relatively cheap agricultural land to highly profitable building plots' (Fishman 1987: 10). That is, the suburb was an idea that first arose in tension with capital but whose subsequent wide dispersion beyond the activity of the earliest bourgeois suburbanites represented capital's prompt colonization and promotion of the idea. Today, most suburban development is deeply saturated by capital; the subdivision form has become, in Debord's terms, a spectacular landscape. But, to reiterate, this is not a necessary relationship; rather, it reflects capital's intractable entrepreneurial diligence.

This last thought leads to a final observation about capital, culture, and urban form that is essential to the argument of this book: the inherently paradoxical character of urban landscape elements produced by capital. Because capital, devoid of ideas, is required to extract its material from living culture, an immanent use value wholly unconnected to capital's logic is embedded in each commodity – and each urban form – it produces. For example, many landscape features of the current-day suburb represent ideas with no necessary contingent link to capital: the subdivision itself, derived from the eighteenth-century 'bourgeois utopia'; the various principles of the 'neighbourhood unit,' derived from early-twentieth-century ideas for creating humane living environments; the single-family house divided into separate, private rooms, derived from ideas of 'home' and domestic intimacy originating in the seventeenth-century Netherlands; the ranch-style or split-level design of many houses, derived from Frank Lloyd Wright's idea for the prairie house; the setting of houses on neat grass lawns bordered by carefully kept flowerbeds, derived from the eighteenth-century aesthetic of the picturesque (Rybczynski 1986: 15–75, Relph 1987: 62–5, SPCMT 1979, Fishman 1987). To repeat, capital's genius is not to have fabricated this myriad landscape from its own ingenuity but to have infused it with its spectacular spirit.

Thus, at the same time that specific, historically situated human desires and use values are embodied in these landscape elements, capital is also immanent in them as commodified forms. The most vivid ironies occur in the case of forms that, like the subdivision, first emerged in counterpoint to the urban landscape of capital. As will be seen, two further examples of this deeper irony are the high-rise apartment building and the contemporary renovated neighbourhood. Grasping the paradox of urban forms like these, originally created as alternatives to capital's city, but then absorbed and refracted by capital, is essential to appreciating the landscape of a city like Toronto.

Modernism and Boosterism in Postwar Planning

Urban Modernism

Edward Relph has written that 'there have been few inevitabilities in the making of the modern city; if other attitudes had prevailed cities now could have very different landscapes' (1987: 24). Certainly, nothing was inevitable about the particular changes of urban form experienced by inner-city Toronto in the 1950s and 1960s. In a context

of rapid metropolitan expansion generated by the economic and political stimuli of the city's thriving economy and pro-growth policies
at each level of government, it is clear that some change would have
occurred. But the precise nature of this change was not predestined
but accrued to specific dominant attitudes toward city-building in
currency at the time. Crucial among these were urban modernism
and the particular form of pro-development boosterism prevalent in
the city's municipal government.

Most tersely defined, urban modernism is an approach to city-
building rooted in a perception of the historical urban landscape as
a problem to be solved by cataclysmic refashioning, an outlook illustrated in Sigfried Giedion's *Space, Time and Architecture*, which
was published in its first edition in the late 1930s. For Giedion, writing
in the wake of the explosive growth of industrial cities, the historic
urban fabric had run its course. He described cities of his era as badly
overcrowded, pathologically chaotic, and overwhelmed by machines
like the automobile and factory that destroyed the logic and amenity
of urban forms inherited from the pre-mechanical age. He argued that
what was required for cities to work effectively in the milieu of the
twentieth century was a fundamental restructuring in accordance with
the metanarrative of a 'universal architecture' dedicated to order,
functional efficiency, and benign colossalism and promoting a 'unified
organization of life' (1967: xxxvi, 25).

An example of Giedion's ideas for urban restructuring is the inner-
city expressway, a form he espoused because it would separate vehicles from pedestrian districts and thus, he believed, create both more
effective movement of traffic and more livable streetscapes; and he
regarded the fact that building these roads would require razing large
swathes of the disorderly and congested old city not a regrettable
outcome of their construction but a positive benefit – a necessary step
in the overall reconfiguration of urban form (1967: 823–33). He also
encouraged segregation of land-use and the development of massive
high-rise projects interspersed with greenbelts like those designed by
Le Corbusier, so that all city-dwellers and not only the well-to-do,
could have access to parks, gardens, and outdoor recreation; and he
celebrated the construction of monumental downtown skyscraper
complexes, like New York's Rockefeller Centre, which he believed
would serve as the modern equivalent of the Athenian agora or medieval cathedral square (1967: 769, 833–56).

Giedion was not optimistic about the city's prospects were its fate
simply left to the 'dismal' ordinary course of urban government. Rather,

he believed that 'it rests with the instincts of the ruling class' to create the restructured city, drawing on the expertise of a technical elite to ensure realization of the new urbanism (1967: 843). In this context, his heroes were the Baron Haussmann, Le Corbusier, and Robert Moses, men who also pursued a radical re-engineering of urban fabric according to autocratic procedures (Clark 1984: 36–41, Fishman 1982: 235–42, Caro 1975). And as for the humdrum of city-dwellers who were not of 'the ruling class,' modernism's impact on their lives was clearly in their best interests and interpreted benignly by its prophets. Thus Giedion, for example, characterized Haussmann's eviction of the working class from Paris and erasure of their neighbourhoods – described by the Baron himself as the 'disembowelling of the ... *quartier* of uprisings and barricades' – as a laudable effort to 'give the great mass of the people a chance to live outside the city' (Clark 1984: 39, Giedion 1967: 773).

Modernist Form and the Agenda of Toronto Boosterism

Giedion described urban modernism as a 'new tradition' in city-building. Clearly, it was a tradition consistent with the postwar reconstruction of inner-city Toronto, a project partly rooted in the ideas of modernism and an antipathy for historic urban form. In his case-study of urban renewal in Toronto in the 1950s and 1960s, Fraser documents attitudes of planners of the period toward the inner city's old residential districts; they appeared to have 'disliked old neighbourhoods simply because they were old ... It is plain that Toronto's planning was being done by men who hated cities,' or at least hated the city fabric of the past (1972: 57).

Partly, this view reflected a vigorous distaste, congruent with modernist thinking, for old, mixed-use downtown neighbourhoods in themselves, categorized by city hall as undesirable by definition (Fraser 1972: 57). The planners preferred new, large-scale forms that separated uses, were structurally homogeneous, and appeared orderly to the eye. Illustrative in this regard was their approach to commercial districts. For example, a 1963 planning document described the city's main commercial strip along Yonge Street as 'busy, prosperous and exciting' but recommended the strip's reconstruction because 'its buildings are old and, though often well fixed-up, they are a heterogeneous jumble bearing little relationship to one another except in general height' (CTPB 1963: 30). A sketch suggested a preferable streetscape that eliminated the strip's visual diversity and its montage of neon lights: a uniform row of modernized storefronts each precisely alike, recalling Giedion's appreciation of Haussmann, who 'simply and without discussion ... spread a uniform facade over the whole of Paris' (1967: 769). As well, though, the planners' disdain for old downtown neighbourhoods seemed to reflect distaste for the kinds of urban places that had been created by the residents now living in these areas – working-class families, recent immigrants, and low-income households.

The Planning Board was extraordinarily clear in its view on the latter issue. A report written in the mid-1940s set the framework in which these neighbourhoods would be viewed for more than two decades: 'decline of a residential area is the simple and direct result of a fundamental change in the character of its residents ... no decline would take place were the original class of residents' – namely, middle-class residents – 'willing and content to remain' (Fraser 1972: 56–7). The actual structural condition of the neighbourhoods was not at issue. Southeast Spadina, for example, had been designated for core expansion and high-rise development despite the fact that, according to the city's own building code, its housing stock was mostly sound. In 1972, after the neighbourhood had already been under the gun of high-density zoning for several years and subject to widespread speculator activity and absentee ownership, fully 71 per cent of its 681 houses were still in 'good condition,' only 26 per cent required any substantial repair, and a meagre 3 per cent – mostly owned by the provincial government, slumlording in preparation for construction of the contested hydro facility (see chap. 1) – were not economically rehabilitable (CTPB 1972b: 39). Similarly, the Alexandra Park neighbourhood was largely in good condition when the city zoned it for clearance. Rather, the issues of principal concern to the planners appeared to be matters of image and of perceptions of economic efficiency: old inner-city neighbourhoods violated their aesthetic and professional sensibilities, and 'better' use could be made of them. Conspicuously, old neighbourhoods in parts of town that had remained middle-class and more cosmetically pleasing to city hall's eye were not designated 'blighted,' 'slumming,' or 'diseconomic' (although this did not necessarily assure their survival; as noted in chapter 1, middle-class districts – like the Annex, threatened by the Spadina Expressway – were not always safe from civic schemes).

Thus, city hall's approach to inner-city planning during the 1950s and 1960s in part derived from the views of urban modernism about appropriate solutions for perceived problems of old urban form and in part represented disapproval of the way in which the social composition of these districts had evolved. In the latter respect, the city's policies were explicit: in future, there would simply be no room in downtown neighbourhoods for working-class or low-income residents apart from public-housing projects like Alexandra Park or Regent Park (CATF 1974: 232). Like the Parisians uprooted by Haussmann, Toronto's less affluent inner-city residents would be forced to relocate elsewhere. In making its determinations about the fate of their neighbourhoods – designating some for high-rise apartments or public-housing development, others for core commercial growth or expressway projects – city hall framed its approach in the language of *technique*, reflecting 'an overriding concern with ... manipulative planning' (Relph 1976: 81). Its planning documents were characterized by such rationalist wording as the imperative 'to replace obsolescent buildings and other uneconomic, deteriorated or improperly located properties' (CTPB 1967: 28), rhetoric echoing Giedion's preoccupation with order and functional efficiency.

Functionalist thinking meant, for example, that although the neighbourhoods at Gladstone-Havelock and north of High Park were residential districts of good quality, they were more suitably designated for high-density housing oriented to the city's new subway system, or that it was appropriate to gut neighbourhoods in the Christie-Clinton corridor or remove old buildings like the Temple Building in order to deploy the space they occupied in more instrumentally efficacious ways. Decisions about what constituted 'diseconomy,' deterioration, or improper location were, of course, best left to the planners: the experts. Relph has a felicitous phrase for this attitude, 'benevolent environmental authoritarianism' – benevolent because the benign prescriptions of planners are assumed to be 'in everyone's best interest,' environmental because at issue is 'the relationship between people and their built environments,' authoritarian because 'all decisions are made by ... the professionally-trained authorities' (1981: 98–100). In this stress on the role of urban technicians, Toronto's style of city-building again shared the approach of urban modernists like Giedion; often hidden from view by the prose of *technique* was the highly subjective and class-bound nature of the planners' cultural and aesthetic judgments.

Toronto's version of urban modernism was shaped and amplified by the specific political context of pro-development boosterism in which it occurred, an ideology underwritten by policies of the federal and provincial governments and vigorously promoted by a pro-growth coalition of local commercial interests, development corporations, and municipal politicians. The currency of Toronto boosterism was the superlative – growth 'at a rate faster than any of us dreamed of,' 'development in the central core of the city that will stagger the imagination' – and represented a zeal, rooted in an unwavering belief in the 'righteousness' of urban expansion, that was nearly religious in its fervour (Colton 1980: 94, 156; Lithwick 1970: 175). The boosters were astute enough to realize, however, that their enthusiasm alone was insufficient to accomplish their purpose. Left solely within the realm of political debate at the local and metropolitan councils, their program for Toronto's future would likely founder on the shoals of neighbourhood hostility to disruptive public works, conflict among the several municipalities that made up the metropolitan federation, and the city's traditional conservatism. But the ally they required was close at hand in the form of the planning apparatus provincial law mandated them to establish.

'My view,' wrote Frederick Gardiner to Ontario Premier Leslie Frost in 1953, 'is that the Planning Board properly constituted is one of the most important elements in the metropolitan administration' (Colton 1980: 153). This conviction was not based, though, on any faith that Gardiner or his colleagues felt for the sort of omnibus urban design process in the social interest envisioned by modernists like Le Corbusier or Giedion. 'To Gardiner and most Toronto politicians,' wrote Gardiner's biographer, Timothy Colton, 'the idea of a planning apparatus or any other state authority moulding the urban form in comprehensive fashion was anathema. Cities were built best by private decisions, and the private decisions that mattered most were business decisions' (1980: 153). But the growth-boosters recognized that the endorsement of a planning staff for the particulars of their program would provide the clout required to overcome political resistance. For example, in reference to one especially contentious local issue – expansion of a sewage plant in the city's east end that was opposed by nearby residents – Gardiner's letter to Frost continued, 'If the Metropolitan Council has the recommendation of a properly constituted Planning Board, it would be most difficult for the Metropolitan Council to vary from such recommendation.'

Thus, the growth-boosters co-opted the planning process for the 'expressly political purpose' of giving legitimacy to their objectives (Colton 1980: 154). Planning would provide a technical blueprint for rapid development that the planners themselves were expected to support unflinchingly. On occasions when they failed to do so and placed questions of the quality of development ahead of the imperative to promote rapid growth, they were ignored (Fraser 1972: 55). When, for example, the city's planners proposed, in 1952, a relatively modest zoning by-law for the core area or, in 1971, recommended guidelines that might have moderated the most ambitious development project in Toronto's history (redevelopment of the old railyards adjacent to downtown), growth-minded politicians simply rewrote their employees' submissions (Frisken 1988: 24–5, Caulfield 1974: 5).*

For the most part, however, such revisions were unnecessary. The planners' commitments to the principles of modernism and to their vision of the 'renewal' of the inner city were highly compatible with the boosters' interest in enhancing downtown Toronto as a site of investment, an objective toward which the restructuring of inner-city neighbourhoods was perceived as a key strategic element (Magnusson 1983: 133, Goldrick 1978: 33). Still, this confluence of architectural and political ideas is insufficient in itself to explain the widespread redevelopment that occurred. For, although some of the elements of the new inner city were the direct work of the state (such as public-housing projects, roadways, and modernist-inspired government buildings), construction of the bulk of the new urban fabric required that capital find this investment attractive both in itself and in the context of the new downtown landscape that the state's activities were promoting.

Capital did find the new forms attractive. Money flowed readily into the development of apartment and office towers throughout the inner city, projects that were particularly remunerative for investors in the framework of Toronto's rapid metropolitan expansion. The coupling of this process of growth with the city's permissive zoning generated redevelopment of block after block of the old downtown fabric with profitable high-density forms that became a key element in a dramatic transition that occurred in the Canadian property industry. During the postwar decades, Canadian property capital altered

---

* In the latter case, Alderman Karl Jaffary, who had fruitlessly defended the planners' recommendations, then moved that city council retitle the document. In place of *Official Plan Statement*, he suggested *Certain Ill-Considered Statements Respecting Metro Centre Which Are Highly Detrimental to the People of Toronto*. Alderman John Sewell dumped an attaché case full of play-money onto his desktop to illustrate his view that the developer had fleeced the city for millions of dollars in property rights.

from an economic sector composed mainly of a catch-as-catch-can multiplicity of small firms at the fringe of the nation's centre of financial gravity (that was based largely around resource extraction) to an integrated field dominated by a small number of powerful multinational corporations at the core of the Canadian wealth, 'a mere handful of ... companies [who] exerted a degree of control over property development ... that probably had no parallel in any other country' (Barker, Penny, and Seccombe 1973; Spurr 1976; Lorimer 1978; Harris 1987: 371). The reconstruction of inner Toronto was only one element in this transition; others included developers' activities in other cities, the profitability of suburban growth, and policies at each level of government that encouraged creation of large pools of property capital (Spurr 1976: 193–4, Goldrick 1978: 31). But Toronto's rebuilding was an essential element, the jewel in the property industry's crown.

The Paradox of Modernist Form

As in the case of the suburban subdivision, there is a paradox here. The modernist urban forms that became part of the basis for a transformation of Canadian property capital were not capital's creation but first emerged as a critique of capital's city. The Futurist and Bauhaus schools that presaged modernism were concerned with what they viewed as the aesthetic and social bankruptcy of the dominant urban forms of their era, styles derived from the past and embodied in such movements as Gothic and classical revivalism that they condemned as functional anachronisms in machine-age cities and typifications of bourgeois commodity fetish. Among the primary roots of early modernist town planning was the Bauhaus concern for efficient mass production of good housing for working people built according to socialist principles (Relph 1987: 102–9).

While urban modernists like Le Corbusier and Giedion were singularly anti-democratic in their political outlook, their program was one of radical social reconstruction that they believed required and would be engendered by a remaking of city form, a truly urban alternative to the anti-urbanist futurism embodied in such ideas as Ebenezer Howard's Garden City and Frank Lloyd Wright's Broadacre City. For Le Corbusier, writes Robert Fishman, 'old cities had become self-consuming cancers because they had degenerated into a means of exploitation, ... a whole environment built by greed' as an outcome of capital-based property relations (1982: 265–6). Giedion was concerned about the technological framework of modern cities, 'the evil ... of industrial machines' that held cities 'at their mercy,' and argued that, if cities were again to serve as the locale of humane and civilized social relations he believed they once had been, their thorough restructuring was required, reconstruction that must be carried out on behalf of all social groups, not only the affluent (1967: 819). Urban modernism's main canons – that functional purity and aesthetic beauty are congruent, that built environments exert vital social and existential influences on their users' lives, that the city must be conceived as an overall unity built for the benefit of all its residents – were utopian in their spirit, the basis for a vision of a future urbanism oriented away from the logic of industrial capital. Thus, capital's penetration of modernist form has been especially ironic. Immanent in the landscape of efficient apartment towers and functionalist office skyscrapers constructed by the contemporary property industry is a vigorous holistic critique of an earlier version of capital's city.

Brent Brolin has argued that modernist form, with its emphasis on functionalism and monumentality, was a highly attractive style of architecture for capital in part because the same economizing and utilitarian principles bound up in the socialist subtext of early urban modernist planning were compatible with the construction of urban form within the instrumentalist context of capital (1976: 15–16). But capital's commodification of urban modernist ideas has yielded a landscape that no more resembles the urban utopias of writers like Le Corbusier or Giedion than current-day subdivisions resemble the suburban ideal of the eighteenth-century middle class. Instead, Toronto's redeveloped inner-city neighbourhoods are a patchwork of buildings like Dover Square and 390 Bay that have little underlying coherence apart from the momentum of capital seeking exchange value.

Similarly, the state's application of urban modernist principles bent them nearly unrecognizably out of shape. Giedion had warned, 'Nothing positive can be accomplished by clearing slums and simply erecting new buildings on the same sites' (1967: 822). But this is precisely what Toronto's city hall did (granting its definition of 'slums') in projects like Regent Park and Alexandra Park. The effect of the metropolitan federation's expressway projects, meanwhile, was not to purge Toronto's streets of the damaging effects of car traffic – the urban modernists' hope – but instead to dump more and more vehicles into the downtown and surrounding neighbourhoods (a consequence occurring in part because neither the modernists nor the boosters fully grasped the voracious dynamic of urban expressways). Under the aegis of Toronto's pro-growth coalition, urban modernism's vision became a utopia deformed, not a surprising outcome given the profoundly anti-utopian nature of capital's monocentric emphasis on its own reproduction and its ideological stress on the needs and desires of discrete individuals.

Conclusion

Chapter 2 has had two purposes. First, it has framed a critical understanding of urban form in a city-building economy dominated largely by capital, which is distinct from economistic approaches. Second, it has explored the forces of urban modernism and civic boosterism that helped shape Toronto's patterns of urban development during the 1950s and 1960s. Chapter 3 concludes the work of exploring the context of Toronto's 'gentrification' by examining a series of forces that influenced inner-city landscape during the 1970s and 1980s. These include the emergence of a popular movement of municipal 'reformism,' arising to contest the city-building practices of modernism and boosterism; heightening patterns of deindustrialization and the parallel growth of the city's corporate economy and culture; and three key facets of inner-city demographic and neighbourhood change.

3

Reform, Deindustrialization, and the Redirection of City-Building

Turning-point

Toronto's Two 'Reformisms'

The popular movement that arose neighbourhood by neighbourhood across Toronto in opposition to the city's patterns of postwar development reached critical mass in the early 1970s. In the 1972 municipal elections, the boosters who had dominated city council through the 1960s were abruptly reduced to a minority at city council. Among early initiatives of the new 'reform' majority were measures that reversed civic policy toward the inner city. Slash-and-burn renewal was terminated, replaced by planning oriented to neighbourhood protection and conservation of traditional urban forms.

The political movement that brought about this shift of direction was not cohesive but encompassed two distinct wings based in discrete clusters of interest (Caulfield 1974, 1988a, 1988b; Goldrick 1978; Freeman 1982: 290–1; Magnusson 1983: 114–26; Frisken 1988: 37). One grouping, characterized by Warren Magnusson as 'urban conservative' (1983: 115) and generally mainstream in its political outlook, derived largely from the city's more affluent communities, mainly in North Toronto, and focused primarily on matters of land-use planning. These included the quality and amenity of local neighbourhoods and the logic that guided the development of the city as a whole, particularly in respect to the style and architecture of the commercial core and the implications for public economy of a monofunctional central business district whose scale was outstripping the capacity of the transit system.

The second grouping, emerging mainly from working-class neighbourhoods, economically or culturally marginal middle-class communities, and inner-city political networks whose attitude was left-of-centre, was left-populist in character, termed by Magnusson 'urban radical' (1983: 116). It was especially oriented to protection of affordable housing in older downtown neighbourhoods, particularly in respect to the violence done working-class and lower-income communities by city hall's 'renewal' policies; and it was highly critical of shortcomings of the public-housing blocks like Regent Park. This grouping sometimes couched its attack on the city's patterns of development in a critique of property capital rooted in socialist principles; and besides housing and development, it developed a related focus on the process of deindustrialization that was occurring at the expense of the livelihoods of many of the city's blue-collar workers.

These differences of interest were not salient features of reformist politics in all circumstances. In many cases, opposition to the destruction of neighbourhoods or support for innovative development encompassed coalitions drawn from both groupings. The Island community, for example, fighting the metropolitan federation for its survival, had a heterogeneous class composition; meanwhile, an association that formed in Donvale to promote a small non-profit housing project in the neighbourhood included both well-to-do, middle-class in-movers to the area and less affluent, longer-term working-class residents.* On city-wide issues, as well, concerns of the two reformist groupings were sometimes congruent. Both higher- and lower-income communities, for example, were threatened by expressway construction and combined to oppose further penetration of the metropolitan federation's planned highway network into their neighbourhoods; and reformists of all dispositions concurred on a policy to overhaul the municipal planning process by involving local residents more actively in shaping the fates of their neighbourhoods. Besides such kinds of cases of common concern, there were also issues on which the groupings supported each other's interest. Left-populist

---

* Class was not, however, wholly irrelevant to the Donvale case. The housing project was opposed by a second group of middle-class residents who perceived lower-income neighbours as a threat to their lifestyles and property values (Dineen 1974). The Donvale co-op is an important example of inner-city Toronto's recent political currents that arises again later in this chapter and in subsequent chapters.

politicians, for example, consistently voted on the side of well-to-do neighbourhoods fighting proposed high-rise projects in their communities. In turn, 'urban conservative' city councillors sometimes voted for non-profit housing initiatives sponsored by community organizations and politicians from working-class neighbourhoods.

In many instances, however, the two groupings collided. 'Urban conservative' politicians, with old-guard booster support, frequently endorsed housing developments that embodied physical planning principles consistent with the new political mood but included solely up-market housing; on these occasions, they were often opposed by left-populist reformists who argued that these developments did nothing to help create more affordable housing. 'Urban conservatives' sometimes joined the old guard to give commercial developments they considered of particular merit, like the Eaton Centre shopping-mall complex that mimicked Milan's Galleria, exemptions from downtown planning regulations against the adamant hostility of left-populists, who viewed the projects as simply developers' money-making schemes undeserving of special treatment. And councillors from more affluent constituencies voted with the old guard to defeat a left-populist proposal to fund community workers in low-income neighbourhoods whose job would have been to help working-class residents organize around local planning and social-policy concerns. The plan's proponents had argued that lower-income neighbourhoods were at a disadvantage in dealing with city hall because, unlike well-to-do communities, they were unaccustomed to organizing to protect their interests, and their population did not include lawyers, architects, and other professionals whose services were available *gratis* and who were able to deal with municipal personnel on their own discursive ground. But councillors from middle-class neighbourhoods were unsympathetic.

On these and other occasions, the two groupings that had come together to fight city hall's former style of doing business battled one another as bitterly as they had opposed the boosters. These instances illustrated clearly that the popular political movement that had emerged in reaction to civic policies of the 1950s and 1960s was not, as a whole, among those 'urban mobilizations' theorized by Manuel Castells that are 'organized around classless lines ... around issues that only indirectly relate to class power' (1983: 68). 'Urban conservative' city councillors and their supporters often perceived their interests as distinct from those of the left-populist grouping, a perception that was clearly inscribed by class.* The 'urban radical' version of reformism, by contrast, drew its support not only from working-class communities but also from certain middle-class groups (presently discussed in more detail), and among its key issues was protection of not only the physical fabric but also the demographic mix of older inner-city neighbourhoods – a concern illustrated by the case of the Donvale co-op. Thus, on a lesser scale than 'reform' as a whole, the left-populist grouping did more closely approximate the kind of cross-class mobilization imagined by Castells, a point of particular relevance to a central argument of this book.

Overall, 1970s reformism acted as a kind of course-correction for Toronto's development. The occasional early alliances of 'urban conservative' reformers with old-guard boosters proved, in the end, a more compatible partnership than the relationship between the two reformist groupings, and over time this alignment became the basis of a new municipal orthodoxy no less oriented to urban growth than the policies of councils of the 1950s and 1960s but guided by new ground rules of neighbourhood protection, architectural conservation, and 'good planning.' Thus, a strong pro-growth coalition of politicians and commercial and financial interests remained in control of the civic machinery and continued to promote the city's rapid development in an ongoing context of metropolitan expansion propelled by Toronto's role as headquarters of the Canadian corporate economy.

The 'new boosterism' (Sancton 1983b: 294) remained, for the most part, committed to the modernist monumentality that had characterized development during earlier decades – a pattern mainly rooted in the fact that high-density forms modelled on Le Corbusier's grand designs remained property capital's most profitable deployment of urban space – so long as old neighbourhoods and notable old buildings were undisturbed. The wider planning context in which these policies were carried out was altered. Now public transit was said to be the basis of the inner-city transportation system, and downtown office and commercial development was placed in the framework of a new metropolitan plan meant to encourage parallel office and commercial development at transit-oriented suburban subcentres (CTPDD 1986a: 4–14, 1986b: 2–11). But within this context, the downtown

---

* Toronto was not unique in this respect; popular political movements opposing old-style civic boosterism and sharing a similar ideological cleavage arose at about the same time in Montreal and Vancouver (Sancton 1983a: 71–4, Gutstein 1983: 200–5).

skyline remained studded with construction cranes and sprouted a constant new growth of office skyscrapers and residential towers.

The changes of municipal policy that occurred under the reformists were not, however, simply cosmetic. For inner-city neighbourhoods, they represented a major shift of officially encoded urban meaning. Old houses along traditional downtown streets, even where they had been allowed to deteriorate through slumlording or blockbusting, were no longer designated as pockets of 'blight' but were now viewed as an urban resource – a valued part of the city's heritage and a desirable locale for living whose social diversity and venerable architecture were celebrated by city hall's revised planning documents. Likewise, old buildings like Union Station and Old City Hall, and traditional retail districts like the Yonge Street strip and Kensington Market, were now hagiologized and secured from the threat of modernist reconstruction. The framework of attitudes in which historical urban fabric was viewed had been reinstituted.

A particular success in the inner city of the left-populist wing of reform was a shift in the city's social-housing policy away from the construction of large bureaucratically run projects like Regent Park and Alexandra Park that destroyed old neighbourhoods, to the creation of mixed-income developments built on formerly non-residential land and smaller projects located in existing, rehabilitated buildings. In many cases, this housing was administered by its tenants as a private-sector, non-profit cooperative. Social housing of this kind fulfilled a number of objectives of left-populist reform: protecting working-class neighbourhoods, creating more units of affordable housing downtown, integrating assisted-housing households into diverse community settings instead of isolating them in low-income ghettos like Regent Park, and giving assisted-housing tenants greater control over their housing (CTHWG 1973). The new housing policies did have ambiguities. Arguably, the new kinds of projects better served the growth-booster interest in enhancing the downtown as a site for investment than white elephants like Regent Park; and because one objective of the left-populist grouping – besides housing – was to try to turn the flight of industrial jobs from the city, its politicians and supporters had mixed feelings about the fact that many of the non-residential sites available for social-housing projects were abandoned industrial land. As well, the left-populist reformists were dissatisfied with the modest volume of affordable new housing they were able to sponsor. But the city's new social-housing policies did have a major

Yonge Street, North York 'downtown.' Downtown office and commercial development was placed in the framework of a new metropolitan plan meant to encourage parallel office and commercial development at transit-oriented suburban subcentres.

impact on the character and development patterns of several inner-city districts.

The Popular Roots of Reform

In the course of a few short years, the threat of demolition of Toronto inner-city neighbourhoods for high-rise construction, public-housing development, expressway-building, and core commercial expansion was largely removed. One root of this turning-point in civic outlook was at the simple political level, involving political and institutional contingencies that helped lead to the defeat of old-line boosterism. These included a 1968 remapping of the city's ward boundaries that gave reformists more viable constituencies from which to mount attacks on incumbent politicians, the success of early reformist aldermen in dramatizing development issues and creating political capital in the media, and the effectiveness of many reformist electoral campaigns (Lorimer 1970: 37–52, Fraser 1972: 161–6, Caulfield 1974,

Sewell 1972, Harris 1976). But of more fundamental importance was the emergence and gelling of popular attitudes about traditional urban fabric that opposed the agenda of old-style civic boosterism. Four sets of attitudes, in particular, were at the roots of reformism. They arose in the contexts of: traditional popular outlooks toward city-building in Toronto; changing values in planning and related professions; the growth of the city's young adult population affiliated with marginal political and cultural groupings; and the increasing number of middle-class households settling in the inner city.

• Traditional popular attitudes toward city communities and the development processes that affected them were felt at each stratum of the city's social structure. Magnusson has described Toronto reformism in the 1970s as 'to an extent ... a return to normality' from the 'aberration' of obsessive postwar civic urgency to promote development. This 'normality' especially reflected the mood of the city's established elites, who in the past had customarily taken a fairly cautious outlook toward urban change, an approach from which the 1950s and 1960s growth-boosters sharply deviated (Magnusson 1983: 119).* While the traditional social elite did support Toronto's commercial expansion and increasing metropolitan importance, it was concerned about the style and apparent headlong pace of change in the city. Members of the old aristocracy, for example, were active participants in the groups that rallied to the defence of Old City Hall and Union Station. Notably, among the earliest of the reformist councillors to arrive at city hall was William Kilbourn, an urban historian whose books have often celebrated Toronto's traditional architectural and social fabric. Kilbourn was first elected in 1969, partly basing his support in the old and affluent Rosedale neighbourhood, and in the pivotal 1972 election he amassed the largest aldermanic plurality in the city's history. Another politician from a North Toronto ward, David Crombie, was also elected to a council seat in 1969 and, in 1972, became the first of two 'reform' mayors who occupied this office through the 1970s.

For its part, meanwhile, the city's middle class had never wholly abandoned Toronto's old inner-city neighbourhoods (compared, say,

---

* This traditional conservatism toward city-building was reflected in the design of Toronto's first real skyscraper, the 1905 Traders Bank, which rose fifteen stories, displacing the Temple Building as the city's tallest structure. In response to popular misgivings about skyscrapers, the bank's top three floors were hidden 'behind a deep cornice, thus diminishing any visual sense of height' (McHugh 1985: 87).

to middle-class city-dwellers in many U.S. cities who overwhelmingly fled the inner city in the postwar period). S.D. Clark has argued that middle-class suburbanization in Toronto was, to a significant degree, supply-side rather than demand-side driven (1966: 223); many participants in the postwar diaspora to the suburbs during the 1950s and 1960s preferred to remain downtown, departing only because affordable middle-class city housing was not easily available. Those who did remain had made an active choice to stay and to live in the inner city. Especially in the midtown district north of the core and near the university, middle-class households composed a significant segment of the population through the 1950s and 1960s, and it was in this part of town, particularly the Annex neighbourhood, that the Spadina Expressway emerged as the focal symbolic issue of middle-class reform. The area had sent to city hall in 1969 an alderman who based his campaign almost solely on opposition to the expressway and, in 1972, elected two reformist councillors.

Finally, the city's working-class communities often had enduring attachments to their neighbourhoods, locales of strong tradition, established kin and friendship networks, and familiar rounds of everyday life. Two of the the most militant early reformers, John Sewell – who later succeeded Crombie as mayor – and Karl Jaffary, came to city hall in 1969 from the Don district east of downtown, which was still dominantly working-class; the area had already been partly disembowelled (in Haussmann's apt word) for high-rise developments like St Jamestown and public-housing projects like Regent Park, and more wide-scale 'renewal' was threatened. Reformists also managed some success in neighbourhoods more heavily dominated by immigrants than the largely Anglo-Saxon Don district; two reform aldermen elected in 1972, who had ties to organized labour and expressed the most explicitly socialist views at city council, based their support partly in west-end Portuguese and Italian constituencies.

• A second set of attitudes associated with the emergence of reform involved the city's planners, a numerically fractional group in the larger scheme of things but one that occupied a crucial position in the process of Toronto's development. Planners arriving at city hall in the late 1960s had been educated in the midst of an attack on urban modernism centred around writers like Jane Jacobs, Lewis Mumford, and Robert Venturi, and the ideas of these critics of modernist form exerted a powerful influence on the young planners' views of downtown neighbourhoods. Their 1971 proposal for renewal of a small corner of Cabbagetown named Trefann Court, for example, a community that had been bypassed by the construction of Regent Park, was clearly based on Jacobs's principles of 'gradual change' and embodied her anti-modernist principles of mixed use, old buildings, and short blocks (Fraser 1972, Jacobs 1961: 152–221). The planners' new scepticism about the wisdom of expressway-based transportation planning reflected Mumford's indictment of such policies (1963), and their new attitudes toward traditional streetscapes and commercial strips were influenced by the values of architectural diversity and respect for vernacular forms promoted by writers like Venturi (1966).*

It was in the context of the critique of modernism that the planning staff had written the 1972 working paper on Southeast Spadina discussed in chapter 1, whose measured prose barely concealed a comprehensive attack on the city's approach to inner-city planning in the 1950s and 1960s (CTPB 1972b: 14–35). As well, the young planners had come of age in a period when devolution of power to local communities was emerging as a central icon of populist ideology, a principle to which many of them subscribed. Thus, in part, the new outlook toward the inner city not only was a consequence of ideas impressed on city hall from outside but also arose from within the ranks of the city's technocratic elite; and the planners' ideas were often strongly endorsed by spokespersons from related professions – architecture, social services, urban social science – who provided briefs and studies supportive of reformist objectives. Overall, there had been a major upheaval in the way that urban 'experts' perceived and theorized inner-city neighbourhoods.

• A third attitudinal element in the emergence of 1970s reform involved the growth of a specific segment of Toronto's population during the later 1960s, young people of middle-class background gravitating toward alternative communities and styles of life to be found in the city – the bohemian, artistic, radical-political, and gay communities. It does seem arguable that the 1960s were in some way an intrinsically vital era for counter-cultural and avant-garde communities. But also – and perhaps as much to the point – the number of potential recruits to these communities rose sharply in this decade as a consequence of the postwar birth-bulge and rapidly rising levels of higher-educational attainment; as geographer Chris Hamnett

---

* Jacobs, Mumford, and Venturi are discussed in more detail in chapter 4.

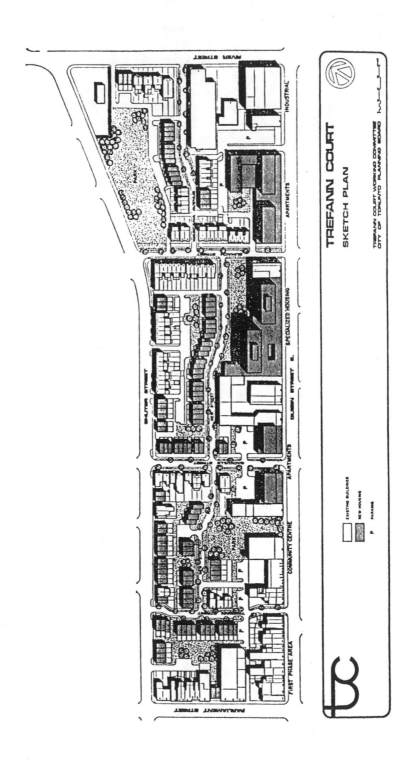

RIVER STREET

INDUSTRIAL

APARTMENTS

SPECIALIZED HOUSING

SHUTER STREET

QUEEN STREET E.

APARTMENTS

COMMUNITY CENTRE

FIRST PHASE AREA

PARLIAMENT STREET

TREFANN COURT

SKETCH PLAN

TREFANN COURT WORKING COMMITTEE
CITY OF TORONTO PLANNING BOARD

EXISTING BUILDINGS

NEW HOUSING

P   PARKING

A 1972 sketch of a planning proposal for Trefann Court (CTPB 1972c: Map 15). The residents of this small working-class district had blocked city hall's original plan to expropriate them and bulldoze their neighbourhood for a southerly extension of Regent Park's public housing (a plan which, like the Spadina Expressway, emerged as an emblematic issue of 1970s reformism; see Graham Fraser's *Fighting Back*). The 1972 proposal embodied principles directly reflecting the ideas of Jane Jacobs. Most of the older housing and commercial buildings are retained, sustaining a closely grained mix of land-use, and the neighbourhood remains tied into the city's grid street-system. Density is raised by infilling new houses consistent with the local fabric along a new street to be created through the midst of the district, while new higher-density housing is located on an arterial road at the district's edge. (Reproduced with permission of the City of Toronto Planning and Development Department.)

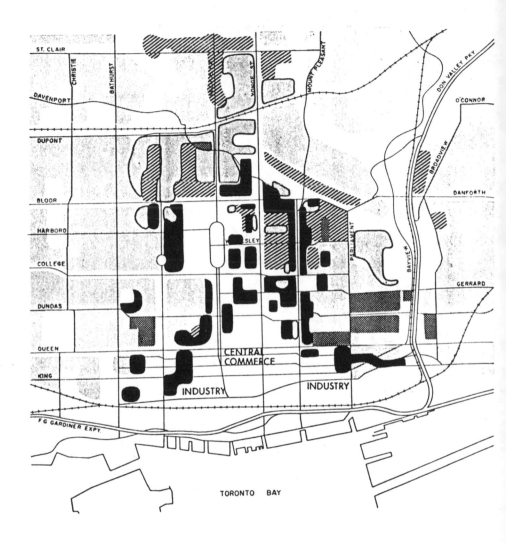

14

SUMMARY OF CHANGES
TO THE CENTRAL TORONTO
HOUSING STOCK

SOUTH-EAST SPADINA   PART II STUDY

0   3000   6000 FEET

CITY OF TORONTO PLANNING BOARD   MAY 1972

REMAINING STOCK OF HOUSES

AREAS OF EXTENSIVE TOWNHOUSING

PUBLIC HOUSING

HOUSES DEMOLISHED TO ACCOMMODATE
EXPANDING CORE USES (PARKING,
INSTITUTIONS, COMMERCIAL)

HOUSES REPLACED BY PRIVATE
HIGH DENSITY APARTMENTS

The 1972 preliminary planning report for the Southeast Spadina district illustrated shifting municipal attitudes toward inner-city neighbourhoods in Toronto. The report placed neighbourhood planning in the context of patterns of change in the 1950s and 1960s that had destroyed wide swathes of older downtown houses, a process of which the authors were explicitly critical and which they summarized in Map 14 (CTPB 1972b: 30). It identified inner-city areas where older housing had been erased for public-housing construction, commercial core uses, and high-rise development and also noted the onset of middle-class movement into downtown neighbourhoods, termed 'townhousing'; the word 'gentrification' was not yet in currency. (Reproduced with permission of the City of Toronto Planning and Development Department.)

trenchantly commented about the growing number of young educated middle-class people in inner cities in Britain, they were there in part because 'there are far more of them' (1984: 305).

A significant measure of the energy of left-populist reformism derived from this demographic group, especially those affiliated with left-of-centre political formations. But while the commitment these young people developed toward municipal reform was in part bred by ideology, it also arose from their immediate experiences. Like the working-class and immigrant inner-city communities in whose low-rent neighbourhoods they often settled, they frequently found themselves under the gun of growth-coalition development practices and forced to fight alongside their neighbours for their turf. The attitude toward city hall engendered by this process, coupled with their support for the cause of the city's less powerful communities and their willingness to serve as foot-soldiers of civic opposition, drew many of them deeply into municipal political activism, where they became a key element in the organizational foundation of left-populist reform.

• A final set of attitudes at the root of the reformist impulse arose among the increasing number of new, more affluent inner-city home-owners, people who by the late 1960s had begun moving into – and in some cases whitepainting – old downtown houses and who were rapidly swelling the ranks of the inner-city middle class. In a 1970 analysis of the prospects for Canadian municipal politics, N.H. Lithwick had argued that urban policies based solely on the priority of generating economic expansion might well engender a revolt among more well-to-do city-dwellers because such policies represented an 'increasing threat to the environment in which they typically work and play' (1970: 18). This prognosis was partly correct. More critically, by the early 1970s, a rising number of more affluent urbanites sought not only to work and play downtown but to *live* there as well, some in the midst of traditional working-class neighbourhoods, others in newly minted pockets of inner-city urbanity in districts like Donvale and Midtown.

The emergence of this group of city-dwellers is the central theme with which subsequent parts of this book are concerned. Here it is simply noted that they were a fourth cluster of actors involved in the defeat of old-style booster dominance and consequent revision of municipal policies toward old downtown neighbourhoods. As the example of the Donvale non-profit housing project illustrates – a case in which a neighbourhood's new middle class was sharply divided on the question of supporting an increased local stock of lower-income housing (Dineen 1974) – the political outlook among these newcomers was not monochromatic. While the more conservative branch of reform found substantial support among them, the left-populist grouping, too, had some roots here.

These four clusters of actors – traditional city-dwellers at each social stratum, the emerging generation of urban planners and professionals, young political and cultural activists, and the city's growing middle class – each contributed to the popular base of civic reformism and the formation of revised civic attitudes toward older inner-city neighbourhoods.

Influences on Cityscape Concurrent with 'Reformism'

Deindustrialization

The parallel reformist critiques of growth-boosterism and its version of modernism were only two of the forces that helped shape Toronto's inner-city fabric in the years following 1972. Other key influences on downtown landscape included deindustrialization, Toronto's growing importance as a headquarters of national and multinational corporate activity in Canada, and certain shifts in the city's demographic and subcultural make-up.

Deindustrialization in Toronto, well underway by the 1970s, occurred in the context of an urban economy in which industrial work was never the central historical feature. Although Toronto did not become the dominant Canadian metropolis until the 1930s, its traditional economic fabric had presaged its more recent function. The city's nineteenth-century economy was rooted in its roles as a commercial centre for colonial agricultural settlement, a seat of provincial government, and a banking headquarters (Nader 1975: 173–4, Careless 1984: 43–69). Manufacturing did increase rapidly during the second half of the century (Kealey 1982); in the thirty years following Confederation, Toronto's industrial workforce rose from 9,500 to 26,000 (Careless 1984: 200). But this was only one aspect of the city's dramatic growth in the period. The non-industrial sector – including corporate and financial activity, wholesale and retail trade, and business, personal, and state services – remained the larger component of the city's economic structure. Since 1900 the pattern has been similar. Even in its peak decades, just after the turn of the century and again in the 1940s, manufacturing absorbed only 35 per cent of Toronto's regional metropolitan employment (Lemon 1985: 197).

But, as the figures suggest, neither was manufacturing an unimportant part of the metropolitan economy, and these industrial firms and jobs were heavily concentrated in the heart of the urban region, within the City of Toronto. In 1951, when postwar deindustrialization commenced, manufacturing accounted for more than half the inner municipality's workforce, employing 156,152 workers in 3,809 firms. In the decade that followed, the number of jobs and firms fell by 25 per cent (to 117,383) and 27 per cent (to 2,765), and in the 1960s, the drop continued at rates of 29 per cent (to 82,764 jobs) and 26 per cent (to 2,031 firms) (CATF 1974: 267). Hence, the pattern of deindustrialization in the City of Toronto in the 1970s – a further 28 per cent decline in the industrial workforce (Muszynski 1985: 14) – echoed a process already twenty years old. It was not until the 1970s, however, that the massive reconstruction of former inner-city industrial and warehousing sites began. In downtown Toronto alone, more than a half-million square metres of industrial space were demolished for redevelopment between 1976 and 1986 (CTPDD 1986a: 98). This timing meant that the creation of a deindustrialized landscape became a process strongly influenced by reformist planning values.

The deindustrialization of traditional North American urban industrial locales is a complex phenomenon. At one level, it has involved simply the dispersal of manufacturing to other locations within an urban region. In Metropolitan Toronto in the 1950s and 1960s, for example, industrial activity within the city and the relative importance of manufacturing in the regional economy as a whole were both declining while, at the same time, the number of industrial jobs in suburban and exurban municipalities was quickly rising; between 1951 and 1971, the ratio of metropolitan area industrial jobs located within the City of Toronto dropped from 78 per cent to 25 per cent (CATF 1974: 276, Lemon 1985: 197). An important force that encouraged this pattern was the emerging dominance of the truck as a mode of transport of goods and of the car for personal movement, diminishing the requirement for propinquity among manufacturing plants, blue-collar workforces, and fixed transportation facilities like railyards, harboursides, and streetcar lines. The new forms of movement opened cheap, formerly inaccessible out-of-city locales for manufacturing activity. In the case of the core of a burgeoning white-collar metropolis like Toronto, this pattern was also encouraged by the push-factor of rising inner-city commercial property values that rendered industrial use increasingly uneconomic and further enhanced the attraction of suburban and exurban location.

A second, more critical connotation of Canadian deindustrialization has been 'offshore' movement of manufacturing activity to the United States, to highly competitive industrial economies like Japan, and to cheap Third World labour-markets, a process intimately tied up with the increasing mobility of multinational capital and the emergence of a global economy. Still a third aspect of deindustrialization – one that relates to diminishing manufacturing workforces rather than a reduction or relocation of manufacturing activity – has been a decline in the absolute number of employees required to make a given product as a consequence of automation and robotization.

The effects of deindustrialization on urban form in inner-city Toronto have been dramatic, particularly along the lakeshore and its parallel system of rail lines, where a century-old manufacturing and warehousing zone has steadily eroded and, by the year 2000, is likely to have all but vanished.

One example of Toronto's deindustrialized landscape is immediately southeast of the central business district, an entirely new neighbourhood named St Lawrence, which is composed of private- and public-sector cooperative and non-profit mixed-income housing. Built largely on disused industrial and warehousing land, St Lawrence became the centrepiece of the activities of city hall's new Housing Department, an agency created following the 1972 reformist election victory in response to left-populist concerns about the decline of the city's lower-cost housing stock and the shortcomings of public housing blocks like Regent Park. The planning of St Lawrence directly reflected specifics of the left-populists' ideas for the development of new affordable housing and for less ghettoized and bureaucratized forms of social housing.

The neighbourhood resembles Regent Park in its scale, covering several square blocks and housing twelve thousand residents at relatively high densities; and like Regent Park, its form follows modernist conventions of functionalist, largely standardized design and mainly segregated land-use. But here the similarities end. St Lawrence's mix of incomes and of tenure types, the tenant-management of its co-ops, and its overall quality of construction and integration into the city's grid street-system wholly distinguish it from public-housing projects of the 1950s and 1960s. It approximates the kind of modernist urban utopia first envisioned by the Bauhaus more closely

St Lawrence. Built largely on disused industrial and warehousing land, it approximates the kind of urban utopia envisioned by the Bauhaus more closely that any other postwar Toronto housing development.

than any other postwar Toronto housing development. Besides left-populist housing objectives, St Lawrence also fulfilled a central planning goal of reform's 'urban conservative' grouping, drawing thousands of new residents into the core to help diversify the area away from monofunctional commercial specialization. And because the site's prior use was non-residential, no old neighbourhoods were wrecked or residents displaced. Recently, the city mooted a major eastward expansion of St Lawrence – named Ataratiri and currently obstructed by the prohibitive cost of environmental clean-up amid a recessionary public economy – to be developed according to many of the same principles; if and when it is eventually built, the area will house another twelve thousand people mostly on abandoned industrial land (CTHD 1988).

Southwest of St Lawrence, immediately beside the lakeshore, is a second new neighbourhood built in a deindustrialized zone, one of a very different kind than St Lawrence: a two-kilometre ribbon of high-density waterfront development that, apart from a cluster of commercial uses adjacent to the central business district at the east end of the site, and a small enclave of non-profit housing co-ops at the area's westernmost edge, is largely composed of up-market high-rise condominiums. Much of the district was built under the sponsorship of a federal corporation named Harbourfront, which purchased the land, formerly occupied mainly by port and industrial facilities, and granted building contracts to private-sector developers. Construction has been governed by zoning ground rules prescribed by the city under the rubric of reuniting Toronto with its lost waterfront (Desfor, Goldrick, and Merrens 1988).

The area has an odd sort of mixed use. Harbourfront includes an antique mart, a crafts centre, spaces for music performances and literary readings, some pubs and restaurants – uses supported partly from revenues generated by the area's residential development and partly from the patronage of affluent shoppers and audiences (who include a large number of tourists). There is, though, a curious shortage of workaday retail uses; for example, there is no supermarket to serve a residential district of several thousand households. Some of the buildings are not new but are converted harbour facilities that exemplify the ironies of deindustrialization. A large dockside warehouse, for example, has been renovated as a venue for luxury professional suites and condominium apartments, exclusive leisure-wear and craft boutiques, and performances by avant-garde dance troupes. Nearby is a building that has experienced a similar metamorphosis: a bulky brick structure that once housed a hydroelectric generator, now renovated as exhibition space for hyper-contemporary art.

The case of Harbourfront illustrates the values associated with the two groupings that made up reformism and the kinds of collisions that occurred between them. Supported mainly by a coalition of old-guard councillors, who endorsed big new developments of nearly any form, and 'urban conversative' reformists who espoused the goals of core-area residential development and linking downtown to the waterfront, it embodies the central principle of boosterism: state sponsorship of private-sector property development. It was opposed, on the other side, by reform's left-populist caucus on the grounds that the project included too little affordable housing. Later, when it was well underway, it attracted the hostility of some of its earlier 'urban conservative' supporters who realized too late that the slablike apartment towers in the style of St Jamestown rising along the project's main boulevard were not quite what they had imagined for the site. In response to their concerns, various government agencies have re-

Harbourfront, Terminal Warehouse. A large dockside warehouse has been renovated as a venue for luxury professional suites and condominium apartments, exclusive leisure-wear and craft boutiques, and performances by avant-garde dance troupes.

cently been reviewing the course of future development for the district.

A third illustration of the reconstruction of disused industrial sites is a kilometre northwest of Harbourfront. Here, Massey-Ferguson (formerly Massey-Harris), a major manufacturer of farm machinery and for several decades Toronto's largest single industrial firm, employing thousands of workers, closed its doors in the mid-1980s (Careless 1984: 112, Lemon 1985: 184). Part of the site has since been redeveloped as a kind of ready-made whitepainted neighbourhood with blocks of brand-new up-market row-houses built to resemble traditional Toronto houses. The remainder of the district is under construction as a fourteen-square-block high-density commercial park, whose major tenants include the Canadian Imperial Bank of Commerce and Bell Canada, firms representative of Toronto's emergent economy of corporate and financial activity dependent on a high-tech

Harbourfront high-rises. Harbourfront attracted the hostility of some earlier supporters who realized too late that the slab-like apartment towers in the style of St Jamestown rising along the project's main boulevard were not quite what they had imagined for the site.

communications infrastructure. The only remnant of the site's former occupant will be one or two modest buildings – Massey-Harris's original 1883 headquarters – preserved as historical relics.

Redevelopment of former inner-city industrial sites also occurs piecemeal at other scattered locations – new commercial complexes near Chinatown replacing garment-district loft-buildings, small private and public-sector housing projects on the sites of abandoned industrial uses along the city's railway rights-of-way, conversion of former light-manufacturing buildings near downtown as retail/ wholesale trade and exhibition space, renovation of smaller factory buildings across the city as studio space for film companies, commercial artists, photographers, painters, and craftworkers. Overall, these patterns have meant significant shifts of function and meaning for a number of old districts throughout the city.

The Growth of the Corporate Economy

Concurrent with deindustrialization has been Toronto's growing importance as the capital of corporate and financial activity in Canada. Again, a battery of statistics is available to illustrate the pattern. By 1983 the head-offices of more than two hundred of the top five hundred Canadian companies and of many major foreign-owned corporations active in Canada were housed in Toronto, and by 1985, 42 per cent of Metropolitan Toronto's workforce was employed in offices, while the white-collar and service sectors as a whole accounted for almost three-quarters of all employment (MTPD 1986: 42, 60). From 1963 to 1980 the value of shares traded on Toronto's stock exchange rose from $2.1 billion to more than $29 billion and, by 1990, had risen to $83.5 billion (Lemon 1985: 198, G&M 1990). During the pre-reformist decade of 1963 to 1973, the amount of office space in downtown Toronto had doubled from 1.3 million to more than 2.6 million square metres, and under the aegis of a new 1976 downtown plan passed by a coalition of 'urban conservative' reformists and old-guard boosters, the volume of office development continued at even more rapid rates, reaching more than 5.6 million square metres by 1990, with another 0.9 million square metres under construction (CATF 1974: 264, Frisken 1988: 66, CTLUC 1990).

Overall, the nature and the scale of shifts in Toronto's economic structure suggest that revision is required in Gilbert Stelter's typology of the phases of Canadian city-building (Stelter 1982). The descriptive and theoretical complexity of Stelter's model makes it a highly useful

Houses on the Massey-Ferguson site. Part of the site has been redeveloped as a kind of ready-made whitepainted neighbourhood with blocks of brand-new up-market row-houses built to resemble traditional Toronto houses.

tool for grasping the essence of Canada's urban history in a range of contexts. But because its final phase is the industrial city – following the earlier phases of the mercantile city and commercial city – it stops short of capturing processes of change lately evident in a city like Toronto, where a fourth phase seems under way.* Urban economies of the new type are often characterized as 'postindustrial,' but this term may seem to connote a kind of evolutionary, ahistorical dynamic; instead, the terms 'deindustrialized' or 'corporate' seem more accurate, the former implying the willed activity of human agents in the

---

* Stelter's typology is discussed in more detail in chapter 4.

process and the latter specifying the dominance of a particular set of actors.*

Rapid growth of Toronto's corporate-service economy has had at least three major effects on inner-city landscape and development. The most obvious has already been identified: massive and continuing construction of office space in the inner core. A good vantage point for viewing this process is from a distance, from an Island ferry crossing the city's harbour. Buildings that dominated the skyline a generation ago – the old Bank of Commerce, the Royal York Hotel – have dropped out of sight amid a mass of modernist office development. (Meanwhile, the city's first cluster of office towers, built shortly after the turn of the century and memorialized in Toronto artist Robert Gagen's 1914 painting *Temples of Commerce*, still remains but is almost entirely hidden.) For a short while in the late 1960s, a 56-storey tower built for the Toronto Dominion Bank was the tallest of the new breed, soon displaced by a 57-storey tower built in 1972 for the Bank of Commerce, quickly surpassed by a 72-storey tower built in 1976 for the Bank of Montreal, which did not quite lose its pre-eminence to a 69-storey tower completed in 1989 for Bank of Nova Scotia. Surrounding the bank towers – that occupy the four adjacent corners at King and Bay streets – are other new towers named for insurance companies, trust companies, and major multinational corporations, buildings that house not only the swelling ranks of company executives and financial managers who guide their firms' fortunes but also a growing army of lawyers, accountants, brokers, consultants, and other professional specialists whose services are required by the massive metropolitan machine.

A second landscape effect of Toronto's new economy has been contingent on this growth of the city's affluent white-collar workforce. The new mandarins of the corporate economy comprised an ever-increasing market for high-end goods, services, and residential accommodations. An indicator of the tastes and resources of this stratum during the fat years of the 1980s was an annual Christmas advertising supplement that began to appear in the newspaper favoured by the corporate elite, the *Globe and Mail*. Named *The Best of Toronto*, it featured such gift selections as $700 ostrich-skin women's shoes, a $9,000 floor-model globe, a $20,000 mahogany china cabinet, and an $80,000 sapphire and diamond necklace. Other indicators included

---

* The writer is indebted to Alan Smart for this observation.

some of the cars that began to be seen in the city's downtown streets and parking lots – BMW's, Mercedes Benzs, and Cadillacs became commonplace in inner Toronto by the 1980s (Oziewicz et al. 1986) – and the growth of the fashionable restaurant trade; the city became a seller's market for establishments satisfying the patronage of diners who sought black truffles, Beluga caviar, boldly *au courant* menus, and $200 bottles of fine Bordeaux (Oziewicz et al. 1986, Carss 1989).

In terms of landscape, the growth of Toronto's corporate gentry meant a proliferation through downtown of these kinds of restaurants and of high-priced shops and specialty boutiques whose exclusive merchandise and impeccably furnished interiors affirmed (*à la* Thorstein Veblen) the taste and discrimination of their customers and clients. One-by-one they were unexceptional places. Toronto had always had its patrician class that sustained a privileged circuit of clothiers and haberdashers, furniture and antique stores, specialty shops and restaurants, decorated according to current moneyed style. But what became noteworthy in the 1980s was their frequency. In sum, they created a pervasive downtown atmosphere of conspicuous wealth and consumption, a landscape of luxury and desire recalling Guy Debord's terse definition of 'spectacle': 'capital to such a degree of accumulation that it becomes an image' (1983: 34). By 1990, according to a study by an international research firm that measured the price of everyday consumer goods and services exclusive of housing cost, Toronto had become the most expensive city in which to live in the Western Hemisphere, surpassing centres like New York (ranked second) and Los Angeles (ranked fifth) (Zarocostas 1990, Duffy 1990).

Spectacle also became evident in the residential landscape created for those members of the corporate and professional elite who elected to live in the inner city. A typical advertisement for a new downtown condominium tower featured a panoramic view of the city's skyline at dusk through the glass wall of a graciously appointed upper-storey salon; an accompanying text described 'an unsurpassed quality of feature and finish,' 'harmoniously proportioned interiors,' and 'wintergarden dens offering cozy windowed retreats.' Elsewhere, streetscapes of newly built or carefully restored vintage townhouses fabricated an appearance of bourgeois domestic tradition (and erased a century of industrial urban reality), homes whose inhabitants comprised a growing market for such goods and services as fine antique furniture, designer wallpaper, customized kitchen cabinetry, and state-of-the-art bathroom fixtures.

Another effect of Toronto's emergent corporate economy on inner-city landscape is less immediately visible and has been more complex: the impact of incipient 'world-class' metropolitan status on local property markets. Toronto's residential and commercial real estate values have risen geometrically in recent decades. An unremarkable old downtown house in an unremarkable neighbourhood, valued at about $15,000 in the 1950s, might have cost $25,000 by the mid-1960s, $50,000 after the city's mid-1970s real estate boom, $100,000 following a second boom in the early 1980s, and $250,000 after still another boom in the late 1980s. Homes in more exclusive locations like Rosedale or more stylish locations like Donvale inflated at even quicker rates, and similar patterns of rapidly escalating values also characterized the office and retail property market.

In part, this appreciation directly reflected increasing demand for metropolitan location – demand for residential or commercial placement within the city's bustling economy and urban lifeworld, but this was only part of the explanation. Another kind of dynamic was at work too, described by a Toronto banking executive as a pattern in which property prices outstripped what might have been anticipated solely on the basis of local incomes and local demand; some support for this view is provided by the relative rates of growth between 1980 and 1987 of Toronto's average gross income – 52 per cent – and average house price: 116 per cent (Salter 1988: 46). What occurred was that the cost of Toronto real estate also became a function of its value as a commodity in the abstract matrix of the multinational world economy. 'One consequence of ... "world-class" status is that it tends to fundamentally change some asset values and the long-term relationship of such values to incomes. Instead of being closely related to incomes, the price of scarce resources, such as prime real estate, will more and more be a function of wealth, foreign as well as domestic' (Gestrin 1990). That is, Toronto property costs came to reflect not only demand for metropolitan placement by potential residential or commercial users but also demand for secure placement by 'world-class' investment capital; as a consequence, prices became 'much more geared to accumulated assets, wealth and savings than to ... what people can afford' (Gestrin 1990).

One effect of this dynamic was a kind of feedback loop through which individual households' fundamental attitudes toward property ownership shifted. 'A generation ago when you sold a house, you didn't necessarily get much more than you'd paid for it; you were satisfied simply that it had retained its value ... Today, the reverse is true. Every upward spiral causes a stampede of buyers desperate to get into real estate before prices move out of reach,' a context in which owning a house became 'the investment of choice for most of the middle class' (Salter 1988: 43, 45). A by-product of this pattern in periods of sudden, competitive demand – for example, during the frenetic price-spirals of the mid-1970s and early and late 1980s – is a speculative practice termed 'flipping': movement into the market of small investors who turn houses over in a matter of weeks, grabbing up windfall profits provided by frightened middle-class buyers anxious to purchase a house while they still can, and further overheating the speculative engine (Welch and Ellmen 1988).

A second effect has been a process of intensification of land-use. By the late 1980s a pattern of reconversion had begun to become evident across the downtown. Turn-of-the-century houses of a type originally built for middle-class family occupancy, which were then converted for multi-household working-class and immigrant occupancy during the economic circumstances of the Depression, Second World War, and early postwar years, were often de-converted back to single-household occupancy when middle-class resettlement of the inner city began to spread during the 1960s. By the late 1980s, however, as the cost of most houses rose beyond middle-class affordability, there was an increasing trend in many inner-city neighbourhoods toward reconversion back to multi-unit use, now for non-family middle-class households.

A third effect of the disconnection of property values from incomes has been a rising incidence of homelessness, a process with its own peculiar landscape effects: the occurrence in the city's alleys, parks, and ravines of temporary living quarters fabricated from corrugated boxes, plastic sheeting, and other makeshift materials, and an increasing appearance of flop-hostels and soup kitchens along inner-city streetscapes. The cheap rooming-houses and rundown walk-up apartments, upon which many of today's urban homeless formerly relied for accommodation, have all but disappeared from inner Toronto.

Inner-City Demographic Shifts

A third main influence on Toronto's downtown landscape during the 1970s and 1980s arose from a series of specific shifts in inner-city demographic and subcultural make-up. Three groups, in particular, were most conspicuous; although they were relatively small communities in the larger metropolitan framework, each exerted an important impact on the forms, functions, and meanings of particular inner-city neighbourhoods.

One was the Chinese community. Following the deracialization of Canadian immigration policy in 1967, Toronto's ethnic Chinese population increased dramatically, mushrooming in the next decade from about eight thousand to nearly seventy thousand, growth that continued apace through the 1980s (Thompson 1979: 310, SPCMT 1984: 54). Many of the metropolitan area's new Chinese did not settle in the inner city. Part of a suburban district named Agincourt, for example (sometimes known colloquially as 'Asiancourt'), has become a kind of suburban Chinatown, populated especially by middle-class immigrants from Hong Kong retreating from the prospect of imminent unification of their homeland with China; the area's local shopping plazas are intense nodes of Chinese commercial activity. But many other Chinese continued to settle or open businesses in traditional immigrant-receptor areas downtown, particularly in the city's main Chinatown in Southeast Spadina, immediately west of the core, and in a corner of the Riverdale district east of downtown.

The main streets of Southeast Spadina are crowded with scores of Chinese shops and restaurants, few of which existed as recently as 1970, that comprise an area of remarkable commercial and cultural vigour patronized by Chinese from across the metropolitan area. The products available are diverse – Chinese groceries, books and videotapes, gifts and novelties, spices and herbal remedies – and the density of shoppers during the district's peak business hours makes it nearly impossible to move along the sidewalks.

One institution located here is the Mandarin Club, a focus of Chinese elite social activity where lawyers, businessmen, bankers, and developers gather for midday lunch and to make useful connections. The club occupies the top storey of a Chinese shopping mall built a few years ago on the former site of a Hungarian Catholic church, a use rendered obsolete by the decline of the local Hungarian community after construction of Alexandra Park. Nearby residential streets also became dominantly Chinese, populated mainly by working-class immigrants who, in the environment of their neighbourhood, were able to carry out everyday life entirely in their own language. The concentration of Chinese retail and residential activity in South Riverdale is much smaller but equally intense. In each case, Chinese immigrants took control of a downtown district and its foreseeable

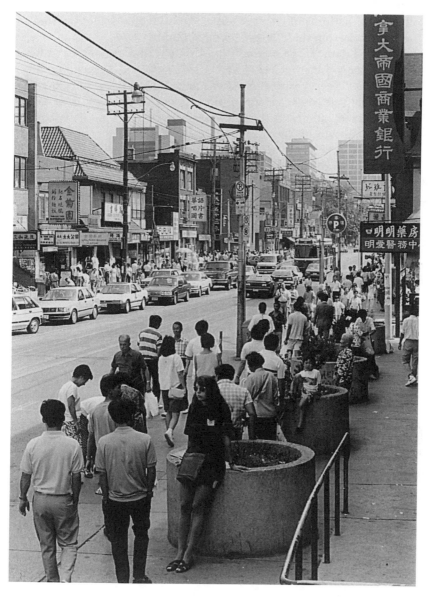

Dundas Street, Chinatown. The main streets of Southeast Spadina are crowded with scores of Chinese shops and restaurants, few of which existed as recently as 1970.

future, and patterns of change that certainly would have occurred in their absence were indefinitely forestalled.*

A second demographic group that influenced a segment of downtown landscape in the 1970s and 1980s was the gay community. Unlike the Chinese, exact figures are unavailable about the extent of homosexual settlement in Toronto; but like the Chinese, their numbers increased rapidly in the later postwar period – partly a consequence of growth of the young, educated demographic cohort from which they were mainly drawn, partly a result of increasing gay migration to Toronto from across Ontario and Canada, and partly a consequence of growing gay consciousness and legal freedom in recent decades. Concentrated in the high-rise apartments and old houses of a neighbourhood centring around Church Street, directly northeast of the central business district, the gay community has created the same kind of liberated space for itself in Toronto that Castells describes in his account of gay settlement in San Francisco – a locale for living and working, and for gay celebrations and gay politics (1983: 138–70).** As they were in San Francisco, gays making places for themselves in Toronto were among the earliest renovators of old downtown houses and came to dominate local residential and retail use in their neighbourhood. Also like the Chinese, many Toronto gays live outside the district but go there on leisure time, sustaining an intense node of bookshops, clothing stores, restaurants, bars and clubs, and other commercial and communal uses.

A third group that helped shape Toronto's inner-city landscape during the 1970s and 1980s were marginal young people associated with the arts and bohemian communities. In the 1960s, the city's bohemian village was centred in a neighbourhood just north of the core, Yorkville, but within a few years the district was overtaken – with city hall's encouragement – by posh commercial, hotel, and residential development. The bohemian community shifted south to Queen Street, below Chinatown and just west of the core, near the Ontario College of Art, and a cluster of small clubs, clothing shops, bookstores, and other uses dependent on the bohemian and arts communities took root here in the 1970s. An almost immediate conse-

---

* As chapter 1 noted, there has been a recent influx of Vietnamese commercial uses to Southeast Spadina, a process whose meaning for the district's future is not yet clear.

**Castells's analysis of San Francisco's gay community will figure importantly in chapter 5.

Church Street near Wellesley Street. Many of Toronto's gays live outside the district but go there on leisure time, sustaining an intense node of bookshops, clothing stores, restaurants, bars and clubs, and other commercial and communal uses.

quence was that the Queen Street West strip became fashionable. This, coupled with the overall inflation of downtown Toronto property values, meant that the district quickly lost its capacity to provide cheap space for marginal uses or to sustain entrepreneurial incubation; these functions began to shift farther west on Queen Street and elsewhere away from the heart of the core. But here, and in a number of other locales across downtown, streetscapes are dotted by stores, coffee shops, bars, and other uses created or patronized by the bohemian and arts communities. Their presence has had clear effects on local landscapes and processes of change in a number of inner-city neighbourhoods.

Conclusion

Part 1 has explored the social and spatial contexts in which recent patterns of middle-class resettlement of older working-class neigh-

Queen Street West. A cluster of small clubs and bars, clothing shops, bookstores, and other kinds of uses dependent on the bohemian and arts communities took root here in the 1970s. An almost immediate consequence was that the Queen Street West strip became fashionable.

bourhoods in downtown Toronto first emerged and, by the late 1970s, became a key aspect of inner-city change.

To be sure, Toronto's 'gentrification' has not been just a local phenomenon but, as chapters 4 and 5 will observe, parallels recent processes of change occurring in cities in a number of societal settings, particularly those whose urban geography in the industrial era was characterized by middle-class diaspora to suburban 'bourgeois utopias' (Fishman 1987) and whose local economies have lately experienced deindustrialization. Moreover (as will be seen in chapter 4), 'gentrification' has been only one element in a wider, apparently interrelated pattern of metropolitan spatial transition in which larger structural forces seem clearly at work.

But, as chapter 2 suggested, urban forms and spatial arrangements are not merely epiphenomena – unarticulated local expressions – of overarching structural determinants but are the creations of social agents situated in particular historical settings. While structural forces may exert clear positive or negative pressures on directions for social action (Williams 1977: 83–9), they are only one aspect of the dynamics of social change. An appreciation of patterns of urban transition in a given metropolitan milieu requires not only an understanding of larger forces that may influence a range of urban places but also a grasp of the local circumstances and local ways in which these patterns are played out by particular social actors. In other words, *structure* denotes only a cluster of necessary conditions (whose coherence cannot be assumed), while *society* denotes a cluster of human possibilities in which the sufficient conditions of social action remain to be uncovered.

Hence, the account of Toronto's recent processes of city-building given in part 1 is not simply a textured travelogue that places 'gentrification' in a setting whose local idiosyncracies are ultimately irrelevant to its occurrence. On the contrary – as subsequent chapters will illustrate – the events, politics, *dramatis personae*, and features of the particular neighbourhoods described are closely bound up in the unfolding and nature of the city's specific processes of change.

Part 2 now turns to a second dimension of the framework that will be established for approaching middle-class inner-city resettlement in Toronto by addressing wider issues of urban development and of social theory. This discussion will be rooted in the general perspective toward urban form framed in chapter 2, which seeks to integrate an understanding of the workings of structure and capital into an appreciation of willed social action arising in the context of the culture of everyday life.

Part Two

THEORY

4

Postmodern Urbanism and the Canadian Corporate City

This chapter focuses on two key aspects of the broader social framework in which Toronto's patterns of city-building since the 1960s have occurred, widely evident processes of metropolitan transition that must be reckoned into an account of 'gentrification' in any specific setting. The first is the advent of postmodernist urbanism, whose genesis and cultural and political meanings the chapter explores. Second, the chapter turns to the emerging residential geography of the corporate city.

Postmodernist Urbanism

Anti-Modernist City Form

In general terms, the direction taken in many parts of Toronto's inner-city landscape during the 1970s and 1980s may be described as anti-modernist or 'postmodernist,' a movement in urban planning and architecture that has entailed a shift away from the ideas of modernist city-building. In particular, postmodernist urbanism has rejected modernism's perception of the historical city as a problem to be solved by comprehensive restructuring according to (in Giedion's terms) a 'universal architecture' committed to a 'unified organization of life' (1967: xxxvi, 25). In contrast, among postmodernist planning's central principles has been a celebration of traditional urban form and social and cultural heterogeneity.

A simple example illustrating the root outlook of postmodernist urbanism are recent North American attitudes toward major-league baseball venues. In the early decades of the century, these were usually single-use facilities constructed in city downtowns or in the midst of built-up city neighbourhoods, and frequently they were named 'Park' or 'Field.' While their architecture was not widely diverse, neither were any two alike; and some were quite distinct in appearance. Because they were situated on the idiosyncratic templates of differently shaped city blocks or available building sites within an existing urban fabric, their dimensions were irregular and unique, a feature that gave games played at each field their own peculiar character. Boston's Fenway Park, for example, with its high left-field wall barely three hundred feet from home plate, contrasted with Washington, DC's, old Griffith Stadium, where the left-field bleachers were more than four hundred feet distant (Bess 1989). As well, the old parks were directly adjacent to streetfront commercial strips and residential neighbourhoods and functioned as one element in dense, closely grained clusters of mixed city land-use. This integration was reinforced by the fact that most fans travelled to the parks by transit or on foot.

By the 1960s, however, ballfield construction had become part and parcel of the process of modernist city-building. New stadiums were typically massive ovals of concrete, megaprojects designed for multipurpose use that could in no sense any longer be called 'parks.' Built to accommodate not only baseball diamonds but also football fields and a range of other functions, they were often placed at suburban locations amid acres of parking lot with immediate expressway access, spatially and functionally disconnected from surrounding patterns of land-use. Their shapes were characteristically symmetrical and identical, devoid of eccentricity; facilities built in Los Angeles (1962), Atlanta (1966), St Louis (1966), and Cincinnati (1970), for example, each had left- and right-field foul-line dimensions of precisely 330 feet. Soon afterward, functional and hermetic domed stadiums became common, facilities whose lighting and climate were matters of mechanical control and whose plastic grass required neither mowing nor watering, places where there was neither day nor night nor yearly seasons – icons of *technique*.

More recently, though, in the emerging culture of postmodernist urbanism, cities have begun to return to the old form of ballfield. The models now most frequently cited for park design are the Chicago Cubs' venerable Wrigley Field and Boston's Fenway, and municipalities planning to sponsor new facilities must often accommodate the vocal sentiments of a body of fans who want them constructed at downtown locations as single-use facilities according to old-fashioned styles of ballpark architecture – an attitude illustrated by the comments of baseball writer Bill James about domed stadiums: 'What is it that attracts people so to the idea of putting a roof over a park? Sometimes people become so problem-oriented, so focused on the worst part of a thing, that they fail to see that in shutting out the bad weather, they are also shutting out the good weather ... An odd psychological mechanism is at work here, the perception of weather as inherently negative, something to be avoided ... Why do [people] want to spend $100-million to play baseball in a warehouse?' (1984: 82). The exemplar of the new era is the Baltimore Orioles' Camden Yards, opened in 1992, a field designed solely as a baseball park and meant to echo the architecture and idiosyncrasy of stadiums of the 1910s and 1920s (Campbell 1990). It *looks* like a traditional park, and among its features is a renovated old warehouse just behind the right-field fence that is used as Oriole club headquarters; Camden Yards has been inserted into a built-up downtown site in which old forms have not been wholly erased (Goldberger 1989).*

In Toronto, postmodernist urbanism has been evident in the preservation and often renovation of older residential housing and neighbourhoods, commercial strips, and downtown office and institutional buildings. Lower Yonge Street, for example, once disparaged by the city's planners as a 'heterogeneous jumble,' is now a protected streetscape. Postmodernist urbanism has been evident, too, in the construction of new housing and retail facilities compatible with, rather than dissonant from, the city's historical fabric. Hence, on the former site of Massey-Ferguson's tractor factories, and in neighbourhoods like Donvale, Southeast Spadina, and the Annex, developers have built batches of brand-new houses that resemble old houses, replicas of Victorian or Edwardian design occupying sites that a decade or two earlier would have been used for high-rise complexes. Meanwhile, many social-housing projects developed since the 1970s – for example, the Hydro Block in Southeast Spadina and the Sherbourne-Dundas complex just east of the core – incorporate old houses on their sites instead of removing them and, hence, remain tied into the visual fabric of their surrounding neighbourhoods. Elsewhere, new

---

* Camden is the exemplar solely among major-league stadiums. The first of the new/old-style parks was, in fact, built not far from Toronto, Pilot Field in downtown Buffalo, constructed in the mid-1980s for use by a minor-league franchise.

Pilot Field, Buffalo. The first of the new/old-style parks was built not far from Toronto, Pilot Field in downtown Buffalo, constructed in the mid-1980s for use by a minor-league franchise. (Photograph courtesy of the Buffalo Bisons Baseball Club.)

The Yonge Street strip. Lower Yonge Street, once disparaged by the city's planners as a 'heterogeneous jumble,' is now a protected streetscape.

stores and commercial and institutional uses have often been built in a hodgepodge of styles consistent with nearby traditional forms. In the milieu of postmodernist urbanism, the Temple Building would remain, restored to its turn-of-the-century elegance.

Even in many recent landscapes largely inspired by modernist thinking, the influence of postmodern principles is often apparent. A major new office complex in the heart of Toronto's core, for example, has been designed to incorporate the façades of a row of (otherwise razed) nineteenth-century commercial buildings. The St Lawrence neighbourhood is integrated with, rather than insulated from, downtown's grid street-system. Harbourfront's high-rise condominiums are interspersed with renovated old dockside buildings. And Toronto's own new sports stadium, though modernist in spirit – a retractably domed, multi-purpose 'concrete whale' echoing parks of the 1960s (Goldberger 1989) – is located in the heart of downtown cheek-by-jowl with its neighbouring uses. With few adjacent parking facilities, it is meant to be reached by transit or on foot, and consistent with postmodernist planning canons, it incorporates a mix of functions, including a hotel, two restaurants, a dance-bar, and an up-market athletic club, intended to diversify its patterns of use.

The Hydro Block housing project. Many social-housing projects developed since the 1970s – like the Hydro Block in Southeast Spadina – incorporate old houses on their sites instead of removing them and thus remain tied into the fabric of their surrounding neighbourhoods.

In cities like Toronto, postmodernist urbanism has been both an intellectual and a popular movement. In the former context – as chapter 3 reported – a vigorous reaction against modernist thinking took hold during the 1960s among many of Toronto's planners and related professionals, who were influenced by such critics of modernist city-building as Jacobs (1961), Mumford (1963), and Venturi (1966). The intellectual basis of urban postmodernism was established by the attacks of these writers against what they viewed as the destructive consequences of modernism for city life and city form. Jacobs, for example, argued that modernist design eviscerated the spatial logic of historical urban fabric and stripped cities of an organic capacity for social vitality and economic regeneration. Mumford condemned modernism's treatment of the city according to the analogue of the machine, an outlook that he believed engendered a ruthless disregard for communal and humanizing qualities of traditional urban culture

BCE Place under construction. A new office complex in the heart of the core has been designed to incorporate the façades of a row of otherwise razed nineteenth-century commercial buildings.

and landscape. Venturi attacked modernism's compulsion for orderly and heroic cityscapes that erased old urban *quartiers* whose diverse architectural forms expressed distinct local patterns of everyday life.

Crucial for these writers was not simply an aesthetic preference for old buildings and old city places but also their ideas about the practical functions of these forms for urban life. Jacobs, for example, viewed old buildings not as obstacles impeding urban development, but as irreplaceable potential locales – 'economic incubators' – for new entrepreneurial activities; and she argued that the finely grained mix of uses characteristic of traditional urban places made them less likely to become crime-ridden environments than the monofunctional landscapes of modernist planning. For Mumford and Venturi, modernist form severed city-dwellers' everyday connections from who they had been, by destroying continuity with urban landscapes of the past, and

The Dome. Toronto's own new sports stadium, though modernist in spirit
– a retractably domed, multi-purpose 'concrete whale' echoing parks of the
1960s – is located in the heart of downtown cheek-by-jowl with its neighbouring uses and is meant to be reached by transit or on foot.

from who they were, by replacing local vernacular architectures with
a monolithic 'internationalist' architecture imposed from outside – a
process described by Linda Hutcheon as the 'destruction of the connection to the way human society had come to relate to space over
time' (1989: 12).

A fourth critic of urban modernism, Brent Brolin, has identified the
crux of anti-modernism as a popular movement: the widespread indifference or hostility to modernist form among the bulk of ordinary
city-dwellers (1976: 8). Views of this kind were clearly part of the
impulse toward 'reformism' in Toronto's local politics during the 1960s
and 1970s, attitudes felt among people who were mostly unfamiliar
with ideas of writers like Jacobs, Mumford, or Venturi but who did
know what they didn't like. Charles Jencks, often credited with coin-
ing the term 'postmodernism' in architecture (Relph 1987: 225), takes
a similar perspective, arguing that modernist urbanism embodied an

elitist architectural language that failed to 'speak' to most city-dwellers (1977: 6–8). Postmodernism too, writes Jencks, has an elitist aspect that addresses an intellectual and architectural cadre who are knowledgeable about the ideas of writers like Jacobs and Venturi and appreciate postmodernist design's theoretical roots and the interplay of vernacular and historical references that characterize its forms. But, he argues, because postmodernism is a double-voiced architectural language that also speaks in traditional dialects that address ordinary city-dwellers, it enjoys much more widespread general appeal than modernism.

Certainly, quite apart from its emergence as the new orthodoxy in urban planning, postmodernism has achieved considerable success as a popular commercial trend. New malls in Toronto's suburbs often feature colonial, Victorian, or art deco façades of a kind Relph terms 'imagineered' or 'quaintified' (1987: 129–30, 253–4). Designs resembling old houses are popular; one recently built professional and retail mall in Toronto's suburb of Scarborough is composed of a pastiche of replicated house-designs from several eras. Beyond the suburbs, meanwhile, old rural villages that formerly housed agrarian communities are retrofitted as up-market shopping enclaves, often mainly occupied by antique stores, craft galleries, and interior-design shops. Throughout the urban area, new restaurants are commonly designed in stylized forms – in the manner of an imagined Tex-Mex road-house or 1940s diner or old-fashioned malt shop, places that resemble movie-sets complete with such authentic props as neon beer signs, jukeboxes, and soda fountains. In this vein, a Toronto restaurant reviewer recently praised 'the nostalgically meticulous return to 50s authenticity' of a west-end brunch establishment (Ayanoglu 1989). A curious feature of this case is that, before its purchase and renovation by new owners, it had been an unadorned 1940s/50s-vintage neighbourhood luncheonette that featured a good bacon, egg, and hash browns breakfast special. Restored to '50s authenticity,' its morning menu includes eggs Benedict and strawberry crêpes. The most recent trends in Toronto supermarket design include aisles named for neighbourhood streets, imitation awnings above the packaged-goods shelves, and butcher, seafood, and delicatessen counters fashioned to look like the small city shops of a district like Kensington. This kind of fetishization of postmodernist styles yields landscapes and interiors that have a kind of Disneyesque quality, again recalling Baudrillard's serene celebration of simulations that 'bear no relation to any reality whatever': copies of non-existent originals (1983: 11).

Suburban Toronto, a new mall. New malls in Toronto's suburbs often feature colonial, Victorian, or art deco façades. Designs resembling old houses are popular.

Approaching Postmodernist Urbanism

The pivotal concerns in the collision of modernist and postmodernist urbanism are best approached in the framework of Fredric Jameson's summary of the bill of particulars levelled against modernism by its critics: 'the bankruptcy of the monumental,' 'the failure of [its] protopolitical or utopian program,' its 'elitism,' and its 'virtual destruction of the older city fabric' (1984a: 55). The second item, in particular, concerning modernist urbanism's 'protopolitical or utopian program,' raises a crucial aspect of the debate, about the nature and agenda of modernism as a belief-system.

A key issue here is whether modernist urbanism may really be judged a 'failure' (Brolin's word) given the circumstances in which its program was attempted. As was discussed in chapter 2, the appropriation of modernist form by capital and by state authorities committed to growth-boosterism excised or deformed the utopian impulse that originally underlay it. 'Here,' Jencks writes, 'we find a strange ... deflection of the modern architect's role as a social utopian, for we ... see that he has actually built for the reigning powers of an established, commercial society' (1977: 26). In other words, it may not have been modernist urbanism that failed us but we who failed it, by allowing its absorption into programs of city-building utterly hostile to its egalitarian objectives. In this context, it is sometimes argued

The fetishized village (Unionville). Beyond the suburbs, rural villages that formerly housed agrarian communities are retrofitted as up-market shopping enclaves.

that critics of modernism have misdirected their attack. Jurgen Habermas and David Harvey, for example, have defended the subtext of visionary humanism at the basis of modernist urbanism as consistent with the emancipatory spirit of Enlightenment reason and called for a renewal of this spirit in the context of a critique of the perverting influences of capital and the state (Jameson 1984a: 58–9, Boyer 1988: 51–2, Harvey 1989).

A second, more fundamental question concerns the underlying premise of modernist utopianism as a way of thinking. Here, the issue is whether *any* a priori model – any coherent vision for enlightened social reconstruction (such as Giedion's 'universal architecture' oriented to a 'unified organization of life') – is desirable in practice or feasible in theory. Many critics of modernism have ranged themselves against 'totalizing models of argumentation' that seek to 'determine what can be said, who has the right to speak, and what will be the logical development of thought' (Boyer 1988: 51). In this framework, modernist urbanism as a comprehensive vision is interpreted as a 'monologic' system that seeks to subordinate the city to the 'ultimate word' of a single 'unified accent' (Bakhtin 1984: 82, 293) – not only totalitarian thinking in the most literal sense of the word but also bad social theory, because it seeks to reduce the complexity of urban reality to the logic of a unitary syllogism. Arrayed by its critics against the ideological closure of such systemic models are values of the singularity of human experiences and plurality of human vantage points – irreducible individual and subcultural differences that compose a 'diversity of generative beginnings' (Boyer 1988: 51). Chantal Mouffe, for example, celebrates the heterogeneity of 'subject-positions' in contemporary social fabric, alterities that cannot be conflated within a model of social life rooted in the hidden premise that individuals, whoever and wherever they are, are homogeneous by nature and, for all practical purposes, interchangeable (1988). In the context of this critique, any recourse to metatext, even one that springs from assertedly enlightened motives, may be viewed as a form of repression of difference and of possibilities for encounter and combination – a way of thinking that presumes the end of history by foreclosing the future. Clearly, one central principle of postmodernist urbanism is to allow, or to consciously create, spaces *for* difference and possibility – spaces as ephemeral as baseball outfields yielding diverse kinds of strategy and play (from which the historical contingency of variable weather is not expunged by a roof) or as crucial as the traditional urban forms argued by Jacobs and Mumford to engender fundamental urban entrepreneurial and political possibilities.

A third issue concerns the specific content of modernist urbanism's utopian vision. For, while the particular utopia imagined by modernist writers like Giedion and Le Corbusier may arguably be rejected as a flawed vision grounded in an infatuation with elitist *technique* and an insensitivity to the social meanings of history, this position does not entail a rejection of urban utopianism itself – a belief in the possibility of achieving enlightened social consensus about the creation of benign urban forms. That is, the diverse subject-positions argued by postmodernist theory to compose contemporary social fabric are not necessarily isolated and ultimately irreconcilable 'discourses.' Rather, they may be capable of what Habermas has termed 'communicative action' (or 'communicative rationality') directed toward *phronesis*: pragmatic, communal reasoning about ethical and political concerns (Aronowitz 1988: 50, Habermas 1983: 8, Mouffe 1988: 36–8, Laclau 1988: 79). Mumford, for example, though he was among urban modernism's most vigorous critics, was no less a utopian than a modernist like Giedion. He believed that cities were, by their nature, utopian institutions – that city-dwellers come together 'not by instinct or [merely] for a common benefit ... but on the basis of reason' to create a more civilized society through processes of shared culture and politics (Gill 1990: 92). Precisely because he believed that modernism was catastrophic for this vision, Mumford attacked it.

Hence, while anti-modernist urbanism is not necessarily anti-utopian, its vision of the city differs from that of modernism in a fundamental way. Modernist urbanism's utopia is a 'voiceless object of ... deduction' (Bakhtin 1984: 83), an uncovered metaphysical truth to which metropolitan life shall henceforth conform. In contrast, postmodernist urbanism conceives of a multiplicity of diverse and reverberating lifeworlds, 'a plurality of fully valid voices' (Bakhtin 1984: 34), whose combination moves toward an *unknown* city. An appropriate metaphor for the latter vision is what Mikhail Bakhtin terms 'polyphony' (1984). This word implies not cacophony but multi-part harmony in which each individual and subcultural city voice seeks a dialogic position in an open-ended heterotext whose seeming disorder is actually a complex form of 'intricate and unique' order – the internal logic of the historical city celebrated by Jacobs (1961: 447). In this context, 'society [is] understood as a vast argumentative texture through which people construct their own reality' (Laclau 1988: 79), and the city itself is simply, yet profoundly, a practical arrangement reached through the subtle workings of true urbanity – an outcome that cannot be deduced from theorized first principles.

One argument of this book is that middle-class resettlement of older inner-city neighbourhoods in Toronto is at least partly rooted in the critical and sometimes utopian subtext of postmodernist urbanism – that among the seeds of 'gentrification' have been, first, resistance among a specific segment of city-dwellers to certain key aspects of the construction of contemporary urban space (particularly modernism and suburbanism as these have been refracted through the interests of capital and the state) and, second, an impulse toward a more humane and more urbane city. From this perspective, 'gentrification' reflects, in part, a rupture in dominant canons of urban meaning and a cluster of social practices, carried out in the context of everyday life, oriented toward reconstituting the meanings of old city neighbourhoods toward an alternative urban future.

To be sure, 'gentrified' housing has also become a highly commodified form as a consequence of its appropriation by the same forces that earlier absorbed such ideas as modernism's high-rise apartment building and suburbanism's residential subdivision. As well, 'gentrification' has illustrated the emergence of a deindustrialized urban economy and the irrelevance of working-class city-dwellers to this process. Irony and paradox, however, are the essence of urban forms. Hence, on the one hand, an appreciation of commodification, spectacle, and structural economic forces that shape urban landscapes are crucial to grasping the nature of 'postmodern' urban forms as they have evolved at large under the aegis of capital. But, on the other hand, middle-class resettlement of older inner-city neighbourhoods cannot be understood apart from a sociology of resistant social practice in the framework of everyday life.

Postmodernism and Urban Social Movements

Further, the book argues that the process of middle-class resettlement has constituted, in part, a critical social movement: a collective social action undertaken in 'resistance to tendencies [of dominant groupings and institutions] to colonize the lifeworld' or in opposition to 'existing forms of closure and repression' (Habermas 1981a: 35, Magnusson and Walker 1987: 29).* In specific reference to the process of city-building, critical social movements are 'collective actions consciously aimed at fundamentally modifying the city's role in society or redefining the historical meaning of "urban,"' or at sustaining a particular historical role of cities or meaning of 'urban' against unwelcomed forces of change (Castells 1983: 71). In other words, they are oriented to 'residual' or 'emergent' urban forms and meanings and in opposition to presently dominant perceptions and values (Williams 1977: 121–7). As chapter 5 will observe, making a link between 'gentrification' and the concept of the urban social movement is not a novel hypothesis. It is, however, one that has remained largely unexamined by writers who have proposed it.

The notion 'social movement' has a specific status in contemporary social theory, emerging as an effort to reconceptualize resistant social practice in response to a key perceived inadequacy of Marxian structuralism. In orthodox Marxian cosmology, meaningful critical social practice may occur solely within the frameworks of class and production. But 'the plurality of current social struggles,' Ernesto Laclau

---

* 'Lifeworld' denotes the relatively coherent and 'intersubjectively shared' reservoir of implicit and non-problematic socially formed understandings in whose context a given collectivity approaches its reality and activities (Habermas 1981b: 70, McCarthy 1981: xxiv).

has observed, 'emerging in a radically different and more complex world than could have been conceived in the nineteenth century, entails the necessity of breaking with the provincial myth of the "universal class"' (1988: 77–8). Social movements are conceived as critical social formations that may transcend class structures and interests.

Among the more persuasive contemporary cases of dominance and resistance cited by social-movement theorists to which the Marxian notion of class seems irrelevant are those of gender and race. In the context of the urban realm, meanwhile, Castells cites a series of historical and contemporary instances of apparent 'multi-class' movements – for example, the emergence of the San Francisco gay community mentioned in chapter 3 (1983: 138–70, 320).* In this connection, chapter 3 described left-populist 'reformism' in Toronto as an urban movement that also cut across class lines – illustrated, for example, by the effort of people of differing class positions to develop a mixed-income housing cooperative in the Donvale neighbourhood. It is the close link between many of the groups that composed the base of left-populist reformism in Toronto and the early phases of defence and retrenchment of older inner-city neighbourhoods that helps sustain the view that middle-class resettlement of these neighbourhoods may in part be conceived as a component of an urban social movement.

This perspective is directly at odds with the outlook of a theorist like David Harvey, who, as chapter 2 observed, views urban forms in the context of a determining economic structuralism; for example, it was noted that Harvey conceives suburbs as simply 'the creation of the capitalist mode of production.' Harvey takes a similar approach to postmodernist urbanism, characterizing it as 'nothing more than the cultural clothing' of the new economic order visible in cities like Toronto – deindustrializing metropolitan areas functioning in the framework of an emerging global economy of flexible accumulation (Harvey 1987: 279). Harvey's outlook echoes Jameson, who describes postmodernism as 'the cultural logic of late capitalism' (1984b). Hal Foster, meanwhile, characterizes postmodernist urbanism as, 'in part, a policy that would reconcile us ... to the chaos of contemporary urban development' in the context of 'the fragmentary nature of late-capitalist urban life' (1985: 127).

---

* As Lawrence Knoop argues, however, neither is class wholly irrelevant to contemporary gay urban politics (1987).

In this outlook, the demise of modernism's utopian metanarrative is seen to constitute the fragmentation of the Enlightenment effort to attain a universal language of emancipatory resistance into a Babel of local dialects, an eventuality said to be highly functional for capital's interest under conditions in which it has shifted away from the secure anchorage of specific forms in specific places toward increasingly mobile and abstract forms. Arguably, the fragmentation of oppositional practice is functional for dominant interests under any circumstances. But Harvey's view is that, in the latter decades of the twentieth century, this eventuality (as represented in postmodernist urbanism) reflects wider cultural and discursive patterns that are, in turn, rooted directly in the organization of capital.

Harvey's view of postmodernist urbanism and allied social movements is not entirely bleak. He does find here 'a progressive angle ... which emphasizes community and locality, place and regional resistances, ... respect for otherness and the like' (1989: 351), and he observes that 'the cultural theses of postmodernity are evidently open to radical interpretation in the cause of greater empowerment of the poor and underprivileged' (1987: 279–80). But, on balance, his view is that postmodernist urbanism ultimately functions as highly affirmative for, rather than in resistance to, currently dominant social groupings, a consequence of the fact that, in the framework of postmodernist social movements, 'it is hard to stop the slide into parochialism, myopia and self-referentiality' (1989: 351). In this respect, postmodernism ultimately represents a regressive step toward a nihilistic relativism that, 'by acknowledging the authenticity of other voices, immediately shuts them off from access to more universal sources of power by ghettoizing them within an opaque otherness' (Harvey 1989: 117).

A somewhat alternative view is that of Castells. Castells celebrates the concept of the social movement as a theoretical improvement on Marxian commonplace and documents various urban social movements as occasions of critical practice that 'have [had] major effects on cities and societies' (1983: 329). In the end, however, he finds such movements essentially 'reactive' because they are 'not agents of structural change' but only 'symptoms of resistance to social domination' (1983: 326, 329). For Castells, local urban movements of a kind that might be characterized as 'postmodernist' are directed at the wrong 'targets' precisely because they are oriented toward specific, more parochial circumstances rather than general, more strategic objectives – say, processes of 'economic production' or the workings of the technocratic central state (1983: 329). Such social movements 'do not relate directly to the relationships of production, but to [local] relationships of consumption, communication and power' (1983: 320).

In their failure to attack the 'right ... targets,' Castells writes, urban social movements are partly rooted in an apparent powerlessness felt by dominated groups in contemporary society (1983: 320). '[W]hen people find themselves unable to control the world, they simply shrink the world to the size of their community ... people go home ... [for] they appear to have no other choice' (1983: 329–31). Implicit in this view is the premise that, in any given political context, there are correct targets for resistance that can be theoretically apprehended in advance by reasoning social actors and that effective oppositional practice will be grounded in an orientation to these objectives. Hence, while this outlook does not remain tied to class as the only meaningful agent of social change, it continues to share with structuralism an a priori privileging of specific realms of resistance – in particular, the realm of production – as the only 'right' paths along which it is possible to 'transform history' (Castells 1983: 328). In this respect, it is essentially hostile to the 'postmodern' political thinking of such writers cited above as Mouffe and Laclau. Unlike Harvey, Castells does not perfunctorily dismiss postmodernist social movements. But he sees their ultimate value mainly in terms of their capacity for 'nurturing the embryos' of later movements that may be more effectively directed – a refuge that offers hope for the future of 'proactive' critical social action – and not necessarily in terms of their own particular values or objectives (Castells 1983: 331).

A quite different approach is taken by Warren Magnusson and Rob Walker, who reject the view that there are 'right targets' for critical practice that can be specified 'in advance' and for whom 'the very notion of a central issue for popular struggles should be suspect' (1988: 59, 66). In Magnusson and Walker's view – in contrast to those of Harvey and Castells – it is the very strength of many contemporary critical social formations that they are rooted in particular local circumstances; they arise as concrete practices in relation to specific dilemmas in a complex world where there are 'many realities, many truths, many revolutions' (1988: 59). Consistent with the notion of *phronesis*, and with Mumford's understanding of the workings of urbanity, these local movements oriented to 'struggles of specificity' are not ghettoized voices fated to remain unintelligible to one another but may become the roots of broader, empirically based movements of 'connection' oriented to drawing links among specific local concerns and to movements of 'imagination' oriented to reconstituting social life in new forms (1988: 61–3). Enlightenment reason has not been abandoned here but rather has been redirected away from seeking a fixed, monologic, and universalizing foundation for resistant social practice toward an 'open-ended horizon' that is dialogically approached through experience (Laclau 1988: 81). Thus, postmodernist critical practice does not necessarily entail a thoroughgoing rejection of modernism but rather emerges from the movement of modernism's vision along a contingent historical trajectory. Laclau characterizes recognition of this contingency and of the pragmatic and empirical nature of postmodernist critical practice as the dual components of a renewed emancipatory metanarrative specific to the contemporary age (1988: 81).

To conclude, a postmodernist urbanism consistent with the critiques of modernism of such writers as Jacobs, Mumford, and Venturi has been a crucial aspect of the social milieu of city-building in Toronto since the 1960s. The ideas of such theorists as Harvey, Castells, and Magnusson and Walker offer distinct approaches to understanding this phenomenon.

The chapter now turns to a second aspect of the contemporary context of city-building in Toronto, the emerging residential landscape of the corporate city.

The Social Geography of the Corporate City

Toronto has been in no sense unique in its general patterns of landscape transition in recent decades. Changes experienced both downtown and throughout the metropolitan region have also been evident in many other urban places; for example, a recent anthology has documented analogous processes of middle-class resettlement of older inner-city neighbourhoods in Canada, the United States, Britain, and Australia (Smith and Williams 1986a). Similarly, the fashionable residential and commercial renovation or redevelopment of formerly industrial and harbour space, typified by Toronto's Harbourfront and Massey-Ferguson projects, has occurred in a number of cities in North America and Europe.

In addition to gentrification and waterfront redevelopment, a third common element of recent metropolitan restructuring has entailed the increasing demographic and functional diversity of suburbs. The main components of the traditional middle-class suburb – low-density subdivisions settled by a relatively homogeneous population of nuclear families, retail and service functions contingent on this residential base, and scattered ribbons of highway-side commercial and industrial use – have been overtaken by increasing socio-economic, ethnic, and life-cycle heterogeneity, widespread construction of high-density housing forms, and the development of dense nodes of primary office and commercial use (illustrated by the new 'downtown' in Toronto's suburb of North York). Emergence of this landscape has led Robert Fishman to argue that the prototypical suburb as it evolved in anglophone culture since the early Industrial Revolution is becoming largely a historical relic, replaced by a polynucleated urban region centred around a form he terms the 'technoburb ... that is neither urban nor rural nor suburban in the traditional sense' (1987: 17, 182–207).*

A fourth feature of metropolitan restructuring is evident at the urban fringe, where deagriculturalization is occurring as a kind of exurban counterpoint to inner-city deindustrialization. Here, desired locales of settlement now include not only exclusive older suburbs or new tracts of 'executive homes' but also old town centres where affluent in-movement and local protectionism often displace former residents and main-street commercial activities in a manner paralleling inner-city 'gentrification': a 'gentrification' of once rural villages.

These aspects of metropolitan change are not unrelated. The popularity of waterfront condominiums seems partly linked to the increasing fashionability of inner-city living that 'gentrifiers' helped to establish, while the rhetoric of marketing both newly built downtown 'townhomes' and waterfront apartments constructed on former industrial sites seeks to appeal to the commercialized postmodernism of what advertising parlance often describes as 'the new urban lifestyle.' Likewise, there is a clear connection between middle-class resettlement of old downtown neighbourhoods and of exurban village centres, whose many similarities of residential and commercial renovation apparently reflect a parallel disposition among segments of the more affluent housing market toward traditional, rather than modernist or suburban, settlement forms. The sandblasting, hues of paint, antique accessories, and brass numbering of the elegant old houses refurbished by small-town resettlers closely resemble styles of whitepainting in fashionably restored areas of downtown, and in both settings value is placed on historically interesting structures. Older

---

* Joel Garreau terms this form the 'edge city' (1991).

houses in one village near Toronto, for example, are designated by local real estate entrepreneurs as 'century homes,' a signifier for architectural age that becomes a signifier for prestige (Spatafora 1988). Meanwhile, the rapidly rising incidence in suburbs of working-class, immigrant, and low-income households – often living in high-rise apartments or public-housing projects resembling St Jamestown or Regent Park – is partly a consequence of the rising cost of the inner-city residential locales formerly settled by less affluent city-dwellers but now priced beyond their means. The concurrent emergence of suburban corporate-office subcentres is partly linked to preservationist values toward old downtown districts and architecture that have helped encourage municipal planning policies of commercial deconcentration (CTPDD 1986a). In these and many other respects, the varied elements of current-day metropolitan restructuring are of a piece, interrelated facets of a coherent process.

However, while this pattern has occurred in a number of societal settings, it is not ubiquitous; not all cities in these settings have experienced similar degrees of spatial restructuring. Writers in Canada, Britain and the United States, for example, have reported a positive and apparently contingent relationship between urban economies based on corporate and white-collar service activity and degrees of inner-city 'gentrification' (Lipton 1980; Berry 1980; Ley 1985, 1986). Likewise, a proliferation of up-market core-area condominiums and of 'gentrified' exurban villages, as well as the emergence of major suburban office districts, are characteristic of cities with deindustrializing corporate economies. It is this apparent connection between an emergent form of metropolitan economy and specific local shifts in urban geography that leads to the observation made in chapter 3 that a fourth stage is required in Gilbert Stelter's typology of Canadian city-building.

The strength of Stelter's 'periodization' is that it draws together the essential features of Canadian urban history in the framework of a political economy of urban function and decision-making power (Stelter 1982). In this context, Stelter identifies three general phases: a mercantile era dating until the early 1800s during which Canadian urban places served as entrepôts and as administrative and military centres and were dominated by the imperial state and its local officials; a commercial era during the mid-nineteenth century in which cities served as regional trade and service centres for largely rural colonization and as sites of small-scale industry and were increasingly dominated by indigenous local commercial elites; and an industrial era originating in the later 1800s during which large-scale industry became the dominant force in urban economies and power centralized toward the head-offices of large industrial firms and toward the nation-state. Thus, as Stelter observes in a later text (1986: 6–10), the typology stops short of encompassing deindustrializing cities of the late twentieth century whose primary functions are corporate management and related financial and professional services in the framework of a global economy and whose processes of city-building are dominated by transnational corporations and highly integrated multinational property companies in a framework of diminishing importance of the nation-state.

In the context of this book, the key feature of Stelter's typology is the typical residential pattern of Canadian cities from period to period. In towns and cities of the mercantile and early commercial periods, for example (consistent with Sjoberg's general model of preindustrial cities [1955]), the core was the primary locale of more elite residence, while the less affluent classes either tended toward the outskirts or lived immediately alongside the upper classes as domestic workers, conscripted functionaries, apprentices, or the like; the early suburbs of Toronto and Halifax, for instance, were working-class and lower-income districts (Armstrong 1988: 31, Careless 1984: 89, Stelter 1982: 9–10). It was not until the industrial period, with rapid expansion of a factory economy centred mainly near city cores and the collateral rapid growth of an immigrant working class, that much of the burgeoning middle class shifted its residential base to streetcar-suburbs. In this context, the current-day resettlement of Canadian inner-city neighbourhoods by higher-status urbanites appears not as a new phenomenon but the reassertion of a traditional historical pattern. For example, the recent movement of many well-to-do Torontonians to waterfront locales has constituted a retrenchment of space that was once theirs, from which they retreated during the early industrial era (Goheen 1977: 86).

To be sure, it is the nature of typological thinking to oversimplify a complex reality. But a typology like Stelter's may also usefully identify key features of this reality. Here, its utility is to highlight historical patterns of residential settlement in Canadian cities, in whose context it is arguable that there is nothing especially remarkable or surprising about recent processes of middle-class reoccupation of the inner city. As David Ley has trenchantly observed:

With the revitalization process of the past decade, sections of the post-industrial inner city have begun a transformation from the home of the laboring classes toward a zone of privilege reminiscent of the innermost ring in Sjoberg's model of the preindustrial city. If present trends continue, the social geography of the nineteenth-century industrial city may even appear to urban scholars of the future as a temporary interlude to a more historically persistent pattern of higher-status segregation adjacent to the downtown core. (1984: 201)

It is in this context that the Introduction described recent processes of middle-class downtown resettlement as the re-'gentrification' of the inner city;* in viewing urban residential patterns in a longer-term historical framework, Ley alerts us to the ethnocentricity of such dominant earlier twentieth-century theories of urban spatial organization as those framed by human ecologists like Ernest Burgess (1925) and Homer Hoyt (1939), whose concentric-zone and sectoral models were relevant mainly in grasping the geography of a specific group of cities at a specific historical moment (namely, twentieth-century U.S. industrial metropolises like Chicago).

The deployment of Stelter's typology suggests that, in addition to the fact that Toronto's economy may be classed as corporate-deindustrialized, there is a second important parameter circumscribing the study of its patterns of residential settlement: it is a Canadian city. For, while there do appear to be structural factors at work in shaping the geographies of deindustrializing or corporate cities in whatever settings they occur – a correspondence that is surely not a matter of happenstance but reflects a common socio-spatial logic – there may also be important differences in the ways that this geography manifests itself in distinct societal frameworks. Specific economic, political, cultural, spatial, and demographic circumstances may be expected to yield differing processes and outcomes in different settings. A number of Canadian writers have argued that emergent residential patterns in Canadian inner cities must be treated in the context of the particular social setting in which they occur (Ley 1985: 29, Filion 1987: 228–9, Dantas 1988: 86, Rose 1989: 119–22). In particular, these writers are concerned to distinguish Canadian cities from

---

* It is arguable that the enduring occurrence of old city houses and traditional inner-city neighbourhoods in the work of Canadian cityscape painters during the industrial era may have clearly augured the advent of re-'gentrification' (Caulfield 1992a).

A Typology of Canadian City-Building (Based on Stelter 1982)

	Mercantile	Commercial	Industrial	Corporate
Urban function	entrepôts; administrative & military centres	regional trade & services; small-scale industry	large-scale man-ufacturing or extractive indus-tries	corporate man-agement; finan-cial & related services
Locus of power	imperial state	local commercial elites	company head-offices housed in major cities; nation-state	multinational corporations
Agent of city-building	imperial state; colonial elites	local commercial interests & property entre-preneurs; local government	industrial com-panies; small & large property firms; local & senior govern-ment	multinational development corporations; local & senior government; joint state/ corporate ven-tures
Settlement pattern	elites at centre; working class at centre and at outskirts		working class at centre & out-skirts; elites & middle class in exclusive inner-city enclaves & suburbs	elites & middle class at centre & in exclusive suburban & ex-urban enclaves; working class in suburbs & in-ner-city public housing

U.S. cities by identifying what may be distinct aspects of the Canadian metropolitan experience, and to avoid the pitfall of what Michael Goldberg and John Mercer have termed 'the myth of the North American city,' in which generalizations based in U.S. cases are uncritically applied to Canadian urbanism (1986).

As has already been noted in chapter 3, middle-class flight to the postwar suburb, for example, was less pronounced in Canada than in the United States, a difference partly rooted in contrasting middle-class perceptions of cities as locales for family life. Canadian cities have generally been viewed 'as more attractive places to raise children than most of their American counterparts' (Rose 1989: 119). Another factor has been the vigorous and widespread survival of working-class ethnic enclaves in Canadian inner cities, whose vitality has often attracted middle-class resettlers but whose stability has sometimes

Ichabod (Eric Freifeld, 1950, watercolour, 54.6 x 74.9 cm, Yaneff Gallery, Toronto). The enduring occurrence of old city houses in the work of Canadian cityscape painters during the industrial era may have augured the advent of re-gentrification.

deterred wholesale 'gentrification' – as in the case, for example, of Toronto's Chinatown. All these elements have created differing socio-spatial conditions of downtown restructuring than the devastated racial ghettos that dominate many U.S. urban cores. The utter abandonment of inner residential districts reported to have occurred in many U.S. cities (described in the case of New York, for example, by Peter Marcuse [1986]) – that, in an echo of the ethnocentrism of the human ecologists, is sometimes typologized by U.S. writers as the ultimate fate of downtown neighbourhoods (Smith and LeFaivre 1984: 49) – is virtually unknown in Canada.

In the realm of public policy, meanwhile, the early viability of metropolitan regional government in Canada – illustrated by Toronto's metropolitan federation, established in the early 1950s – has created differing political conditions for urban restructuring than the municipal fragmentation common in many U.S. urban areas. Metro's planning powers and infrastructural authority have permitted it, for

Backyard on Baldwin Street (Albert Jacques Franck, 1964, oil on canvas, 75.9 x 60.7 cm, permanent collection, Rodman Hall Arts Centre, National Exhibition Centre, St Catharines, Ontario)

instance, to legislate the creation of primary commercial subcentres in suburban locales and to frame a comprehensive attendant transit policy. As well, Canadian metropolitan authorities have by and large taken significantly more progressive approaches toward both public transit and social housing than most U.S. urban governments, further differences that have helped forge an alternative path toward metropolitan restructuring.

In respect to cultural circumstances, meanwhile, Neil Smith has argued that resettlement of the downtown 'urban frontier' in U.S. cities is linked in popular consciousness to the national myth of settlement of the wilderness frontier (1986), a proposition that is clearly inapplicable in the Canadian setting, where a myth of this kind has never been in general currency. Smith's view is buttressed by the fairly frequent use in U.S. accounts of 'gentrification' of the term 'urban pioneer' to refer to early middle-class in-movers to inner-city neighbourhoods (Holcomb and Beauregard 1981: 42, DiGiovanni and Paulson 1984). Further, the subtext of race that has deeply permeated U.S. urban culture as a consequence of near-majority or majority non-white settlement of most major U.S. cities (and, as well, of widespread racist attitudes) has not been a central feature of Canadian city life (Sancton 1983b: 229–305, Goldberg and Mercer 1986: 45–7).

To be sure, there are a number of common features of postmodernist city-building in Canadian and U.S. inner cities – 'gentrified' neighbourhoods, redeveloped waterfronts, the conservation and celebration of venerable and vernacular architectures. Clearly, corporate urbanism in Canada and in the United States has been shaped in part by a similar underlying logic. But the particular route toward change, the processes through which it occurs, and the meanings of specific aspects of urban transition for the social actors involved are not reducible to a single model. Conclusions of a case-study of urban restructuring in a Canadian or U.S. locale are not necessarily transferable across the border.

Finally, a third parameter that must be taken into account in studying residential settlement patterns in Toronto – in addition to the 'postindustrial' nature of its economy and its Canadian societal setting – is its British cultural heritage. As was noted in chapter 2, this factor is relevant in approaching popular attitudes toward cities and suburbs. Suburbanization as it has occurred in anglophone Canada and in the United States (an aspect of North American urbanism that does cross the border) evolved from a historically situated response to the dilemma of the industrial city that originated in Britain, specifically

London, described by Fishman as the 'birthplace' of the suburban 'bourgeois utopia' (1987: 18–38). This particular adaption to the emergence of industrial urbanism was not universal; in Paris, for example, Baron Haussmann solved the problem by banishing industry and its workers to the outskirts while maintaining downtown as bourgeois terrain (Clark 1984: 23–78, Fishman 1987: 107–16). An understanding of the historical roots and the nature of the anglophone suburb is important to grasping current-day residential patterns in a city like Toronto insofar as 'gentrification' may constitute a rejection of traditional suburbanism among a segment of contemporary middle-class city-dwellers – precisely the argument that will be made in subsequent chapters of this book.

Conclusion

Chapter 4 has explored the emergence of postmodernist urbanism and of the residential geography of the corporate city, broader processes in which middle-class resettlement of older inner-city neighbourhoods in any given setting must be placed. Chapter 5 now examines various interpretations and theories of 'gentrification' and seeks to develop a framework of understanding consistent with the general perspective of critical urban study, a task that was undertaken in preparation for the fieldwork reported in part 3.

5

Everyday Life, Inner-City Resettlement, and Critical Social Practice

The Riddle of Culture

Stage-Models and Marginal Gentrifiers

As a theoretical concept, 'gentrification' has been elusive. The term has generally been used to denote middle-class resettlement of older inner-city neighbourhoods formerly occupied by working-class or underclass communities. But participants in this process have been highly demographically diverse. In Toronto, they have differed along a number of axes:

Visibility and tenure. They have ranged from owner-occupiers of dilapidated old houses to tenants of developer-built batches of brand-new infill structures designed to resemble elegant old houses.

Occupation and income. They have ranged from marginally employed creative workers (artists, musicians, actors, writers) earning their main income in part-time service jobs (as bike couriers, temp. secretaries, restaurant waiters, and the like) to high-salaried professionals and corporate managers.

Political outlook. They have ranged from people committed to movements of the political left (unionism, feminism, ecologism, as well as radical municipal reformism) to individuals whose ideological outlook is vigorous free-market conservatism.

Cultural affiliation. They have ranged from members of institutionally semi-complete subcultures, like the gay or bohemian communities, to people whose everyday lives are wholly mainstream.

Household composition and lifestyle. They have ranged from cos-

mopolitan one- and two-person adult households to strongly familistic couples with children.

And there are no easy congruences among many of these variables:
gays may be lawyers or paper-hangers; professors may live in shabby
bungalows or up-market townhomes; feminists may or may not have
children. There is no 'typical' middle-class resettler in Toronto.

Most theorizations have concurred that *some* of these resettlers are
gentrifiers – those whose home renovations are highly visible (Jager
1986); or those who are directly tied to the white-collar corporate
economy (Hamnett 1984); or those who are said to participate in a
culture of conspicuous consumption (Ley 1980, 1985); or those whose
settlement patterns are linked to dramatic reversals of what Neil Smith
has termed the 'rent gap': a difference between existing and potential
property values that 'creates the opportunity for the revalorization of
... "underdeveloped" section(s) of urban space' by capital (Smith 1979,
1986: 24, 1987a: 165). In other cases, gentrifiers have been theorized
as individuals who share some distinct mix of these features. But
where theorists of gentrification have found a conundrum has been
in the case of middle-class inner-city resettlers who share *none* of
these traits. This dilemma has generally been resolved in one of two
ways: deploying a phase-model, or the 'chaotic concept' approach.

The first strategy labels nearly *all* middle-class inner-city resettlers
'gentrifiers' and subsumes differences among them in a stage-typol-
ogy of gentrification, an exercise with both neoclassical and structuralist versions.

Examples of the former are the approaches of H.B. Holcomb and
Robert Beauregard, who have counted among gentrifiers less affluent
gays as well as other individuals with 'unconventional life-styles'
(1981: 42–4), and of David Ley, who has included 'avant-garde artists'
and others 'non-conformist in their lifestyle and politics' (1985: 23,
123, 131–6). These groups are said to dominate in the first phase of
a three-part local cycle that is initiated by movement into a neighbourhood of economically or culturally marginal middle-class resettlers drawn by cheap space, local colour, and a tolerance or enthusiasm
for social difference; is then continued by more mainstream middle-
class in-movement oriented toward neighbourhood fashionability and
security of investment; and is concluded by a conjuncture of inflating
prices, still more affluent arrivals, and emerging neighbourhood elite
status. Each phase is accompanied by the increasing involvement of
real estate entrepreneurs, and demand-side consumer forces are viewed
as crucial to the process.

The principal structuralist stage-model has only two phases. Bohemians and artists, acting as a Trojan Horse for property interests and for municipal boosters who have paved their way, move into a debilitated neighbourhood. Then, as real estate values – influenced by avant-garde presence – quickly inflate, developers and affluent in-movers are fast to supplant their unwitting colonists. In this approach, demand-side forces are viewed as largely epiphenomenal. All that really matters are the workings of property capital and of the local state, which is reduced to capital's pliant branch-office (Zukin 1982a: 173–205, 1982b; Deutsche and Ryan 1984). Neil Smith, the most widely-known structuralist analyst of gentrification, has not framed a stage-theory himself but has cited Sharon Zukin's model and else-where implied an underlying framework of sequential phases (1986: 31–2, 1987a: 160).

The second strategy eschews stage-models, arguing that unquali-fied use of a single term – 'gentrifier' – to describe the diversity of old city neighbourhood resettlers creates a 'chaotic concept' that 'com-bines the unrelated' (Sayer 1982: 71). For Bruce London and John Palen, for example, use of 'gentrification' to describe activities of peo-ple who 'may be only marginally middle class [and] hardly ... "gentry"' smacks of abuse of language (1984: 7). For Damaris Rose and for Beauregard (writing five years following his collaboration with Holcomb in a different vein), gentrification involves different actors working in different ways for different reasons and producing dif-ferent results, so that we cannot really talk about 'the gentrification process' (Rose 1984: 57–8, Beauregard 1986: 40). Rose has coined the term 'marginal gentrifier' to denote those whom stage-models usually class as first-phase, individuals who are generally neither conspicuous whitepainters, affluent members of the corporate economy, nor spec-ulative investors in the 'rent gap.' Smith, meanwhile, seeking to retain a coherent structuralist concept of gentrification, has acknowledged Rose's point and argued that 'marginal gentrifiers' should be wholly 'decoupled' from gentrification's 'central defining characteristics' (Smith 1987a: 160).

Each of these strategies has strengths and weaknesses. The strength of stage-typologizing is its basic logic, sensing that in some important way the diverse elements of middle-class resettlement of older inner-city neighbourhoods hang together as a unified process. But in its particulars, because it seeks to describe specific patterns said to occur in specific neighbourhoods, stage-typologizing poses problems. In Toronto, for example, three gentrifying districts adjacent to downtown elude the three-stage model. The Annex never had phase one, York-ville skipped phase two, and Southeast Spadina has seemed for well more than a decade unable to shift to phase three. In each case, there are exculpating circumstances. As was observed in chapter 1, the Annex never really lost middle-class status in the first place, and Southeast Spadina has been entrenched by a stable, working-class Chinese community. Yorkville, meanwhile, is adjacent to one of the city's exclusive retail and commercial districts, centred along Bloor Street. But counting these and other cases, more Toronto neighbourhoods significantly vary from the model than conform. While, to be sure (as will be subsequently noted), there are often fundamental differences between earlier and later groups of middle-class in-movers, and while the three-phase typology is sometimes a useful heuristic device, it describes only a fraction of actual cases with any precision.

A fourth Toronto case, Donvale, did experience the three phases but is immediately adjacent to Regent Park – the city's largest public-housing project – where, according to Ley's stage-based model of Canadian gentrification, it simply should not be (1985: 97). A fifth Toronto variant of the process has occurred in areas like the residential section of the former Massey-Ferguson site that are 'gentrified' in a single phase as non-residential uses are replaced with complexes of newly built, old-fashioned, up-market townhousing. A similar lack of fit between typologized phases and what actually seems to occur in downtown neighbourhoods has been observed in the United States, where a study of the experience of gentrifying districts in six cities concluded that 'many of the trends ... observed in the revitalizing neighbourhoods do not correspond very closely to the descriptions of the process contained in the various stage models' (DeGiovanni 1983: 35).

The structuralist phase-model fares no better. In many Toronto neighbourhoods – among others, Donvale, Dufferin Grove, Southeast Spadina, Quebec-Gothic, and South St Jamestown – 'first-phase' gentrifiers fought on the side of existing communities, often successfully, against developers whose notion of 'highest, best use' was not chic renovation but wholesale demolition for high-rise construction. For the property industry, *this* was the most profitable reversal of the 'rent gap,' plans embraced wholeheartedly by municipal boosters. By encouraging civic policies of neighbourhood protection, early-phase gentrifiers did in several cases help to pave the way for later more affluent in-movers, but not at all as structuralist canons prescribe. Gentrification occurred *in spite of* property capital's expressed and real interest and contrary to city hall's first intentions.

Before turning to the strengths and weaknesses of the chaotic-concept approach, it is useful at this point to digress in order to explore more closely a central principle of the structuralist approach, Smith's rent-gap theory. The rent gap has been a focus of intense debate in scholarly literature concerning gentrification, and neighbourhoods of the type just described, where gentrification cut against the grain of both property capital interest and booster municipal planning, illustrate one of the most serious difficulties with the concept.

Smith's theory is rooted in the tenet that undervalued urban space will be inexorably colonized by property capital toward '"highest and best" use (or at least a "higher and better use"),' a dynamic that emerges as 'the product ... of the specific needs of capital' and one to which consumer forces, while 'not completely irrelevant,' are ephemeral in any way that seriously matters (Smith 1986: 23, 31; Smith and LeFaivre 1984: 53). Like Harvey's attitude toward suburbs, or the neoclassical 'economic ecology' from which Walter Firey demurred, Smith's outlook toward gentrification is rooted in a determinist perspective that reduces the construction of urban space solely to the logic of the economic sphere, a way of thinking reflected in the subtitle of his first article on the topic: 'a back to the city movement by capital not people' (1979).

Among Smith's critics, Hamnett has taken what is sometimes termed a 'production-of-gentrifiers' approach. He focuses on the increase in recent decades in the supply of potential middle-class resettlers of older inner-city neighbourhoods, a consequence, on the one hand, of postwar population shifts and, on the other, of the emergence of corporate urban economies; and he argues that 'gentrification is not an inevitable byproduct of the depreciation of capital in nineteenth-century, inner-city neighbourhoods ... [but] was and is contingent on underlying changes in employment and demographic structure' (1984: 313). Ley, meanwhile, on the basis of data derived from twenty-two Canadian cities, has concluded that 'evidence is entirely lacking for the rent gap thesis' and concurs with Hamnett that gentrification appears linked to the growth of 'postindustrial' urban economies (Ley 1985: 57, 1986: 529, 1987a: 465–8).

Two researchers working in Toronto, nevertheless, have argued that their data clearly support the rent-gap theory (Kary 1988, Sabourin 1988: 232). The difficulty with their studies, however, is that they are based solely on an inspection of house prices and the economics of housing renovation. Using only this data, rent-gap theory does appear vindicated; the rising cost of old inner-city homes supports an argument that their potential value was earlier unrealized, making them a magnet for property capital (assuming a strategy could be devised to exploit their 'real' value). But as Blair Badcock has illustrated in the case of Adelaide, 'gentrification represented the third-best response [to the rent gap] so far as property capital was concerned' (1989: 132).

In Adelaide – and in Toronto – property capital's preferred investment in 'devalorized' inner-city space was high-density commercial development, and its second preference was high-rise apartment or condominium construction (Badcock 1989: 133). Investments associated with gentrification – house renovation, townhouse construction, associated local commercial projects – only became a palatable alternative when other possibilities were foreclosed. This foreclosure occurred in Toronto as a consequence of the municipal reformist movement and subsequent legislation of neighbourhood protectionism, activity that can clearly not be reduced to promoting property capital's immediate best interest. It *may* be contended that certain aspects of the up-market renewal of older downtown neighbourhoods are somehow vaguely congruent with 'capital-in-general' 's interest in securing a particular form of inner-city social geography in the 'postindustrial' era, but this is an entirely different argument – one that imagines capital writing off possible fruits of the rent gap in order to achieve more subtle hegemonic objectives. In any case, the economics of gentrification itself do not offer especially strong evidence for a totalizing absorption of urban space by advanced property capital. The rent-gap theory appears more applicable to developments like Harbourfront's condominium towers or to the commercial section of the old Massey-Ferguson site than to the refurbishment of venerable inner-city neighbourhoods.

It is partly in this context that the model outlined in chapter 2 may offer a more satisfactory approach to the construction of urban landscapes than the economic determinism of either structuralism or neo-classical ecologism (ways of thinking Mark Gottdiener has characterized as the 'straightjacket' of contemporary urban theory [1985: 263–91]). In the model, the socio-economic infrastructure through which specific urban forms are produced – suburban subdivisions, modernist apartment complexes, 'gentrified' neighbourhoods, or any other – is only one of two basic elements at play in the shaping of urban space. To be sure, this infrastructure has, in the case of Toronto, been largely rooted in the logic of property capital, frequently in intimate conjunction with civic boosterism. But Smith and the structuralist writers appear to imagine that this is the only force that matters and pay little heed to the second element proposed in the model, the autonomous emergence of specific ideas about landscape forms in situated contexts of the culture of everyday life. It is insufficient to fudge the case, as Smith does, by qualifying 'highest and best use' with the vague parenthetical sobriquet 'or at least a "higher and better" use,' but then leaving the forces that may mitigate property capital's interest as an enigmatic black box. Harvey produces a similar mystery when he reduces these forces to epiphenomenal status by dismissing postmodernist urbanism as 'nothing more than the cultural clothing' of emergent urban economic structure, a matter apparently requiring no further serious inquiry once capital's interest has been asserted. An alternative view of gentrification, consistent with the model, that does not conceive gentrifiers as 'the mere bearers of a process determined independently of them' (Rose 1984: 56) but seeks to account for the questions left unexamined by structuralist analysis will be explored presently. First, however, the chapter will return to reviewing various theorizations of gentrification.

In the case of the chaotic-concept approach, its strength is the recognition that the notions 'gentrifier' and 'gentrification' as they are often used are not reducible to a common denominator. But this disaggregation of 'marginal' from mainstream gentrifiers is also the approach's weakness; it leaves only disconnected pieces. The root logic of stage-typologizing, that the varied elements of middle-class inner-city resettlement are somehow related, is lost.

The issue that arises from this critique of stage-models and of the chaotic-concept approach is whether, once distinct types of city resettlers and courses of resettlement are 'decoupled' from beneath the monologic rubrics 'gentrifier' and 'gentrification,' there is a right way in which these people and processes may be recoupled as elements of a pattern that is not chaotic but coherent. The solution here is not to try simply to frame a more flexible typology of neighbourhood phases. At best, this might offer a clearer sense of how varied groups of gentrifiers relate sequentially; it would not address the underlying social logic of the process. A more fruitful path is proposed by Smith, who, in the wake of several attacks on the determinist nature of rent-gap theory, suggested that the riddle of gentrification may turn partly on 'explaining ... why central and inner areas of the city, which for decades could not satisfy the demands of the middle class, now appear to do so handsomely' (1987a: 163–4). Smith was writing in a U.S. context, where, as has been observed, the scale of postwar middle-class abandonment of the central city was much more pronounced than it was in Canada, and hence this shift in popular taste may have been more conspicuous. Still, the question does also have relevance in Canada, where inner-city neighbourhoods, as locales that now embody what Ley has termed new 'canons of good taste' in Canadian urbanity (1985: 24), have clearly become more favoured by middle-class households in recent decades than they were, say, thirty years ago.

Although still couched in a structuralist framework, Smith's question appears to raise the issue of the culture of everyday urban life – to suggest that only by exploring the resettlement of old city neighbourhoods in cultural context can the relationship among different groups of resettlers, and hence the nature of what has been termed 'gentrification,' be more fully grasped. In this regard, it is a question that leads onto terrain that is not well mapped, a largely blank area in the literature that led Peter Williams to observe that 'the failure to comprehend the importance of culture ... represents a central weakness in the gentrification debate' (1986: 68). Many writers have acknowledged that, somehow or other, culture is a salient part of the middle-class inner-city resettlement process, but they have usually left its exact role – the role of philosophic or aesthetic values, or everyday desires, or structures of feeling about daily life – a puzzle.

One Vital Clue

Some writers, for example, have argued that the forms of gentrification are closely tied to contemporary processes of class-constitution; but they have then left unexamined the question of why this should be so. Smith, for instance, having made a structuralist distinction between the *fact* of gentrification (a 'systematic component of a larger economic and social restructuring of advanced capitalist economies') and its forms (which embody 'a search for diversity as long as it is highly ordered, and a glorification of the past as long as it is safely brought into the present'), has argued that these forms represent 'patterns of consumption' that are 'clear attempts at social differentiation' by the new urban corporate elite (1986: 21, 1987a: 168). In a similar vein, Michael Jager has followed a route sketched by Thorstein Veblen and Jean Baudrillard and found the aesthetics of gentrification and the 'attempt [by gentrifiers] to appropriate [the] history' of old neighbourhoods as 'central to processes of class constitution' (1986: 78–81). For Williams, meanwhile, 'the very act of living in areas "with history"' reflects the activity of middle-class groups 'seeking a clear

identity' (1986: 68). It might be argued that, insofar as this perspective
overlooks the diversity of old inner-city neighbourhood resettlers, it
is embedded in precisely the kind of monologic notion of gentrification that Rose has labelled chaotic. It might be replied, however,
that this objection is small beer inasmuch as these writers have something important to say about a key group of gentrifiers – members of
the upwardly mobile 'postindustrial' middle class – to which the question of conceptual chaos is largely peripheral. But a more basic issue
still remains.

In addressing a possible social function – class-constitution – of the
forms of gentrification, Smith, Jager, and Williams still leave the forms
themselves a riddle. Why do *these* forms have this function? Why do
resettlers not accomplish their purposes in architecturally modernist
structures built where old neighbourhoods are razed? Why, instead,
are old neighbourhoods gentrified? Or, come to that, why bother to
resettle in cities at all – why is class status not constituted in some
variant of the suburb? Smith's answer is the rent gap, but at least in
the case of Toronto (quite apart from other difficulties posed by the
rent gap), middle-class resettlement of old city neighbourhoods vigorously survives the rent gap. So how does an hypothesized affection
for 'diversity' and for certain historic architectural styles come into
the picture?

Similar questions arise in respect to Beauregard's and Ley's char-
acterizations of gentrification as a form of conspicuous consumption
in which particular 'amenity packages' – stylish restaurants, art galleries, fashionable architecture – act as demand-side stimulators of
old-neighbourhood resettlement (Beauregard 1986: 43–4, Ley 1985:
23–5). Were postwar suburbs, after all, any less rooted in a culture
of consumption? What else is to be made of their landscape of house-
pride, late-model cars, convenient appliances, and massive retail malls?
Isn't the key question how to account for the *new* 'canons of good
taste' Ley outlines? And are these simply matters of ungrounded demand-side whim – in which case should social science retire from the
field and allow market-research to provide its understanding of gentrification? No, there is not much help here with the dilemma of why
inner areas of cities now seem to satisfy middle-class aspirations for
which they were perceived as largely ill-suited only a generation ago.

Zukin, like Smith, has taken a structuralist view: that urban spatial
restructuring, of which gentrification is one element, is an investment
strategy put in place by 'corporate-sector capital' in which 'sponta-
neous market forces' are largely illusory (1982a: 174, 1982b: 256).

But she does not wholly foreclose the role of individual agency; 'the heart of the city' may 'exert an irresistible social and existential appeal' for artists and bohemians while, for more mainstream resettlers, the inner city may offer space for living which 'reflects real middle class needs and desires' (1982a 174–5, 185). Here, though, we reach a blind alley. What *is* the city's existential appeal? What 'desires' draw middle-class people into old neighbourhoods, and what is their genealogy? But Zukin's concern is a critique of capital's manipulation of desire, not desire itself, and she is silent about these questions.

Rose, too, writes about 'needs and desires' – those of marginal gentrifiers – and is quite specific about the kinds of 'needs' she has in mind: those of moderate-income single mothers who may have 'difficulties ... carrying on their particular living arrangements in conventional suburbs,' or of structurally unemployed young people who 'congregate in inner-city neighbourhoods where certain kinds of self-employment and informal economic activities are an essential means of "making do"' (1984: 63, 65). She is less clear, though, about 'desires' gentrifiers may feel – motivations toward old-neighbourhood resettlement rooted, not in practical matters, but in cultural or (in Zukin's word) 'existential' dilemmas. How do we account for the movement into old neighbourhoods of, say, middle-class people who have the means to live wherever they choose, who by any demographic measure would two decades ago have settled in suburbs, and today seek the city? Or of educated young people who are not job-market casualties but deliberately forgo mainstream employment in favour of inner-city marginality? What is coded in the word 'desire'?

These are examples of a consensus among diverse treatments of gentrification that in some way culture does matter. Beyond this, however, the picture is fuzzy. Several of these writers do, though, leave one vital clue to their thinking: that gentrification may be 'in part a reaction to the perceived homogeneity of the suburban dream' (Smith 1987a: 168), 'a rejection of the suburbs as a place in which to earn and spend' (Williams 1986: 69), a response 'to the perceived blandness and standardization of the suburbs' (Ley 1985: 24) involving people 'repelled from ... suburban time-space rhythms of separate spheres of work and daily life' (Rose 1984: 62). Other writers, too, cite feelings toward suburbs as a stimulus to old city neighbourhood resettlement (Holcomb and Beauregard 1981: 58, London and Palen 1984: 2, Allen 1984: 30). The issues they raise are not the relative transportation convenience of core-area housing for downtown workers, or supposed 'lifestyle' tendencies that are said to draw non-'familistic' urbanites to inner-city locales – factors sometimes cited as key residential sorting mechanisms embodied in gentrification. Rather, these writers' concern, albeit in language that is more suggestive than precise, is city-dwellers' feelings about the culture of everyday life afforded by varied metropolitan settings – a perception that, in some basic way, inner-city and suburban places, contemporary and traditional urban places, are very different.

Marginal Social Movements and the Culture Industry

Middle-Class Resettlement and Everyday Life

The attitude reflected by the latter writers is consistent with the notion that social practices oriented toward perceived emancipatory possibilities of older inner-city neighbourhoods – possibilities arising from specific use-values city-dwellers find in these residual locales – may have been among the vital seeds of gentrification as it has emerged in Toronto. These social practices may, in part, be conceived to originate at society's margins among social formations least under the dominance of hegemonic culture, from which their content then spreads on the one hand by diffusion, sustaining its resistant character, and on the other hand by rationalized commodification, as affirmative practice often largely stripped of its seminal meaning.

This outlook is not entirely new in treatments of Canadian gentrification. Ley, for example, a key Canadian writer in the field, has taken a perspective in many ways similar (1980: 238–43); but there are also differences. Ley's analysis of threats to 'the personal world of values and meaning' in current-day urbanism is framed in the context of a theorized dichotomy between the corrosive force of the 'rational, bureaucratic and secular world view' embodied in a dominant 'instrumentalist' ideology and the resistant reflex of an 'emotional, spiritual and aesthetic' world-view emerging from an 'expressive' ideology (1980: 242, 1987c). The approach taken here, however, relates perceived threats to 'values and meaning' to patterns of modernist and capitalist urbanism. Ley locates the origins of avant-garde resistance to current-day city-building in bohemian movements of the 1960s (1980: 237–43); but while the 1960s were, to be sure, a period of social ferment, marginal inner-city settlement may be traced earlier. Finally, Ley treats the connection between earlier and later-stage gentrifiers as a matter of demand-side preference: 'The sensuous and aesthetic philosophy released by the counter-culture has been appropriated in various forms by the growing numbers of North America's leisure class' (1980: 242). In the perspective taken here, this connection is explored in the context of the relationship between marginal cultural practice and processes of commodification.

Two further Canadian writers whose approaches have common features with the perspective taken here are Damaris Rose and Caroline Mills. As this chapter has already reported, Rose's analysis is predicated on differentiating marginal inner-city resettlers from the more affluent in-movers usually classed by stage-models as later-phase gentrifiers. In this context, her concerns include the personal needs and desires that make downtown neighbourhoods more satisfactory residential locales than other types of urban environments for economically or culturally marginal groups. In particular, her interest is the dilemma of women seeking placement in the city – for example, middle-class single mothers for whom inner-city resettlement may constitute a preferred locale of everyday life in both practical and more holistic terms: 'a deliberately sought out environmental solution' to issues of gender and single parenthood (1984: 66, 1989). But while she does address the critical possibilities of older downtown neighbourhoods for these actors, she does not explore connections that marginal gentrification may have with other forms of inner-city resettlement.

Mills's analysis closely parallels the perspective taken here. She has characterized the postmodernist celebration of residual urban form as 'both a reaction against corporate visions of the city, and a confirmation of the vigour of the commodity form' (1988: 169). But her theorization of the relationship between resistant marginal cultures and dominant commodity culture is limited to the argument that the latter is 'capable of incorporating potentially oppositional cultures' (1988: 172). In contrast, the argument here is not just that commodity culture *may* absorb marginal forms but – consistent with the discussion of the logic of capital in chapter 2 – that commodity culture *requires* the emergence of autonomous ideas susceptible to its appropriation. That is (echoing Baudrillard), capital's production of exchange values is contingent on a prior production of use values.

Perhaps the most trenchant evocation of the emancipatory objectives and use values sought by marginal middle-class groups in the resettlement of older inner-city neighbourhoods is Castells's account of San Francisco's gay enclave: 'not only a residential space but also a space for social interaction, for business activities of all kinds, for leisure and pleasure, for feasts and politics' (1983: 151). San Francisco's gay community sought space that was a *place*, that was distinct and physically and 'ontologically' secure, and that offered its users 'autonomy, familiarity and ... meaning within the private realm – space of 'existential' and 'empathetic insideness'* (Seamon 1979: 148–9, Saunders 1986: 280). San Francisco's gay community sought space for an everyday life of a kind Roland Barthes has termed 'erotic,' where 'subversive forces, forces of rupture, ludic forces act and meet' and where 'buried possibilities for expression and communication' may be recovered (Barthes 1986: 96, Habermas 1981b: 36). It sought space for occasions of festival, 'drinking, laughing and dancing in the streets,' and for the 'ceremonial meeting place' that Mumford argued was a 'first germ of the city' – space among whose possibilities was expressing a 'carnival sense of the world ... turn[ing] oppression into creation, and subvert[ing] established values by emphasizing their ridiculous aspects'** (Castells 1983: 141, 162; Mumford 1961: 10; Bakhtin 1984: 107).

What is valuable in Castells's analysis of San Franciso's gay community for a more general appreciation of 'marginal gentrification' is not only his account of the community's subculture and its creation of a particular spatial setting for this subculture but also his treatment of this process as an example of an urban social movement. His account suggests that the concept of the 'social movement' may have particular relevance for theorizing middle-class resettlement of older inner-city neighbourhoods, at least in its initial stages, a view in which he is not alone. London and Palen, for example, observed several years ago that, while the social-movement 'approach ... is, paradoxically, the least well-developed in the literature ... it may hold the greatest potential for providing a synthesis of the multiple causes of the phenomenon,' a view later echoed by London and two other co-authors (London and Palen 1984: 21; London et al. 1986: 383). The idea that 'marginal gentrification' may at least partly be theorized as a social movement is also implicit in the accounts of several other

---

*The latter terms are Edward Relph's. 'Existential insideness is that in which a place is experienced without deliberate and self-conscious reflection yet is full with significances ... Empathetic insideness demands a willingness to be open to significances of a place, to feel it, to know and respect its symbols' (1976: 54–5).
**Bakhtin describes 'carnival' as oriented to 'free and familiar contact among people ... in a concretely sensuous, half-real and half-play-acted form ... counterpoised to the all-powerful socio-hierarchical relationships of non-carnival life' (1984: 107, 123).

writers, including three principal Canadian analysts discussed above, Rose, Mills and – in some work – Ley.

As was reported in chapter 4, Castells developed his model of urban social movements in response to what he argued were the theoretical limitations of orthodox Marxian structuralism. To reiterate, he describes them as collective social practices that are oriented to the forms, the functions, and the meanings of cities and city landscapes and are irreducible to the totalizing workings of capital or the dynamics of class; and while he conceived them as essentially 'reactive,' he also argued that they may function as agents of critical urban change (1983: 291–305). In particular, he views them as oriented to three specific categories of objectives: within the economic realm, 'to obtain for its residents a city organized around its use value'; within the cultural realm, 'the search for cultural identity, for the maintenance or creation of autonomous local cultures'; and within the political realm, 'the search for increasing power in local government, neighbourhood decentralization, and urban self-management' (1983: 319–20).

The left-populist grouping of Toronto's 1970s municipal reformist movement has already been cited as an example of the kind of formation Castells has in mind. (Of concern here is solely his definition of such movements; his verdict that they are ultimately misdirected because they are not mobilized against correct 'targets,' discussed in chapter 4, is a quite separate issue.) What underlay left-populist reformism, besides certain notions of distributive justice, were visions of urbanism and of city-building that transcended local political concern and also transcended class interest, an alternative to the agendas of modernist urbanism and civic boosterism that conceived of a socially and architecturally diverse city holding cultural meaning and social possibility for its users (Salsberg 1970). Embodied in this vision were the focal elements theorized by Castells as the basis of urban movements: specific use values of urban space, the cultural integrity of the city's communities, and such institutions of local self-management as neighbourhood councils and cooperative housing projects.

Likewise, these three objectives have been aspects of the practices of groups in Toronto that might be aggregated within Rose's notion of 'marginal gentrifier,' many of whom were closely allied to the emergence of left-populist reformism and whose choice to live in the inner city has been rooted not simply in instrumental consideration of pragmatic needs but, like San Francisco's gay community, also in a perception that such qualities as *place*, polyphonic sociability, and carnival are impoverished in the spaces of current-day city-building but may be sustained in traditional city places. In pursuing these qualities of life through their settlement patterns and politics, marginal middle-class resettlers of older downtown Toronto neighbourhoods sought to resist perceived threats to specific use values of the inner city, to their subcultural integrity, and to their power to manage their own lives.

Within the institution of intellectual practice, there are two main bodies of critique of current-day city-building: a humanist view concerned with perceived consequences of modernist urban design, and a Marxian view that stresses a perceived pervasion of urban life and landscape by commodification and capital. As was discussed in chapter 4, the humanist polemic against modernism has particularly condemned its reduction of the city to the analogue of the machine, a way of thinking that is said to yield 'depressing' and 'monotonous blocks of urban sameness,' a 'placeless' and 'absurd landscape we experience as ... apart from us and indifferent to us' – the outcome of a 'paternalism' devoted to *technique* that, paradoxically, creates places that are 'dehumanising because they are excessively humanised' by a calculating rationality (Cox 1968: 424; Kalman 1985: 37, 44; Mumford 1963: 174; Relph 1976: 90, 127; 1981: 63–105). The Marxian critique, in contrast, is oriented to the penetration of urban life by capital, both as a form of social control and in the form of the commodity, for which modernist design is believed to act as a kind of camouflage. For Marxian urbanism, the modern city becomes transformed into an abstraction, a 'collection of ghettos' and a 'space of variable flows ... of capital, labour, elements of production,' which is dominated by 'monofunctional instrumentality ... as the centre of ludic communion disappears' and as daily urban life is increasingly colonized as 'society of spectacle' (Lefebvre in Martins 1982: 171; Castells 1983: 314; Gottdiener 1985: 235, 1986: 301; Debord 1983). Both versions of critique, however, concur about certain perceived consequences of the urban forms they attack. In each perspective, particular use values of city space, including such qualities as *place* and liberated sociability, and individuals' and communities' capacity to sustain their cultural identities and to manage their own lives, are said to be critically threatened in contemporary city-building.

Unlike the writers cited, most city-dwellers do not record their ideas according to conventions of intellectual practice. They may share the same feelings, however, and seek to enact them in other ways. Many artists, for example, have grappled with the city within the same structures of feeling as various social critics, at least since Edouard Manet, whose work records scepticism about Parisian social life and landscape in the wake of Haussmann's reconstruction (Clark 1984, Jeffrey 1978, Whitford 1985). City-dwellers may also express their feelings within the realm of their everyday lives, where they are able, individually or collectively, to pursue practices through which they seek to elude domination of hegemonic cultural structures and to constitute alternative conditions for experience. For the marginal middle class, resettlement of older inner-city neighbourhoods has been among these activities; and this has not been just a recent occurrence. While the process labelled marginal or first-phase gentrification was clearly evident among counter-cultural movements of the 1960s (Ley 1980: 238–43, Zukin 1982a: 191, Palen and London 1984: 2), it did not originate there. Lower New York, for example, became a bohemian district much earlier, and the San Francisco gay community's roots may be traced at least to the 1940s (Castells 1983: 140–1). In Canada, inner-city niches populated by artists, gays, and other culturally marginal groupings have existed for decades. The process termed marginal or first-phase gentrification has occurred, in fact, throughout most of the era of modernist/capitalist city-building.

In summary, it may be necessary to stand on its head the commonplace about gentrification that it is based in a 'longing for a ... halcyon past,' for 'custom and routine in a world characterized by constant change and innovation' (Holcomb and Beauregard 1981: 55, Rybczynski 1986: 9). On the contrary, affection for old urban forms may be rooted in longing, not for a flight into the past, but for a subjectively effective present, in a desire, not for routine, but to *escape* routine – a routine of placeless space and monofunctional instrumentality (Lefebvre 1971). Old city places may offer difference and freedom, privacy and fantasy, possibilities for carnival amid the 'relief of anonymity' where 'the ultimate word ... has not yet been spoken': 'anything can happen here – and it could happen right now' (Raban 1974: 62–3, 201, 225; Kahn 1987: 13, 15; Bakhtin 1984: 166; Berger 1977: 62). These are not just matters of philosophic abstraction but, in a carnival sense, of 'the desire for pleasure, understood in its most material and sensual form,' a force that Walter Benjamin believed was among the most vital stimuli to resistance against domination (Buck-Morss 1981: 64). 'A big city is an encyclopedia of sexual possibility' (Raban 1974: 229), a characterization to be grasped in its widest sense.

The city, a realm of intimate communities and familiar subcultures, but also a world of strangers, is 'the place of our meeting with the other' (Kahn 1987, Lofland 1973, Barthes 1986: 96).

The Appropriation of Cultural Practice

Often people do not fall easily into nominal categories. Concepts like 'conservative' or 'familistic' or 'white-collar' are firm at the core but softer at their edges, and it is toward these edges that a plurality of social actors are situated. Likewise, the meanings of 'avant-garde,' 'bohemian,' and 'culturally marginal' are clear, but what is their perimeter? Many people share some avant-garde values but not all, or engage in only some aspects of bohemian lifestyle; they have a foot in both mainstream and marginal cultural camps. Many gays, for example, have marginal leisure-lives but conventional work-lives. It is across this blurry zone at the edge of the avant-garde that the emancipatory attraction of old city places spreads by diffusion to people not immediately or obviously thought of as marginal gentrifiers, people whom stage-typologists might label second-stage or transition-phase gentrifiers. Groups like hard-core bohemians or militant gays may, in their settlement patterns, act as a kind of 'cultural vanguard' for middle-class people who, if not unreconstructedly marginal, are only ambivalently mainstream (Castells 1983: 160). Here, the values underlying resettlement of old city neighbourhoods may be diluted. People with some essential ties to dominant structures will have less inclination than cultural expatriates to create highly distinct places and rounds of life and may do so less vividly. Included may be many city-dwellers who pursued cultural or economic marginality when younger but, as they grow older and perhaps have families, gravitate toward greater security and stability. But the resettlement of older inner-city neighbourhoods does sustain some of its emancipatory character among these people – individuals who, not for reasons of exogenous style but of *desire*, find suburbs and modernist spaces unlivable.

This diffusion does not account, however, for the current popularity of older city neighbourhoods well beyond groups that might be reasonably termed culturally marginal or quasi-marginal – the fashionable retrofitting of old neighbourhoods for invasion by up-market middle-class resettlers and by the well-to-do. This restructuring of the city as what Smith has dubbed a 'bourgeois playground' (1986: 32) is not simply a matter of spreading consumer demand for inner-city settlement forms initiated by marginal groups in which, as it turns more mainstream, the emancipatory content of the forms merely becomes more diluted. Something quite different than just demand-side dynamics is at work – a process rooted in the logic of what Thomas Crow (after Max Horkheimer and Theodor Adorno) has called 'the culture industry' and in the relationship of this industry with marginal groups:

> In our image-saturated present, the culture industry has demonstrated the ability to package and sell nearly every variety of desire imaginable, but because its ultimate logic is the strictly rational and utilitarian one of profit maximization, it is not able to invent the desires and sensibilities it exploits. (Crow 1983: 252)

In this context, the avant-garde serves a crucial function by 'search[ing] out areas of social practice which retain some vivid life' and acting as 'a kind of research and development arm of the culture industry.' Hence, the avant-garde's activities, 'which come into being as negotiated breathing space on the margins of controlled social life,' may ultimately become 'as productive for affirmative culture as they are for the articulation of critical consciousness' (Crow 1983: 251, 253).

In vital respects, modern property entrepreneurs are part of the culture industry. They seek to produce, advertise, and market not just functional space but desirable places for everyday life. As much as housing, their product is lifestyle. But like the rest of the culture industry – and like capital in general – they cannot invent desires they commodify but need to extract them from living culture. Earlier, they adapted the shells of the bourgeois dream of the domestic suburb and the modernist dream of an egalitarian city. More recently, confronted on one hand by the rent gap and by the 'larger economic and social restructuring of advanced capitalist economies' (Smith 1986) and on the other hand by 'insurmountable ... opposition to the slash-and-burn tactics' of neo-modernist city-building (Zukin 1982a: 176) – opposition that was partly rooted among early-phase gentrifiers – property entrepreneurs required a new style of marketable desire.

The forms of marginal urbanism, resonant with *place* and erotic sociability and already diffusing through the edges of the middle class, were appropriated, stripped of their disreputable taint of deviance, and bundled in a Disneyesque wrapping highly palatable to 'post-industrial' urbanites (and highly profitable to the entrepreneurs, though not so profitable as their initially preferred high-density forms). These are spaces of simulated insideness in the traditional social life of the historical city, locales of synthetic eroticism and prefabricated carnival comprising a landscape of postmodernist commodity units – new houses designed to *look* like old houses, *cinema-noir*-styled diners that serve designer chili, boutique malls in modes of Victorian and art-deco elegance. Here, trapped in a matrix of spectacle, old city neighbourhoods from St John's to Victoria become identical as fast-food burgers and reliable, unthreatening, and placeless as any modernist space.

Consistent with the perspective toward capital outlined in chapter 2, it is important not to reduce this process of appropriation to the monologic workings of structure but rather to maintain a sense of the paradox of urban forms. Among the most prescient reflections about 'gentrification' is Zukin's observation that

> the basic problem ... is not, as the Frankfurt School of social critique warned back in the 1940s, that capitalism eventually transmutes all ideas into commodity fetishes. Rather, the danger is that the realization of ideas in urban space re-creates an unequal distribution of the benefits these ideas represent. (1982a: 190)

That is, it would be incorrect to theorize the 'social and existential appeal' of inner-city locales and their capacity to fulfil 'needs and desires' of the corporate city's bourgeois as simply an illusion of use value rooted in capital's manipulation of images; the impulse of these city-dwellers to occupy 'the heart of the city' is not merely epiphenomenal (Zukin 1982a: 174–5, 185). Within each commodity fetish is a historically produced use value whose immanence constitutes the irony of exchange value. But what does seem to occur under the aegis of capital is that the realization of use value in urban space remains the privilege of individuals who, in a milieu where individualism and use value themselves become fetishized, have the material resources to exert control over their lives. Meanwhile, other city-dwellers – mothers on welfare, the working poor, the walking wounded of skid row – become victims of the process.

Zukin's observation raises the question of the political meaning of gentrification, an issue that generally centres on the fact that the so-called 'revitalization' of old inner-city neighbourhoods has often been based on the devitalization of less affluent communities. Canadian data in this respect are fragmentary but do seem to point to a clear pattern of forced displacement, particularly of low-income tenants in districts caught up in the speculative frenzy of widespread white-painting (Ley 1985: 144–52, 1987b: 16–17; Howell 1987: 25–9). (Working-class homeowners in Canadian inner cities have not generally been similarly victimized; they usually do not sell out unless they prefer to cash in their property in order to move to a suburban locale, typically earning substantial appreciated value as beneficiaries of a shrunken rent gap.) In the case of Toronto, for example, processes of de-conversion associated with gentrification – the refitting of multi-unit houses to single-household use – may have accounted for the loss of as many as seventeen thousand moderate-cost rental units in the decade from 1976 to 1985 (Layton 1987).

This process is often more complex than a simple gentrification/displacement model may suggest. In a number of Toronto neighbourhoods, the thrust toward devitalization was carried out not by middle-class resettlers but by high-rise speculators following a block-busting strategy of planned destabilization, an important observation because it clarifies the real agents of the dissolution of many working-class communities (Sewell 1972: 141–62). But the end results are evident. Old housing does not 'trickle down,' and groups on fixed incomes are squeezed into an increasingly tighter housing market (CTHD 1987: 7–31). Immigrant-receptor areas frequently lose this function, fragmenting new immigrant groups to the suburbs, out of touch with the kinds of intimate communities of integration that have traditionally served as the fabric of immigrant everyday life (SPCMT 1979). Cheap rooming-house districts are erased, aggravating the problem of homelessness.

Some structuralist critics of gentrification seek to hold both marginal and more affluent gentrifiers equally responsible for this displacement. The former are said to be 'complicit' in the dislocation of low-income residents. Marginal gentrifiers may think that they are only 'pushing into niches here and there,' but what they 'really' do is 'activat[e] ... a mechanism of revalorization [of] patrician terrain'; presumably, they should read their Gramsci and mend their ways (Deutsche and Ryan 1984: 102, Zukin 1982a: 178). This view has a seductive quality of unsentimental ideological vigour. Certainly, in their search for place and for traditional city sociability, marginal gentrifiers are not acting according to prescribed revolutionary canons. But whether they are simply engaged in the class project of keeping the workers down is another question. The evidence from Toronto is that marginal resettlement of old city neighbourhoods has not been reducible to bourgeois politics but rather, in neighbourhoods like Dufferin Grove, Southeast Spadina, Kensington, and South St Jamestown, has been an effort by groupings of city-dwellers, together with their neighbours, to seek a measure of control over their lives and living spaces.

It is uncertain, for example, that the 'early-phase' gentrifiers of Donvale who allied with local working-class residents to create a non-profit housing co-op may be lumped holus-bolus with the affluent later resettlers who bitterly opposed them (Dineen 1974). Nor is it clear that people in a community like Toronto's Island neighbourhood, who fought more than a decade to prevent the bulldozing of their homes, can be held accountable for the fact that with changing property fashions their cottages, once labelled squatters' shacks, have run the risk of becoming prime waterfront property. Irony, yes; dupish complicity, no. The real agent of displacement in Toronto has not been the gradual activity of marginal middle-class resettlers, who are usually happy to live side-by-side with older residents and often act as a bulwark against the eradication of old neighbourhoods. Rather, it has been the emergence of concerted entrepreneurial interest in traditional city space, activity oriented to consumers whose self-image and property values are threatened by survival of any traces of a neighbourhood's unfashionable past (Jager 1986).

It is in this context that the class-constitution analyses framed by Smith, Jager, and Williams become salient and that the ultimate irony of the process becomes evident. The commodification of 'gentrification' displaces not only working-class and underclass communities but also erases the locales of marginal inner-city settlement (Simpson 1981: 4–5). In Toronto, for example, affluent whitepainting has increasingly squeezed visual and performing artists out of their traditional downtown living and working spaces to the degree that little available housing or studio space now remains for them (TAC 1988, Holden 1988, Drainie 1989, Nunes 1990). Less affluent members of the gay community are unable to secure placement within the pink ghetto, while younger members of bohemian and political-activist groupings are expatriated from their former downtown enclaves. The search of economically and culturally marginal groups for urban place breeds, through the workings of the culture industry, their own displacement.

Gender, Urban Form, and the Inner City

Gender is an aspect of disaffection from suburban environments and of middle-class resettlement of older inner-city housing that requires explicit theoretical reckoning. Like class, race, and other constructed social distinctions in given cultural settings, gender is materially embodied in the landscape of the contemporary Canadian city. As Liz Bondi has observed, what is at issue here is not the way that certain urban forms or architectural styles are sometimes said to reflect 'feminine' or 'masculine' traits – formulations usually rooted in naturalizations of female and male that function mainly to reinforce prevailing ideologies of gender (a way of thinking that Bondi illustrates by Jencks's use of patriarchal gender-typing in his account of postmodernist architecture [Bondi 1990: 4, Jencks 1977: 73]). Rather, what is of concern are the consequences of these ideologies for the production of urban space. The most relevant aspect of gender in the case of urban forms in a city like Toronto is the institutionalized pattern of male dominance and female oppression that has historically characterized Canadian social relations. Toronto's suburban landscape of segregated domestic use, for example, is a form contingent on a particular mode of the reproduction of labour – the nuclear family – and on the designated role of women as indentured custodians of this domestic realm; the Canadian suburb may be characterized as intrinsically patriarchal (Fishman 1987: 33–8, MacKenzie and Rose 1983).

Because of the centrality of gender to social relations – arguably no less pivotal in contemporary societies than capital – it may be anticipated that shifts in understandings of gender will significantly affect perceptions, production, and uses of urban space. In the case of present-day Canada, the phenomenon of feminism, not just as a political idea but as an emergent force in individuals' self-constitution and relationships to everyday life, is altering perceptions of gender in crucial respects. Canadian feminism is very much a social movement in process whose consequences for social fabric are currently neither fully understood nor achieved. Clearly, however, feminist thinking and sentiment have been key forces at work in the popular reaction among a segment of city-dwellers against traditional suburban environments and living arrangements and in related urban demographic shifts. It is precisely this view that has helped animate Rose's seminal contribution to the study of gentrification, work that partly focuses on 'changes in women's employment situation [that] may often be *constitutive* of gentrification' (1989: 133). (With Zukin and Mills, Rose illustrates the conspicuous presence of women among pioneers in inquiry about gentrification.) In an article felicitously titled 'A Woman's Place Is in the City,' Canadian sociologist Gerda Wekerle argues that the emergent logic of gender in contemporary urban society is rendering 'suburbs ... increasingly dysfunctional' and 'will

require major changes in the land use patterns of American cities'
(1984: 11, 17). 'Women are a major impetus for the revitalization of
North American cities. The dramatic increase in women's participation in the labour force in the seventies has created a new demand
for urban housing and for services that can only be found in cities'
(1984: 11).

There are two aspects to the pattern Rose and Wekerle describe.
Most obvious is its demographic dimension. Economically self-suf-
ficient middle-class women compose one component in the growing
market for downtown housing identified by the 'production-of-gentrifiers' perspective, accommodation that includes apartments, condominiums, and old houses that women may own individually or in
partnership or where they may live as tenants. But while the increasing presence of such women in metropolitan areas is a necessary
condition for the emergence of this settlement pattern, it is clearly
not a sufficient condition. Like the rent gap – which created an availability of affordable housing for specific demographic groups – the
'production' of particular categories of potential inner-city resettlers
by present-day processes of social formation explains only a structural
component of their settlement pattern. It does not account for the
underlying logic of their preference in metropolitan settings like Toronto, where comparably priced or less costly housing is available
elsewhere and the choice of downtown living is made from among
several possible options.

This preference is the second aspect of the patterns identified by
Rose and Wekerle – the sufficient condition for women's settlement
of downtown housing, and a choice that appears to involve both
pragmatic and cultural concerns. Among the former are matters of
locational convenience that, for groups like single mothers or working
mothers, are crucial factors in managing their workaday living arrangements. The latter include an apparent affinity of some women
for the everyday lifeworld of the inner city, an environment they
seem to find more congenial than other equally affordable housing
locales.

Hence, gender is a key factor to be accounted in theorizing 'gentrification.' In specific respect to city life and city form – and in concert
with one of the main arguments of this book – feminism has been
highly consistent with Castells's model of urban social movements.
Among the principal objectives of women who have sought to combat
or elude patriarchal social relations in the context of urban space have
been use values of this space (such as the requirement for daycare

centres near workplaces and the freedom to use public spaces secure from threat of assault), cultural identity as a distinct collectivity with specific spatial requirements (such as places for women's commercial activities and health services), and political control of their affairs both as individuals and as a group with specific spatial needs (such as affordable co-op housing and crisis hostels). Residential choice is one of the realms in which the feminist movement – in part, as a distinctly urban movement and as one key component of the middle-class resettlement of older inner-city neighbourhoods – is playing itself out.*

Conclusion

Chapters 4 and 5 have sought to establish a theoretical groundwork for considering 'gentrification.' The advent of postmodernist urbanism – as a force in both urban design and urban politics – and the emerging morphology of the 'postindustrial' metropolis, discussed in chapter 4, are both important parts of the picture for historically situating recent patterns of middle-class movement to the inner city. Meanwhile, the work of the writers discussed in chapter 5 provided a foundation for reflecting on 'gentrification' and developing propositions for inquiry. In particular, this chapter has sought to connect 'gentrification' to the culture of everyday life and – consistent with the approach to urban form set out in chapter 2 – to Crow's account of the culture industry. Hence, the chapter sought to address the issue identified by Peter Williams (1986: 68) by treating the workings of culture as a key element of 'gentrification.' As well, chapter 5 has sought to view middle-class inner-city resettlement in the context of Castells's notion of the urban social movement.

The ideas and processes discussed in part 2, together with the interpretation of Toronto's recent patterns of city-building discussed in part 1, were the basis for the fieldwork now described in part 3 – the culmination of the book. The fieldwork sought to approach a particular group of middle-class inner-city resettlers in Toronto – who will be identified in chapter 6 – in the contexts of the local urban circumstances described in part 1 and the theoretical perspective developed in part 2.

---

* A recent interpretation of 'gentrification' that dovetails with much of the perspective of this chapter, particularly in reference to the question of gender, is Warde (1991).

Part Three

FIELDWORK

6

Fieldwork Strategy and First Reflections

This chapter introduces a group of middle-class resettlers of older inner-city neighbourhoods in Toronto who were interviewed about their residential preferences and everyday lives. It is important to stress from the outset that these individuals in *no* sense represent 'gentrifiers' in general as the term has usually been used in academic or popular literature. Nor was the objective of fieldwork to explore comprehensively the emergent social fabric of the inner city of corporate-era urbanism. Rather, fieldwork sought to focus solely on the questions of whether the preferences of a segment of middle-class inner-city resettlers about their housing locales and everyday lives reflected a pattern of critical social practice and whether the residential choices of these city-dwellers might validly be viewed in a context of urban social-movement theory.

While chapter 5 argued that phase-models of 'gentrification' are a conceptual tool of only limited theoretical utility, it also noted that such typologies do have some descriptive use so long as they are carefully applied. In the framework of a phase-model, the individuals interviewed in the fieldwork reported here would almost all be categorized as transition-stage – or early- and mid-stage – 'gentrifiers.' They included a preponderance of downtown homeowners aged thirty to fifty employed in middle-class occupations, but virtually none of whom would be grouped as culmination-phase (or third-stage) 'gentrifiers' as this group is usually described and theorized. The specific demography of those interviewed is outlined later in the chapter; as well, some common general attitudes among them are sketched, material that helps define their identity empirically rather than taxonomically. First, however, the chapter describes the procedures by which the interviews were carried out – the methodology of fieldwork.

A Sample of Inner-City Resettlers

Sample and Interviews

The resettlers in question – in total, sixty-three – were asked to participate in interviews dealing with their lives in downtown neighbourhoods and their thoughts and sentiments about this residential locale. In the parlance of social science, they acted as 'respondents.' The interviews were unstructured, designed not to elicit a series of discrete answers to a scheduled sequence of questions but rather to approximate as much as possible ordinary conversation – conversation in which it was understood that respondents were to do the bulk of the talking. Thus, apart from a handful of questions about general themes that comprised the skeleton of the interviews, and a small number of demographic and biographic queries required to sketch an aggregate description of the respondents, each interview followed its own course. Thematic questions focused on such issues as how respondents happened to move to their present home; their feelings about their housing, neighbours, and neighbourhood; their attitudes toward other possible residential alternatives (such as suburbs or high-rise apartments) and toward various processes of change occurring in inner-city Toronto (in particular, 'gentrification'); and, finally, in the case of parents, their views about child-rearing in downtown locales. Demographic queries concerned such information as respondents' occupations, length of residence at their present address, household composition, the main locale in which they lived with their parental households, and so forth; tabulations of some of the latter data will be reported shortly.

Interviews were conducted during winter and spring 1989 and ranged in length from about one hour to nearly three hours. Each interview was tape-recorded and subsequently, within forty-eight hours, closely reviewed and transcribed in edited form. For the most part, interviews were conducted at respondents' homes on weekday evenings or weekend afternoons, an approach intended not only to encourage informal conversation but also to permit observation of the condition, degree of renovation, and style of decor of the homes, important considerations in the study of 'gentrification.' In the case of the small number of respondents who preferred to be interviewed away from their place of residence, the researcher later carried out observation of the exterior of their homes, gathering at least some partial knowledge of their condition and appearance. Each respondent understood that his or her remarks were to be used in research concerning middle-class resettlement of older inner-city neighbourhoods (or, in a few cases, that they were participating in a pilot rehearsal of the interview procedure), and the confidentiality of interview contents was assured.

The main rationale for a loosely structured interview design is that this format offers a research instrument sensitive to particular features of individual cases. One advantage of this strategy is that many decisions about what themes to raise and to stress, and about how to approach and to contextualize these themes, are not prescribed by a standardized researcher's agenda but are made by respondents themselves, in conjunction with the researcher, during the course of interviews. In the case of the fieldwork reported here, for example, several respondents independently raised the topic of non-profit cooperative housing, an issue of some importance that will be discussed toward the close of this chapter. Among the researcher's key tools in interviews of this type are noncommittal follow-up questions – questions like 'Anything else?' or 'Is there anything more you want to say about that? – and the techniques of deflection and tracking (Hoffman 1980).

Through this approach, a researcher is better able to develop a grasp of the systems of meaning and understanding that inform respondents' views and also to have greater confidence in the internal validity of interview data than is possible using more highly structured techniques. To be sure, this method does exact a price insofar as it does not furnish easily manoeuverable numeric information of the type offered by survey-interviewing methods oriented toward statistical analysis. However, more structured approaches are not suitable in many research contexts. In opting for loosely structured interviews in the present research, two considerations were of particular relevance.

The first arises from the general status of research concerning 'gentrification.' Less structured interview methods are often associated with exploratory research in areas where there has not yet been much systematic empirical study. Their goal is to provide groundwork for subsequent, more schematic observation. Although there is a substantial literature concerning 'gentrification,' middle-class inner-city resettlers themselves have been conspicuously silent amid the theoretical treatments and demographic analyses that compose this literature's bulk. There has been little attention to what 'gentrifiers' themselves have to say about their activities. Hence, the interviews were, in part, conceived as exploratory research.

The second consideration concerns the researcher's predisposition. The research discussed in this chapter arises in the framework of an outlook toward social science that envisions individual actors as salient units of study not only in the context of demographic categories and interaction networks – that is, as 'cases' of larger systems – but also as unique agents: irreducible and idiosyncratic cases in themselves. This outlook in no sense diminishes the importance of class, gender, kinship, community, or of any other aggregate unit in the genealogy of social action. Indeed, the discussion that follows will make reference to each of these 'variables.' Rather, this outlook also directs attention toward social life as an ongoing construction constituted by discrete, acting individuals who are themselves in a constant process of self-constitution. At issue in contrasting this outlook and allied research activities with more systemically or statistically oriented approaches is not the relative legitimacy or validity of different perspectives but, within the patchwork quilt rather than whole cloth that comprises social science, simply matters of emphasis. It is in a context of this kind that art historian Michael Podro observed,

> ... the fact a position is partial, that it is not comprehensive, is a necessary virtue. If it is to be a position in any useful sense at all, it must make some features salient rather than others, engage with the work in one way rather than another ... What is needed is that we should be able to both grasp the point of the enterprise and to observe the objects with which it is concerned. (1982: 213)

The point of the enterprise reported here was to gather intensive information about a relatively small number of individual actors who, in themselves and in their residential settlement activities, are the 'objects' with which research was concerned.

The goal of securing frank and familiar conversation with respondents was further pursued by the system of 'sampling' employed – that is, the method used for identifying a group of individuals who might in some sense be said to be representative of a larger universe of similar cases. Respondents were gathered by the procedure of 'snowball' sampling: accumulating new contacts through the agency of existing contacts. A series of three-tier snowballs was initiated through individuals personally known to the researcher, who then suggested one or two individuals outside the researcher's sphere of acquaintance who might agree to participate in an interview, who in turn suggested one or two additional interview prospects – a procedure yielding snowballs looking something like this:

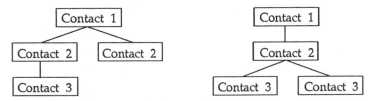

A key advantage of this sampling technique is that, in each case of second- or third-tier contact, the personal reference of an individual already known to both researcher and respondent is available to help establish rapport. As well, personal references were instrumental in securing interviews; only four prospective second- or third-tier respondents declined to be interviewed. Hence, the sixty-three completed interviews were drawn from contacts with sixty-seven potential respondents.

An issue suggested by these diagrams of the typical kinds of snowballs pursued is the extent of contact among second- and third-tier respondents, a concern that arises in respect to snowball sampling inasmuch as the external validity of research may be truncated if respondents are interconnected members of a single extensive interaction network. In the case of the present research, this was not the case. In following up second- and third-tier contacts, the researcher specifically sought to move in differing network directions and avoid individuals known to one another. Hence, the respondents discussed are members of a series of distinct networks –

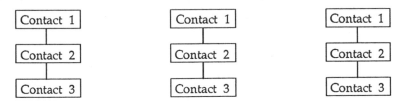

– rather than one large network:

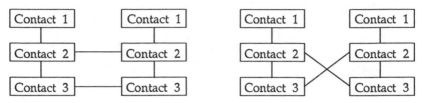

Apart from some cases of network links among first-tier contacts, or a few cases in which a second-tier contact was personally known to two first-tier contacts, respondents were generally unacquainted with one another.

As well as being drawn from multiple interaction networks, respondents were drawn from a diversity of neighbourhoods in inner-city Toronto, as indicated by the map of their distribution on page 157. The plurality of west-end respondents partly reflects the fact that 'transition-phase gentrification' was, at the time of interviewing, more widespread in west-end than east-end inner neighbourhoods. A large section of the inner east end – bounded on the map by Jarvis, Bloor, Queen streets, and the Don Valley – is mainly composed of high-rise apartments, public-housing projects and highly affluent culmination-phase 'gentrification,' and the district immediately north of this area (where no respondents were drawn) is the venerable, wealthy enclave of Rosedale. As well, no respondents were drawn from the corridor just north of the central business district, largely an area of office, retail, and institutional uses and high-rise apartments. (An interesting, though not especially relevant, finding that emerged in sampling was that west- and east-end respondents tended to refer the researcher almost exclusively to snowball contacts on their own side of town.)

In conclusion, the sample was in no sense 'random' – a probability sample to which each transition-phase 'gentrifier' in inner-city Toronto had equal likelihood of selection. While random sampling is highly useful in many research contexts, it was not employed in the present case for three reasons. The first was tactical; random sampling would not have permitted developing interview contacts based on personal references, a method that – as noted – parsimoniously generated a network of respondent leads and helped establish good researcher-respondent relations. Second – as has also been noted – the purpose of research was not to examine 'gentrification' in general but

DISTRIBUTION OF RESPONDENTS IN INNER—CITY TORONTO

	FEMALES	MALES	TOTAL
PARENTS	16	15	31
NON—PARENTS	16	16	32
TOTAL	32	31	63

WEST END - 37

EAST END - 26

rather to uncover and document certain values and outlooks that might be found among a segment of middle-class inner-city resettlers and might be germane to the relevance of social-movement theory in conceptualizing their residential activities. In other words, the researcher approached the field with a particular interest and focused attention in directions where that interest might most fruitfully be explored – a procedure that is not tautological but analogous to the practice of an astronomer who believes a given phenomenon is most likely to be observed in a particular sector of the sky and aims a telescope there rather than randomly or at other sectors. Finally, because random selection assumes the availability of a fairly complete and up-to-date list of the universe of all cases from which respondents will be sampled, its use was precluded in the research described here. There is no list, nor any approximation of a list, nor any satisfactory way of constructing one, in reference to middle-class resettlers in inner Toronto neighbourhoods whose housing activities might be conceptualized as critical social practice. Hence, the research required the use of non-probability sampling.

The Respondents

As has already been stressed in this chapter, the sample was mainly composed of individuals who would be grouped in stage-models of middle-class inner-city resettlement as 'transition-phase gentrifiers.' On the one hand, respondents were not, for the most part, currently members of the kinds of economically or culturally marginal groups that have typically been associated with 'first-phase' resettlement, although several had been participants in politically or culturally marginal inner-city groups when they were younger. As this tabulation of their ages indicates, at least half the respondents were young during the socially volatile years of the later 1960s –

	Parents	Non-parents	Total
Age Group			
21–30	–	9	9
31–40	13	12	25
41–50	15	9	24
50+	3	2	5

– and a number of these older respondents still maintained at least some affiliation with activist political organizations or avant-garde cultural groupings. On the other hand, neither were the respondents highly affluent participants in the mainstream of Toronto's emergent corporate economy – the stratum most closely associated with what stage-typologies envision as culmination-phase 'gentrification.' While most respondents did have white-collar or 'service' jobs, none was employed in Toronto's corporate/financial sector. Although the sample did include eight lawyers, all but one worked for social service agencies, non-profit institutions, or in small practices largely oriented to various forms of social advocacy. The exception was a gay male who commuted to a corporate-sector job in a smaller Ontario city – the sole corporate-sector employee in the sample:

	Parents	Non-parents	Total
Occupations			
Social services, government	8	9	17
Law, other professions	8	4	12
Teaching, academic, library	4	5	9
Journalism, media, publishing	5	4	9
Arts	4	3	7

	Parents	Non-parents	Total
Student	–	3	3
Clerical	–	3	3
Real estate	1	–	1
Small industrial management	–	1	1
Full-time parent	1	–	1

As the tabulations suggest, one concern in sampling was to contact a relatively equal number of parents and non-parents. This was not because it was anticipated that these groups composed relatively equal segments of the target population. Although the number of parents among middle-class inner-city residents appears to have risen substantially during the 1980s, it is likely they were and still are a minority among resettlers (patterns that no up-to-date data are available to document in any precise way). Rather, for reasons that will subsequently become clear, parents are a key group to include in any analysis of middle-class inner-city resettlement that is concerned with issues of critical social practice and social-movement theory.

In terms of household type and housing form, the bulk of both parent and non-parent respondents lived in one- or two-adult households, and they almost all lived in older houses. All but one parent – a long-term resident in a non-profit cooperative – were homeowners. Non-parents, meanwhile, were about evenly split between homeowners and tenants (who generally rented either apartments in old houses or, in a few cases, whole small houses):

	Parents	Non-parents	Total
Household Type			
1-adult	3	13	16
Male-female couple	27	10	37
Other 2-adult	1	4	5
3- or 4-adult	–	5	5
Housing Type			
Older house (pre-1930)	30	27	57
Newer house (post-1960)	–	1	1
Converted small warehouse	–	2	2
Old low-rise apartment	1	2	3
Tenure			
Homeowners	30	14	44
Tenants	–	17	17
Housing cooperative	1	1	2

For the most part, respondents' housing was not fashionably renovated. Most of the houses (or apartments) where they lived were maintained in their old condition. In many cases, this had involved some repair or reconditioning – in a few instances, quite extensive work – but this had mainly been done either for required maintenance or to modify room-layouts. Few were 'whitepainters.'

Parents were generally not highly mobile. About three-quarters had been at their current address longer than two years, while six of eight who had lived at their present location for less than two years indicated an intention to remain for the foreseeable future. Non-parents, meanwhile, were about evenly split in respect to mobility, with an expectedly strong correlation among younger age, more recent movement, and greater likelihood of movement in the near future:

	Parents	Non-parents	Total
At Current Address			
> 5 years	11	7	18
2–5 years	12	9	21
1–2 years	5	7	12
< 1 year	3	9	12

The sample did not represent Toronto's multicultural, multiracial demography. All but three respondents were either Canadian-born or immigrants from the United States or Great Britain, and only one (Canadian-born) was a member of a visible minority:

Place of Birth	
Ontario	34
Another province of Canada	16
Immigrant from United States	8
Immigrant from Great Britain	2
Immigrant from continental Europe	2
Immigrant from South Africa	1
Visible Minority Status	
Not member of visible minority	62
Member of visible minority	1

As well, a majority of respondents had surnames that would generally be stereotyped as Anglo-Saxon or, in several other cases, as Jewish.

In respect to personal history, respondents were mainly from middle-class urban or suburban backgrounds:

	Parents	Non-parents	Total
Class of Parental Family			
Middle/upper-middle class	23	23	46
Working class	8	9	17
Parental Family Residence			
Mainly in cities	11	9	20
Mainly suburbs	12	13	25
Mainly small towns or rural	5	7	12
Multiple locales	3	3	6

Finally, the sample generally fell into three groups in terms of the neighbourhoods in which it lived and its patterns of settlement in these neighbourhoods:

– about half (thirty-two respondents) were residents of inner-city enclaves that, at the time of interviewing, were either dominantly working-class or a fairly evenly split hodgepodge of middle- and working-class residents;

– twenty-seven respondents had been early middle-class in-movers (in some cases, to a nearby address from which they had moved to their present address*) to formerly working-class neighbourhoods that had subsequently 'gentrified' around them;

– a few respondents have moved into neighbourhoods that were already largely middle-class at the time of their arrival.

Clearly, the sampling method cannot be claimed to have exhausted all of the kinds of 'transition-phase gentrifiers' who may be found in inner Toronto. As well, there is a good deal that the research did not learn about the sample. As has been noted, for example, no effort was made to compile extensive statistical material; and while a lot of casual information was gleaned about the typical daily rounds and interaction patterns of many respondents, no systematic time-budget or network data were gathered. As well, the information reported represents respondents' outlooks at only one point in time, with no

---

* In most cases, respondents' immediately preceding housing location – both tenants and homeowners – was in downtown Toronto:

Preceding Address	
Downtown Toronto	55
Suburban Toronto	4
Small town/rural	1
Other city	3

'longitudinal' dimension (comparing, say, their views shortly after moving to a neighbourhood with their views several months later). The interview instrument used in William Michelson's 1970s study of residential preference (Michelson 1977) remains in many ways the standard in the field of housing research in Toronto, in comparison to which the procedure used in the present study was highly limited. The research strategy does generally establish, however, sound plausibility for the findings that are reported within the limited realm for which generalization is made.

Respondents and the Inner City: First Reflections

Before turning to the main body of findings generated by the field-work, a few first reflections are appropriate insofar as they help to offer a clearer understanding of the sample and to place the findings overall in social context. As well, these reflections bear on the issue of the degree to which respondents may have a kind of 'utopian' vision of the inner city as an urban living environment.

As was observed in chapter 4, the latter issue is relevant in grasping the nature of postmodernist (or anti-modernist) social practices and in understanding distinctions that may exist among different forms of these practices. One common usage of the word *utopian* in reference to space is to connote an ideal but unrealized locale for everyday life shaped by an interplay of imagination with critical and practical reason, and the housing perceptions and preferences of most of the sample are not consistent with this definition. None of them would desire a wholesale reconstruction of the city along the lines of the early urban modernists' vision. Rather, their sense of urban 'utopia' is akin to that of such critics of modernism as Jacobs and Mumford – not the vision of an ideal of community in the mind's eye that may be fashioned at some future time but of a locale for living whose infrastructure is already at hand within the framework of the residual form of the historical city. Often, they are highly critical of distributive features of current-day Canadian urbanism; they frequently have vividly unfulfilled visions in this respect. But they also have a strongly positive image of old downtown neighbourhoods. In the words of one inner-city Toronto resident (not a respondent),

> Our community represents a little utopia of sorts. People from the whole spectrum of cultural, religious, lifestyle and economic backgrounds live on our street in relative harmony. Our community is so strong because

of the ideal we share of a strong community, regardless of the differences
in our backgrounds. (Freedman 1991)

The qualifier 'of sorts' is noteworthy here insofar as it suggests an
understanding that the 'utopia' in question is more modestly conceived than what is implied by the word's often more apocalyptic
usage.

The first reflection, then, concerns the degree of respondents' commitment to inner-city living, an attachment that for some of the sample is ambivalent. The latter respondents also envision an alternative
kind of place in a rural or small-town environment that they might
find desirable. In the words of an artist/designer living a stone's throw
from the downtown core,*

> I would like someday not to live downtown. I would like to live
> where there are trees and woods. (D15)

Or of a staff-lawyer with a provincial government agency:

> I'd like living in the country as well. My wife and I lived there for a
> year; it was fantastic. (B16)

Others enjoy living mainly in the city but want to spend at least some
of their time in another setting – for example, two editor/typographers
in their early forties, one employed by a small publishing house, the
other by a downtown weekly newspaper:

> I would certainly like to live some portion of the year in a place
> where I could step out the door and not see anybody but my family,
> not hear anything. (B11)

> Every penny I'm saving is to buy a little place in the country. (C5)

Some respondents raised the possibility of living out of the city part-

---

* The interview excerpts reported in this and subsequent chapters are, for the most
part, verbatim transcriptions of respondents' remarks. In some cases, wording has
been tightened or altered to remove repetitions, ambiguities, or mannerisms; in a
few cases, the sequence of wording has been reordered for the sake of clarity; and
in two cases, wording was reconstructed from fieldworker's notes because the relevant remarks were not taped. Each excerpt is coded. Those prefixed 'A' and 'B'
denote female and male parents respectively; those prefixed 'C' and 'D' denote female and male non-parents.

or full-time because they are inclined in this direction for themselves. Parents also think in terms of their children:

> Our kids do miss being in the country ... We realized we had to consciously get out to the country more. (B3)

> I lived in the country as a kid, and I never thought I'd ever leave the city once I became acclimatized, and now I'm looking at [son] and saying more and more that it might be better for him in a small town. But it will be one or the other, either the city or a small town. (B2)

Among both parents and non-parents who raised this issue, these alternatives were repeatedly paired:

> I prefer to live either in the city or the country. (A4)

> Either the country or the city, not anything in between. (A2)

It would be highly inaccurate, in this context, to portray the respondents collectively as individuals torn between urban and rural life, harbouring romantic notions of bucolic bliss. Only a minority raised the subject at all, and like the father above, several who spoke about the possibility of leaving the city had, in fact, at least partly grown up in rural or small-town environments, and hence were personally familiar with the advantages and disadvantages of these kinds of locales. Moreover, only a couple of respondents actually expressed an intention to alter their living arrangements in the foreseeable future. For the others, the idea of departing the city seems to have a kind of chimeric character. What is noteworthy, rather, are two other points.

First, while the inner city does have a kind of utopian quality for many respondents – a majority of whom never dream of leaving the city except to go to another city ('I'm a city mouse,' said one [D3]) – others partly perceive urban life as a compromise necessitated by the vicissitudes of earning a living along the particular career-paths they have chosen, careers that usually cannot be pursued away from an urban setting (for example, as media-workers or specialized professionals). For these individuals, the city is an environment that sometimes pales when measured against the imagined possibility of out-of-city living, and their enjoyment of the city is occasionally diminished by the idea of a quite different kind of residential locale.

Second and more importantly, however, small towns, rural environments, and other cities are the *only* alternatives respondents considered in discussing where they might live if not inner-city Toronto. Unanimity is a rare occurrence in social research, even in a targeted non-probability sample of the kind pursued here. In the present fieldwork, however, *not a single respondent interviewed* would move to a suburban locale under foreseeable circumstances. The logic of this attitude, and respondents' views about suburbs, will be explored in chapter 7. In conclusion, while some respondents prefer inner-city housing mainly within the specific framework of the metropolitan setting – given the alternatives of either downtown or suburb – most of the sample prefers this residential locale measured against any possible alternative.

A second general reflection relating to the nature of respondents' decisions to live in the inner city concerns the validity of theorizations of residential settlement patterns that stress the importance of such hypothesized role-based 'lifestyles' as 'familism,' 'careerism,' or 'consumerism.' Wendell Bell, for example, has argued that individuals' rational choices to emphasize one or another (or some combination) of these roles and to seek appropriately supportive residential environments are an essential factor in urban housing preference (1968). The data reported here, however, call into question this kind of approach, suggesting that at least some city-dwellers – represented by the overwhelming bulk of the sample – find in their residential settings holistic qualities of life that pervade their full rounds of activity. For these individuals, it is only within the context of broader frameworks of preference expressing fundamental values that such factors as 'familism,' 'careerism,' or 'consumerism' become salient.

Bell did observe that 'the three ... lifestyles did not seem adequate to account for all the responses given' in his own fieldwork, and he framed a residual category he termed 'quest-for-community' to encompass many of the square pegs that did not fit the round holes of the theory (1968: 157). But he found this pattern of choice sufficiently unimportant that it remained peripheral to his central thinking. In the fieldwork reported here, in contrast, the nature of respondents' residential preferences runs preponderantly against the grain of 'lifestyle' theory. Their choice does not reflect preference for a particular role-emphasis but rather the desire for a *lifeworld*. ('Quest-for-community' is an aspect of this choice for many respondents but, as will be discussed, is only one of a number of considerations germane to their thinking.) This finding helps to sustain the view that an impulse toward a kind of ideal living environment – not simply a pragmatic

question – is at play in the housing-location decisions of the bulk of
the respondents, and it raises a key theme that will recur in reporting
the fieldwork.

A third reflection relevant to respondents' general perceptions of
the inner city arises from concerns many of them express about the
current course of development and property markets in Toronto's
downtown neighbourhoods. For example, the complexity of inner-
city demography, including the presence of a range of economic groups,
is – as will be seen – among the main features respondents value
about this residential locale. In recent years, however, this diversity
has been rapidly diminishing as working-class households, bohemian
communities, and other less affluent groups have been displaced from
their former neighbourhoods. Only a small handful of respondents
did not express at least some anxiety about this process, and among
those who did, many support state activity to help sustain downtown's social mix. For example, fully one-fourth of the sample (sixteen
respondents) voiced a belief that non-profit housing cooperatives of
the type initiated by Toronto's 1970s municipal reformists are essential to maintaining the kind of demographically varied communities
in which they want to live.

As this chapter noted earlier, the topic of non-profit housing was
unprompted by the researcher. The interview contained no routine
probes concerning respondents' attitudes toward government housing
policy. However, seven of the respondents in question were in some
way linked to the co-op housing movement – two as employees in
the non-profit housing sector, two as activists working on behalf of
co-op housing in community groups in their neighbourhoods, two as
long-term residents of inner-city co-ops, and one as a lawyer who
frequently represents housing co-ops. (Notably, these seven respondents were unconnected within the snowball structure of the sample.)
The remaining respondents who talked about co-ops were simply
individuals familiar with and supportive of non-profit housing:

I see the cooperative housing in the neighbourhood as its saviour, because there is quite a bit of co-op housing around here ... At least
that guarantees that the neighbourhood is going to be respectably diverse. (D14)

To be in any way effective or have any kind of significant impact [in
maintaining inner-city demographic mix], we have to build many,

Donvale, the Spruce Court Co-op. Respondent B3: 'The interesting communities will be where there are co-ops, because that's where the diversity will be – because everything else will be insufferably bourgeois.'

many times more units than we are of non-profit, non-commodity housing. (D11)

This is why I'm really in favour of non-profit housing co-ops, because I think that's the only way people like young artists are going to be able to stay in the inner city. (C7)

The interesting communities will be where there are co-ops, because that's where the diversity will be – because everything else will be insufferably bourgeois. (B3)

The key point about these attitudes toward co-op housing is that they illustrate an important way in which many respondents' vision of the inner city is increasingly an imaginary, as the real locale of their choice becomes the absent locale of their nostalgia (a word whose literal meaning is 'homesickness'). To the degree that this is the case – that a contradiction has emerged between the city they seek to inhabit and the city as it is – their image of downtown neighbourhoods as an ideal residential environment is no longer based in the perception of an existing reality but in the dream of a possible reality, one that can be accomplished only by active intervention to sustain and strengthen the inner city's residual social fabric. Hence, their attitude toward the city is not *laissez-faire* but rooted in a specific idea of the city that has become problematic. (Respondents' concerns about the changing character of downtown neighbourhoods are addressed in detail in chapter 8.)

In conclusion, most respondents do have a kind of ideal sense of the living locale they expect and desire the inner city to be. Although some of them feel an occasional inclination away from the city toward an alternative, more rural living environment, few plan to make this change, and *none* can imagine choosing to move to a suburban locale. As well, the holistic nature of most respondents' perceptions of inner-city life renders role-emphasis (or 'lifestyle') models of residential choice largely irrelevant to their housing activities. Finally, many respondents have found that Toronto's downtown neighbourhoods are becoming increasingly inconsistent with their vision of inner-city life.

These first reflections help set the stage for fieldwork findings discussed in chapter 7: reasons reported by respondents for their decision to live in older inner-city neighbourhoods.

7

Middle-Class Resettlers and Inner-City Lifeworlds

This chapter explores the main reasons discussed by respondents for their decision to live in inner-city neighbourhoods, reasons that are distilled to four distinct qualities of life they believe may be found in these locales: (i) a closely grained mix of, on the one hand, community and, on the other, the city as 'a world of strangers'; (ii) demographic diversity; (iii) a tolerance and nourishment of non-traditional and marginal values; and (iv) spatial and architectural features of downtown and its neighbourhoods.

Private Realms and Public Realms

'Community' and the Inner City

Respondents repeatedly echoed the view that inner-city neighbourhoods have qualities of 'community':

> To me, downtown is very similar to living in a small community. It's like living in a small town where people know each other. (C6)

> We have a great local shopping street that's like the main street in a town. On the weekend you can never go there without seeing people you know. (A6)

> We live on a park where a lot of parents come and sit with their children, so I've met a lot of people from sitting there with my own children. There's a skating rink in the winter, so everybody's out there

skating all the time; and in the summer they play baseball. It's a social centre – it feels a little like a village. (A12)

I have the strong sense of this neighbourhood as being like a little
village. We have lots of friends around here, so that [daughter] knows
half a dozen people along this street, and half a dozen people along
the next street, and on the street after that. When we go to the store
there's lots of people saying hello to one another. (B14)

It's like living in a small community – like the small town I grew up
in. (A10)

A few non-parents interviewed were indifferent or even hostile to the
value of community-of-locality and did not share this outlook – for
example, two younger single women:

It's not something I particularly care about one way or the other. No
... that doesn't interest me. (C8)

I would say on my own street there's a low sense of community,
partly because there's a lot of single people ... I don't miss it, and it's
not something I necessarily look for. In fact, one of the reasons why I
left a small town was because it had that strong sense of community;
I found it suffocating. (C11)

But they were exceptions. Virtually every parent interviewed and a
majority of non-parents identified the perception of 'community' as
a main reason why they like living in downtown neighbourhoods.
   Respondents' meaning of 'community' does not necessarily entail
social relations with immediate neighbours that arise solely from
proximity. But such contacts do often occur. For example, a social-
agency lawyer from a working-class background found that she saw
more of her neighbours after she became a parent:

Now I spend a lot of time in my neighbourhood, and these are the
people I relate to ... It's my neighbours that I pass the time of day
with and sit and have a beer with after dinner. The street I grew up
on was very similar – people of all different ethnic backgrounds,
working people – and this street makes me feel right at home ... One
guy up the street is as right-wing and red-necked as they come. But
that's okay – you sit out there and have a beer and argue with him.
(A13)

Neighbourhood park. Respondent A12: 'We live on a park where a lot of parents come and sit with their children, so I've met a lot of people from sitting there with my own children. There's a skating rink in the winter, so everybody's out there skating all the time; and in the summer they play baseball. It's a social centre – it feels a little like a village.'

A single mother from a suburban middle-class background reported similar frequent contacts with working-class neighbours:

> The area that I'm in now is a working-class area ... The neighbours know each other, they help each other. If we're doing work on the backyard, the neighbours will come and help us do the work, and we help them ... If I had to go out in a rush, I could leave [daughter] with the neighbour. If you need a shovel in the wintertime, some-body has a shovel ... I have my own life separate and apart from the street, but the street's still part of my life ... I like the feeling I'm part of [it] ... It's the feeling of community. Like the guy up the street, his daughter got married, and he came down and brought us all wedding cake – us, the neighbours, the neighbours across the street; everybody got wedding cake. If people have baseball tickets they can't use,

they'll go up and down the block to see who wants to use them.
(A16)

Many non-parents, too, reported social relations with working-class
and immigrant neighbours:

> One of the reasons I like this street is that it's a place where people
> say hello to each other ... where kids are playing on the street ...
> When I wanted to get some digging done around the house [to repair
> a drainage problem], I went to talk to the guy across the street and
> said did he know anybody on the street who needed work who
> would be able to do that kind of thing, and he said, yeah, he knew
> so-and-so and so-and-so. (C3)

> This street is a village; we watch out for each other ... People keep an
> eye on each other's houses and trade plants for the garden and help
> each other get jobs done. They know that I used to be a nurse, so
> sometimes I get called with little health questions ... It's not like we're
> great friends, but there's that kind of community contact. (C4)

> We know the neighbours here. Our street is very stable. – – – next
> door has been here sixty-four years, and the – – – s, two doors down,
> have been here sixty-seven years, and – – – has been here for twenty-
> five years, six doors down ... I guess [wife] and I are the only people
> on this block with professional kinds of jobs ... [and] I sometimes get
> called if there's a disturbance on the street, if a house is broken into
> ... Sometimes when people want to report something, they call me
> and ask me to call the police. (D3)

But while these kinds of interactions do involve more than only saying
hello to familiar faces, they are usually not especially intimate, consisting for the most part either of occasionally passing time outside
the home chatting with neighbours or of relationships of reciprocal
aid involving such matters as street-surveillance, home maintenance,
or childcare.

Not all respondents report neighbouring relations of these types.
Others have only incidental relationships or none at all with working-
class or immigrant neighbours:

> In the spring, as soon as the weather's nice, people are in their yards.
> People are always dropping by to chat when you're working in the
> front yard ... but really there's very little in common ... Beyond five

or ten minutes over the fence about gardening – well, it's hard to get past that; a lot of people don't have much in the way of English. (B3)

I know the other people who live in my house – there's four apartments, and we borrow things from each other, stuff like that ... [But] I don't feel that close to the Chinese people; I don't know any of my Chinese neighbours. (C7)

We don't communicate very much with people of different ethnic backgrounds ... People around here who are our friends are people of our own background. (A2)

Overall, the data revealed certain predictable patterns with respect to neighbouring. Respondents who were long-term residents of their neighbourhoods, had children, were homeowners, worked at least partly at home, and seemed to have relatively extroverted personalities were more likely to report frequent contact with neighbours on their street than more recent or childless residents, tenants, or people who worked solely away from home or appeared to have more introverted personalities. Yet, whether or not respondents have sustained ties with immediate neighbours based on simple proximity was largely immaterial to their perception of local 'community.' A woman who reported only occasional contacts with adjacent neighbours said of her street:

The community feeling is based on seeing people day-by-day and sharing a common patch of city space with them. (C9)

Another respondent explained why he likes living in the 'community' of a west-end working-class district:

A lot of what develops in terms of community is that people live their lives in the open, on the street, in sight of each other. It's a gas walking up this street on afternoons in the summertime and seeing everything that's going on on people's porches. In a couple of hundred yards you can see a hundred people enjoying themselves. I like life being visible ... We know hardly anybody on the street ... but there is a cohesiveness that's here whether we're completely part of it or not. (D5)

An index of community, which may serve as a test of respondents' perception of the presence of community in the absence of networks

of sustained social ties between working- and middle-class neighbours, is what occurs when neighbourhoods are threatened. In this
respect, three areas from which respondents were sampled had recently experienced local controversies: in one case, burgeoning drug
traffic on a nearby arterial street; in another, the prospect of a noxious
land-use adjacent to a cluster of houses; in a third, a proposed housing
development whose density worried its neighbours. Each was an area
in which respondents reported that there had not previously been a
conspicuously high degree of close contact between working- and
middle-class residents, but in each case a substantial number of residents of both groupings turned out at community meetings to discuss
the issues and try to take mutual action. A respondent in the first of
these neighbourhoods described this process:

> When it started happening, and people started feeling oppressed by it
> on the street, the neighbours would all talk, and we had a couple of
> large meetings. Eighty or a hundred people showed up at the recrea-
> tion centre to talk about it and to set up a steering committee; com-
> munity action was there when necessary. (B3)

As a consequence of this organizing, the neighbourhood was able to
exert pressure on city hall and the police department to help combat
the drug trade. In the case of each neighbourhood, a strong, nascent
community seemed simply to have been waiting for an occasion to
coalesce, a pattern reflecting the sentiment of a respondent who said
of his street:

> People who live around here – you know that you share certain
> things with them, important things about how you want to live your
> lives, shared likes and dislikes about the way you live. I think there's
> an important unspoken bond between people around here. (D1)

Distinct from the question of relations with neighbours based on
simple proximity, most respondents reported having friends in their
immediate locality:

> My best friends happen to have moved here, all around the same
> time, some coincidentally, some to follow their friends ... so it's a
> whole network of people walking by and stopping in and visiting.
> (B6)

I don't know any of the Portuguese, but that doesn't mean I feel isolated here. I have a lot of friends all within a short distance, all within five or ten blocks. (D6)

I socialize with some of the neighbours, but I don't really know them that well. But I have a sister who lives in the neighbourhood, and I have friends who live nearby, and I like the idea that I'm accessible to my friends and my sister. (A16)

And virtually every respondent reported a network of friends within the inner city generally, beyond their immediate neighbourhoods (networks based largely in the east end in the case of east-end respondents and in the west end among respondents living there). These networks were composed in large part of people whose homes were within relatively easy walking or cycling distance, and in this connection, some respondents spoke about 'neighbours' and 'neighbourhood' in a partly despatialized sense:

You have neighbours in the city, but they're not necessarily on your street ... [they're] not necessarily a geographic network. (D5)

Ask me who I actually come into contact with in the course of a week, and my neighbourhood is very different from the neighbourhood here ... My friends are scattered in various places in the city, my attention is scattered all over the place. (D14)

A sense of community, then, is among the main qualities of life respondents find in inner-city neighbourhoods. For many, this 'community' does partly entail social contacts grounded in shared space, often with working-class or immigrant neighbours, a form of sociability that respondents frequently connect with the working-class or ethnic social infrastructures still present in many of their districts (though as will be observed in chapter 8, these infrastructures are often increasingly attenuated). As well, most respondents' sense of community involves sustained participation in networks of friends who live both within their immediate area and across the wider arena of the inner city generally; and they report that many of these friends are also middle-class resettlers of older downtown neighbourhoods who share their particular outlooks and values toward the city.

The Inner City as a World of Strangers

Concurrently, however, with their sense of inner-city community –
the city as a world of neighbours and friends – many of the same
respondents celebrate the city as a world of strangers:

> One of the main reasons why I choose to live in the city is that
> there's a lot of people around – I like a lot of strangers ... I like the
> chance of meeting strangers. (B13)

> When I walk around in the streets downtown, I'm probably not
> gonna see anybody I know – it's a surprise if I see anybody I know.
> So I just walk along, pleasantly by myself, the same way that I like it
> in the country. There's a pleasant anonymity in the city – it's not al-
> ienating. (B11)

> I like the anonymity. I can walk down the street any time of day, any-
> where I want, and no one knows who I am. I can do anything I
> want, and I don't have to worry about anyone's impression – I mean,
> what do I care? I don't even know these people. (C11)

> I like the feeling at night that just a few blocks away people are wide
> awake, the taverns are open. I like to know there are people there;
> there's a kind of life around me. (A5)

One of the main locales in which this juxtaposition of city as community and city as a world of strangers is played out is along the
commercial streets that make up the edges of the inner city's residential neighbourhoods. Nearly every respondent identified their local arterial streets as one of the features they liked best about living
in their part of town – views that will be treated in more detail later
in the chapter in discussing respondents' attitudes toward the inner-
city spatial environment. Respondents enjoy walking on these streets,
shopping on them, stopping in at the restaurants and bars – on the
one hand, meeting friends and neighbours; on the other, encountering
crowds of strangers:

> I like the hustle and bustle on Bloor and Spadina. You walk down
> Bloor on a Saturday afternoon or a Sunday, and it's packed with peo-
> ple walking around, out on the street ... a parade of people going by.
> (A12)

> We lived close to College Street, and we went to the cafes a lot ... We

would go out for a *cafe au lait* at night, and you'd walk along College Street and see groups of people just standing on the corner talking – they'd come out of the Portuguese Club, or they would just be walking down the street, or they'd drive up to the cafe and a whole pile of people would get out and just hang around for a couple of hours ... People got to know us. When they saw us coming, they knew who we were and what we usually ordered ... I like it when people spend a lot of time outside their homes and out on the streets. (C2)

There's action on Bloor Street. I like walking down to the restaurant or to my pub to meet people I know. And on the street are all of these different kinds of people all going about their city lives. (B15)

Another respondent expressed similar sentiments about riding the trolley-bus:

I like cities. I've always felt a desire to be close to ... a lot of human energy ... I don't like the financial district, so I don't mean that. I can't stand the Eaton Centre. Downtown means somewhere around Spadina and Bloor or Yonge and Wellesley to me. I like to see people close together, lots of different activities going on ... I think of riding the trolley-bus somewhere in the west end, like maybe Ossington or Lansdowne – you just see ordinary people, a million different lives doing different things, all intersecting on a bus platform. And I find that enriches my daily life, to feel connected and part of a large group of people ... even though I don't know them. (D11)

Observing the emergence of the modern metropolis, Georg Simmel observed that beneath the cosmopolitan veneer of urban public life 'is not only indifference but, more often than we are aware ... a slight aversion, a mutual strangeness and repulsion, which will break into hatred and fight at the moment of closer contact ... under certain circumstances, one nowhere feels as lonely and lost as in the metropolitan crowd' (1988: 21, 23). Certainly, in some settings and for some individuals, this characterization may be correct; a central lesson that has emerged from decades of social research about urban environments is the variation in individual and subcultural responses to the city's social and perceptual stimuli. Simmel's characterization does not describe, however, the outlook toward the world of strangers along the main streets of the inner city felt by most of the respondents discussed here. Rather, they often find satisfaction and pleasure in their contacts with anonymity.

Waiting for the Ossington bus. Respondent D11: 'I like cities. I've always felt a desire to be close to ... a lot of human energy ... I like to see people close together, lots of different activities going on ... I think of riding the trolley-bus somewhere in the west end, like maybe Ossington or Lansdowne – you just see ordinary people, a million different lives doing different things, all intersecting on a bus platform.'

The Inner City: Diversity and Values

The Inner City and Social Diversity

The second and third qualities of life respondents believe may be found in inner-city neighbourhoods are social heterogeneity and a tolerance and nourishment of non-traditional and marginal values. In this section, these two qualities will be treated together.

Nearly every respondent identified demographic complexity as a primary attraction of inner-city living. They particularly cited the ethnic and racial diversity of Toronto's downtown neighbourhoods (mentioning, among others, the city's Italian, Chinese, Portuguese, East Indian, Greek, Korean, Latin American, and West Indian communities). As well, many cited the mix of working- and middle-class households in many inner-city neighbourhoods. And several made reference to the visible presence of various marginal subcultures, including bohemian and gay communities and artistic and political-activist groupings. In a number of cases, the latter affinity was partly rooted in respondents' own affiliation with one or more of these subcultures, a theme that will be raised in the context of discussing the inner city and non-conventional values. For the present, however, these instances in which respondents were themselves linked to specific marginal groups will be left aside, as will cases in which respondents' personal circumstances connected them to a particular ethnic community (including, for example, two who were non-anglophone European immigrants, some who claimed non-anglophone heritage through one or both parents, and a few who had spouses or housemates who were 'ethnic' Canadians). Given these exclusions, and treating solely respondents' outlook toward cultural or social groupings from which they were outsiders, what is to be made of their attraction to living amid downtown's social and cultural diversity? Are they simply *flâneurs* – cultural voyeurs – who enjoy the erotic spectacle of urban social complexity?

The argument here, based on the fieldwork reported, is that this is not the case; rather, respondents seek to participate in the social kaleidoscope of the inner city as what Edward Relph has termed 'existential' or 'empathetic insiders,' terms defined in chapter 5 that Relph uses in particular reference to individuals' relationships with spatial landscapes but that may also be applied to their relationships to urban social topography. The central evidence in support of this argument was the outlook expressed by parent-respondents toward the question of social diversity and their children. But before turning to this evidence, it is necessary to consider in more general terms the issue of families with children among middle-class resettlers of older inner-city neighbourhoods – people who, according to many conceptualizations of 'gentrification,' should not be there at all and whose presence is central to the argument of the book.

'Gentrification' and 'Familism'

'Gentrification' has often been theorized as activity rooted in what one Canadian writer, Barton Reid, has termed 'a non-familial culture' of everyday life (1988: 36). In Britain, for example, Hamnett has identified gentrification with adult households 'created by later marriage or deferred childbearing' (1984: 302). In the United States, Palen and London, in a mainly demand-side context, have counted as the central players in gentrification childless and one-child households drawn by proximity to downtown jobs and 'adult amenities'; Beauregard, taking a production-of-gentrifiers approach, has cited the 'consumption needs of career-oriented one- and two-person households' created by recent demographic, economic, and social trends as key to the emergence of 'potential gentrifiers'; and Smith, in a structuralist framework, has described gentrification as an urban form oriented to 'the proliferation of one- and two-person households and the popularity of the "urban singles" life-style' (Palen and London 1984: 259, Beauregard 1986: 43, Smith 1986: 30).

In part, this outlook seems to arise from a penetration of social theory by ideology, a process Roland Barthes has termed the naturalization of myth (1973: 109–59) – in this case, the myth that suburbs are the appropriate locale for child-rearing, an attitude urban analysts sometimes appear to lend axiomatic theoretical status. Bell, for example, partly framed his 'lifestyle' theory of residential choice in the observation that 'there is no need to enumerate ... the advantages of the suburbs over many of the neighbourhoods of the central city as a place to rear children' (1968: 151). In the literature concerning gentrification, Williams has described 'the suburban environment' as 'more conducive to childrearing' than city neighbourhoods; Ley has juxtaposed the 'adult-oriented lifestyle' of downtown with 'suburban familism'; Lipton has identified suburban locations with 'amenities that are child-related'; and Beauregard and Hamnett seem to assume that once delayed child-bearing gentrifiers shift life-cycle phases, they will mostly depart for the suburbs (Williams 1986: 69, Ley 1985: 18, Lipton 1980: 58, Beauregard 1986: 43, Hamnett 1984: 301–2).

Lost in this mythology is recognition that not all middle-class parents subscribe to the vision of the suburban familial utopia. Bell himself, for example, characterized as 'familistic' nearly half the cases in a sample of more affluent residents who chose to live in an inner Chicago neighbourhood; Michelson, based on research done in Toronto, alerted housing-choice theorists several years ago to contrasting views among suburban and downtown parents about the supposed child-rearing benefits of out-of-city environments; Irving Allen has observed that inner-city parents appear to find there a 'milieu of social and cultural diversity [that they believe] represents a childrearing advantage over "homogeneous suburbs"'; and Rose has linked the settlement patterns of downtown parents – particularly women – to a rejection of the hegemony of the 'traditional patriarchal household' embedded in the suburban myth (Bell 1968: 158, Michelson 1977: 299–301, Allen 1984: 31, Rose 1984: 51).

With respect to gentrification, one consequence of the insertion of suburban mythology into theoretical thinking seems to have been a kind of ecological fallacy – an approach rooted in the implicit premise that preponderant areal associations are the primary patterns that need to be analysed. Certainly, childless households have been a main component of gentrification, while a majority of families with children in such societal settings as Canada, the United States, and Britain do continue to settle in suburban locations; the occasional inattention to parents among 'gentrifiers' was in part less a matter of neglect than an effort to focus on apparent dominant features of the process. But an account of modal cases of a phenomenon cannot lead to a grasp of the phenomenon overall. In the case of patterns of residential choice, a comprehensive understanding of a given tendency requires a reckoning of *all* types of households involved; and middle-class resettlers of older inner-city neighbourhoods have persistently included many households with children.

This has been especially the case in Canada, whose cities (as was observed in chapters 3 and 5) did not experience wholesale middle-class abandonment in the postwar decades – a period during which Canadian suburbanization appears to have been as much supply-side as demand-side driven – and where, in contrast to the United States, city neighbourhoods have generally been viewed 'as more attractive places to raise children' (Clark 1966: 223, Rose 1989: 119). One implication of the persistence in Canadian cities of middle-class neighbourhoods which include many households with children is that the more recent presence of families among middle-class resettlers of largely working-class districts has not been an especially eccentric pattern. The activity of these households has not represented a sharp break from past practice but only an extension of already settled inner-city middle-class family terrain.

The widespread presence of these households has been increasingly remarked in Canadian literature in the field. Ley, for example, who at one time found it anomalous that 'even families are being drawn to the inner city,' later shifted ground to number households with children as a main component of middle-class in-movement to old city neighbourhoods; Alison Dantas has identified families as key to the middle-class resettlement of a prototypical 'gentrifying' neighbourhood in Toronto, Riverdale, and concluded that 'in theoretical terms' discovery of these families 'requires a broadening of conventional concepts of gentrification'; and Rose has called particular attention to the presence of many single-parent families among middle-class inner-city resettlers (Ley 1985: 22, 1987: 14–15; Dantas 1988: 82–4).

In the context of this book's general argument, that middle-class resettlement of older inner-city neighbourhoods in Canadian cities in part constitutes a form of critical social practice, the importance of correctly identifying the kinds of households involved becomes quickly apparent. For, if families are not involved – if the core of the gentrification process entails mainly only childless individuals whose housing choices may be said to be associated with particular career or consumption concerns – the picture is very different than if a large number of households with children are also involved. In the latter case, simple 'familism' ceases to be a useful sorting mechanism for distinguishing who does and does not settle in older inner-city neighbourhoods, and household-type loses its salience as a variable in seeking to account for this pattern of housing choice. Instead, analysis is forced to confront issues of social values and meanings that may transcend life-cycle stage and to examine the question of why a broad range of middle-class households, including many families with children, settle in old downtown neighbourhoods.

One argument, of course, is that parents who settle in the inner city are, in fact, not 'familistic' – that although they do happen to have children, they prefer to orient their lives and housing choices to career or consumption concerns rather than to family matters. Using, for example, Bell's definition of 'familism' – framed in the United States in the 1960s – this would appear to be the case. For Bell, 'familism' denoted a 'lifestyle' involving 'marriage at young ages, a short childless time span after marriage, child-centeredness' and high fertility (1968: 147, 150), characteristics that do not describe the bulk of the parents interviewed in the present fieldwork, most of whom did not marry young, postponed child-bearing, do not claim to centre their lives solely around perceived needs of their children, and typically have only two children. (Of the thirty-one families sampled, twenty had two children, four had three, and the remaining seven had one; among the latter, two parents said it was likely they would have a second child at some point in the future.) However, it is also strongly arguable that the lived meaning of 'familism' is highly socially contingent – that 'familism' is a cultural construction whose satisfactory definition in one social setting may be quite inapplicable in another. In this context, it is useful to turn to what some parents in the present sample had to say about their orientation to child-rearing and family life – three mothers and three fathers whose attitudes were generally typical of the parent-respondents:

> I can't imagine anyone more family-oriented than me. Our idea of a good time is to come home and be with the kids. (A12)

> I know I can't give my daughter the kind of time or attention a non-working mother or a mother with a nine-to-five job would be able to give, so in that way, yeah, I'm less family-oriented. But in another way I'm very family-oriented. I see my parents two or three times a week, I have my sister living with me right now, my daughter sees my brother and his kids every couple of weeks – I mean it's not either/or, eh? (A16)

> I like home-making, I love children. When they were little, it was very important for me to be with them. But I also had the feeling that I had to be out there in contact with other adults, in some way participating in adult life. (A5)

> I enjoy my work a lot, and I'm out frequently for evening meetings or working till seven or seven-thirty. But I don't know if that's any different from people who enjoy their work who live in suburbs. I love coming home, I love the family. (B3)

> My family is very important to me. I haven't worked full-time since the first kid, three and a half years ago, and neither has my wife. I've taken off extended periods of time just to stay home with the kids when they've had some [health] troubles. (B8)

> I wouldn't say we're less family-oriented than people in suburbs. We do some things as a family; but we also do things as individuals. We *are* a family, but everything doesn't revolve around that. We're not totally on top of one another all the time. (B4)

Perhaps the most serious question in connection with a definition of familism like Bell's is its implicit premise that a woman with a career is axiomatically non-'familistic.' Certainly, a middle-class Canadian woman who marries young and immediately commences bearing several children (Bell's criteria) is unlikely to have much time for other serious pursuits until middle age. (In contrast, Bell's definition seems to assume that 'familistic' middle-class fathers *will* have careers.) In respect to the present fieldwork, however, this kind of assumption emerging from patriarchal conceptions of gender is not the main issue of interest in regard to 'lifestyle' residential theory. Rather, as has already been noted, the findings reported here call into question the entire central crux of the 'lifestyle' model of housing choice inasmuch as the interviews suggest that questions of role-emphasis are largely irrelevant to respondents' preference for living in inner-city locales. They are not seeking suitable locations for the expedient conduct of specific activities but rather have based their choices in more holistic concerns. Their perceptions of environmental settings occur in a context of fundamental values that influence the entire range of pursuits that make up their lives, including where they choose to live. This finding helps sustain the argument that a form of social movement is at least partly at play in middle-class resettlement of older inner-city neighbourhoods. As well, it underscores the importance of correctly identifying and understanding the activity of parents with children involved in the process.

Perceived Values of Social Diversity

Returning, then, to the question of parents, children, and inner-city socio-cultural complexity, nearly every parent interviewed mentioned social diversity as a feature of downtown life they strongly valued for their children:

> You should look at her class picture, a whole slew of people from different backgrounds, Jewish kids and Chinese kids and Portuguese kids and Italian and black. I like it that she sees the world as it is. When I was a kid [in the suburbs], I never ran into a black person. (A2)

> [Daughter] can say a few words of Chinese, which I certainly couldn't when I was her age ... I came from a pretty straightforward suburban upbringing, a white middle-class upbringing, and I think this [for a child to live downtown] is – well, for one thing, it's more fun. And in the long run it will perhaps be more useful to her, since she's going to be living in a multicultural world. (B14)

> This area is fairly multicultural ... I think that's good, that exposure, for the kids. It's a complete head start. I think kids who are brought up in connection to other cultures, other races, will not have to learn

later about human rights and non-discrimination. It will just be acquired. (B6)

The mix of people downtown ... gives a kid a better understanding of the world ... The way I look at it is partly related to my own experience. I grew up in a Jewish neighbourhood – it was thoroughly Jewish; people who weren't Jewish were very much a minority. (B9)

My sister's kids live in the suburbs. They have no concept of how privileged they've been; they haven't a clue what it's like not to have a lot of money. I'd like [daughter] to have a more realistic perception of what the world is like for most people. If you're exposed to people from many income levels, you know from a very early age those differences exist. (A4)

I have very conscious reasons why I don't want my children in suburbia ... My wife has family who live in the suburbs, and I have friends there, and I think it's very bad for children to be brought up where there's nobody except their own financial class. (B13)

My husband and I come from working-class backgrounds, and it's important to us to somehow keep our kids in touch with their working-class heritage and the values that are inherent in that. I'd be afraid of raising my kids in the suburbs – I'd end up with a couple of eighteen-year-olds who I had nothing in common with. (A13)

Finally, a mother who grew up in a downtown ethnic village, lived for a number of years after marriage in a suburban locale, then moved back downtown with her husband when the kids were aged three, five, and six, spoke of social mix in a different sense:

I wanted them not to think in terms of only mothers. All you see in the suburbs during the day is mothers and kids; there's no males or teenagers in sight. To me the suburbs are nothing but bedrooms. It gives kids a false idea. (A5)

This chapter will turn later to parents' views about suburbs and certain stereotypical perceptions that may seem embedded in their attitudes. Here, the key point is that their outlook toward inner-city social diversity is not reducible to a kind of *flâneurism* or an interest in a simulacrum of cosmopolitanism. Rather, it is rooted in a desire to expose their children to a more complex social reality than they believe is likely in other residential settings – a belief often grounded in their own experience of suburban environments as children.

As well, parents value the social diversity of the inner city for themselves, as do non-parents. An illustration of their outlook relates to the availability of ethnic groceries and restaurants in their neighbourhoods, an example mentioned by many respondents in seeking to articulate why they like living in a multicultural setting. The meaning of this example, however, is not simply that they like different kinds of food. Rather, in the context of the interviews, food became a handy metaphor for social difference – for illustrating encounters with social phenomena that were foreign to respondents' own cultural backgrounds and experience and that are an ordinary part of inner-city everyday life. Other respondents talked about the kinds of exterior renovation and yardscaping done by groups like Italian and Portuguese immigrants – 'mediterraneanized' houses, intensive vegetable gardens, small grottos with statutes of religious figures – or about the parades of religious banners, brass bands, and crowds of parishioners from local Italian and Portuguese churches that sometimes wend their way along neighbourhood sidestreets on summer Sunday afternoons. Others mentioned the diverse kinds of clothing and personal styles constantly visible on city streets or the babel of languages audible in food-markets and streetcars. The point of these examples was not their curiosity or quaintness, or some disembodied *ambiance* of urbanity they are perceived to provide, but rather the way that they create a particular texture of daily experience that is perceived to enrich respondents' lives and that they believe would be unavailable in other metropolitan settings. The respondents' interest was not so much the mix of food, languages, or cultural styles in themselves but the polyphony of *people* and human voices in the inner-city lifeworld.

The Inner City and Marginal Values

A further quality that many respondents find in inner-city neighbourhoods is a tolerance and nourishment of non-conventional values, a facet of life they directly relate to the diversity of peoples and cultures, whose close proximity in the inner city they believe necessarily breeds liberality of attitude. Some respondents used logic nearly identical to Louis Wirth's in explaining the 'relativistic perspective' they believe city-dwellers develop under the circumstances of size, density, and heterogeneity: 'the juxtaposition of divergent personalities and modes of life tends to produce ... a sense of toleration of difference' (1938: 20). In respect to support and encouragement for non-traditional values, a key feature of downtown social complexity that respondents mentioned was the presence of a range of middle-class subcultures:

> Being in the city, even though there's anonymity in terms of the general population, if you search it out, you can find a huge population of other people who are very similar to you in their weirdness ... I know there's a large population of people who are very similar to me in terms of their values and beliefs. (C11)

Roughly one-third of the sample (twenty-two respondents), for example, identified themselves as having political outlooks that in one sense or another would be classed on the left – as, say, socialists, radical feminists, or militant environmentalists. A large proportion of the others also seemed clearly, in one way or another, to share such kinds of outlooks, attitudes reflected in their expressed views about such issues as social housing, gender, or municipal politics. But unprompted by any specific question from the interviewer, at least twenty-two explicitly stated such an orientation, and many of them spoke about the inner city and non-conventional values in this context:

> Almost every elected politician from around here is NDP, and I like that – that my community elects progressive people. You don't find that in suburbs. Part of what makes the city vital is that there's political diversity and some possibility of political change ... You can find a sufficiently large nucleus of people who want to do something different. (B3)

> I came to the city wanting to express my [left] political ideas in some active way ... and I was able to find a group of people interested in the same things ... I was able to create a life for myself. (B10)

> Downtown, I think I'm much more likely to find working-class or middle-class people with socialist intentions or beliefs. For me, the inner parts of cities are places where you can do things in terms of working together with a variety of people. (C3)

> Politically, I'm out of the mainstream. Most of what I believe would be considered to be on the left ... For me, the city has tended to be

the motor of social change. This is where the people are, this is where lots of things can happen. (D13)

Others talked in terms of gender and sexual orientation:

> Part of the reason that I moved downtown – I was still in the process of coming out – was, I thought, well, I'm sure to meet some gay people down here eventually. If I sit on a park bench long enough, someone will come along. And they did. (D14)

> When I first moved to the city, it was because of the women's movement. I had the mobility to move to a metropolitan area where I could put myself in the thick of it ... Suburbs are sexually policed; that's what they're for – institutionalized heterosexuality ... [But in the inner city] lesbian women can connect up with organizations that represent their kind of lifestyle, and they can live as lesbians without feeling surveilled or threatened ... There's a wider range of acceptable behaviours here. (C5)

Respondents committed to particular bohemian or avant-garde sub cultural groupings expressed similar kinds of views.

In summary, respondents find downtown other people like themselves who share and help sustain their particular ways of looking at the world – networks of special importance for those whose political, sexual, or cultural practices are non-conventional. They also find a high degree of social diversity, of which they enjoy being part and which they believe fosters a tolerance for difference. Further, among respondents committed to some species of social change, the inner city is perceived as a good seeding ground for pursuing their activities.

Inner-City Landscape and Spatial Field

Perceptions of Suburbs

A fourth feature of older downtown neighbourhoods that respondents cited in explaining their preference for these housing locales is the character of inner-city landscape. One way to approach this theme is to contrast respondents' impressions of downtown with their perceptions of suburban spatial field, an environment they generally dislike.

In part, respondents' outlook toward suburbs is rooted in perceptions of suburban social character – views that surfaced earlier in the chapter in connection with parents' feelings about how inner-city demographic diversity may benefit their children. The topic of suburbs was probed in each of the interviews, and respondents' comments often turned to their attitudes about the cultural basis of suburban life:

> When we bought this house, two years ago, we considered going out to the suburbs. We drove out, and we drove through the streets, and we left. We didn't even look at a house. It was totally incompatible – the expectations and the connotations of being a suburbanite, the traditional values. I tried to imagine myself pushing my little stroller around in this suburban area – I mean, that would just be over the edge. (A13)

> I'm of a generation that equated going to the suburbs with putting my head down, having many babies and never thinking again for the rest of my life. I was desperate to get out of that kind of life. (A4)

> My sense from growing up in a suburb, and of visiting friends who live in suburbs, is that they're fairly bland places, that a very narrow range of people live there ... that there are opportunities for a broader range of experiences downtown than there would be in the narrow political spectrum of the suburbs. (B3)

> I have all these negatives around what a suburb means and what people are like in a suburb. I see it as straight and restricting and conforming ... There's a conforming kind of middle-class attitude ... [and] certain expectations around how you're expected to behave. (A16)

> People who move to the suburbs are pulverized by a dominant culture that defines what the normal, acceptable lifestyle is ... For us to go and live in a suburb would be, in our circle, abnormal. I mean, they'd figure, shit, what happened to them – have they gone off their rocker? It would be thought of as extremely bizarre. (B7)

> I'm a woman, I live alone ... If I lived in the suburbs I would really be socially isolated, because suburban life is couple life. You know – people meet in their homes, they have dinner, they have drinks, and they play bridge, and stuff like that. (C4)

> I grew up in a suburb – a very nice suburb ... lots of space around us, big houses, big gardens, curvy streets with big trees ... [But] every-

thing looked the same. When we were growing up, everyone was my parents' age with kids my age – that's my image of the suburbs. (C14)

I grew up in a suburb ... I suppose there are suburban streets where you get people who get to know each other and who do things to-gether – who organize for some sort of political reason or some kind of community event. But I don't think that happens very much. (D3)

I used to visit a friend in the suburbs ... and I'd look out, and there would be an Indian family over here and a black family over there and a white family over here. But you look at them, and they all are grey; one's the same as the other. I found it very hard to get into any kind of reasonable conversation out there. (B12)

Many respondents were uncomfortable with the stereotypical na-ture of their initial responses about suburbs and added quick dis-claimers that they did realize they were partly trading in somewhat obsolete popular images, that they were aware that a number of To-ronto suburbs have lately become quite demographically diverse. But they also tended firmly to believe that instances in which suburban areas display the same qualities of social life that they value about inner-city neighbourhoods are exceptions. Their suspicion is that, apart from public-housing projects, most of the suburbs' statistical heter-ogeneity is illusory, that suburban rounds of life are inexorably rooted in a subtext of values they describe as 'conventional' and 'traditional' with which they are largely out of sympathy. Beyond this – and it is here that the issue of suburbs' spatial landscape arises – many of them feel that whatever residue of social difference may exist in sub-urbs is subverted by the low-density, segregated-use, automobile-based, and mall-centred character of suburban form. They believe the built environment of suburbs undermines community life, and in this regard, they repeatedly echoed similar concerns – there isn't much streetlife in suburbs, you can't walk to the corner for a carton of milk, malls only have chain stores, suburban landscape is relentlessly new and uniform – that add up to a critique of a setting for everyday life perceived to foster homogeneity and isolation, one that they believe contrasts sharply with older inner-city neighbourhoods.

The Spatial Environment of the Inner City

The features of downtown landscape that respondents value are not complicated. They like the density and the sense that there are a lot of people around. They like the mix of uses. As noted earlier, they frequently cited the proximity and character of traditional retail-commercial strips as among the most positive features of their housing location:

> I live right up the street from Bloor Street. I've been there fifteen years. A lot of the groups that I'm part of [several feminist organizations] – our meeting places and offices are on Bloor ... [And] I meet people there, in the restaurants and bars. My political life and my social life both sort of revolve around it ... It has a lot of energy to it, there's a lot happening on it. Just walking out my door, there are a lot of things happening that, if I lived in a suburb, probably wouldn't be. It's a head-space thing – people coming and going, the political posters up on the postboxes. When I walk down the street, I run into people I know all the time ... The bookstores are there. On Sunday, I can just walk out and go to a bookstore, and I'll probably run into someone I know who's doing the same thing or is on their way to somewhere ... There's a sense of community that Bloor Street gives me – not meaning exactly neighbours, but community. On Bloor Street I can be connected to the world I like to be connected to ... And I can see the ways that the city is changing there too. (C13)

As well, respondents like the age and the look of old city houses, the 'feel' of downtown neighbourhoods, the juxtaposition of different architectural styles along inner-city streetscapes. They like living in a place that, unlike most suburbs, has a history and has ghosts – a past that downtown's old buildings make tangible. And they like *walking*. Again, there was near-unanimity in the sample: almost every respondent said that s/he enjoyed walking to the corner-store, walking to local restaurants or pubs, walking to friends' houses, or just walking for the sake of walking:

> It gives me a chance to get a sense of what's happening. It's a forty-five minute walk from the heart of the business core to where we live, and a walk through the city at different times of day can be very informing. I get a good sense of what's happening on the street, how it feels. Something I like to do is walk the Yonge Street strip every

Bloor Street West. Respondent C13: 'I live right up the street from Bloor Street. I've been there fifteen years. A lot of the groups that I'm part of – our meeting places and offices are on Bloor ... I meet people there, in the restaurants and bars. My political life and my social life both sort of revolve around it ... There's a sense of community that Bloor Street gives me – not meaning exactly neighbours, but community. On Bloor Street I can be connected to the world I like to be connected to.'

> once in a while ... I know that street fairly well; I've known it fairly well for about thirty years. So how is it changing, and how does it feel? The only way you can really find that out is on foot ... I've never owned a car. (D5)

Among the most illuminating examples of respondents' perceptions of the contrast between suburban and downtown landscapes are their attitudes about shopping malls and the differences between using malls and using inner-city commercial streets – a theme raised by several respondents that illustrates not only their perceptions about spatial landscape in varied urban environments but also their feelings about the differing economic cultures of different metropolitan settings:

> I am really repelled by the idea of a shopping centre with just one franchised hardware store, one franchised bookstore ... One of the things I really like about living down here is the different individual stores. (D1)

> In the suburbs, you've got to get into your car, you have to go to the plaza ... There's no feeling of community there. You don't see the guy who works in the corner grocery store walking down the street in front of your house or living next door to where you live ... When you go to the shopping plaza, they're almost all chain stores. They're really impersonal places. (B8)

> In the suburbs, if I wanted to go to the store, or I wanted to go to a movie, I'd have to go to the plaza. Who *likes* plazas? They're not built for people to enjoy; they're built to make money. I don't want to have to go there, and I don't want to have to drive everywhere. Whey can't I just stick on my boots and go down to the corner? ... I like to wander along Queen Street and see old things and new things and odd things. You have the old second-hand stores, the local florist, a shoe-repair. There's an old local gym up at the corner that a lot of people from the community use,* and up there a couple of blocks is a really first-class woodwork and refinishing place. (D7)

> Today 1 went to take my boots in. A fellow's opened up a new shoe repair place. They distributed flyers around the neighbourhood and had grand-opening discounts, and I thought, yeah, this is somebody who's in the neighbourhood now that I will go to, somebody to get to know, a shoe-repair guy ... If I lived in a suburb, I'd probably end up going to the mall for everything. It would be a mall culture, and I'd have to get a car ... It would be absolutely different. (C9)

As observed earlier in this chapter, a common interpretation of middle-class resettlement of older inner-city neighbourhoods stresses the hypothesized 'convenience' of downtown living: the propinquity of jobs and 'amenity packages' for individuals who are theorized to be oriented to career and consumption concerns (Ley 1985: 23). At

---

* The gym in question is mainly a weightlifting club patronized by a largely working-class clientele.

first glance, data gathered in the present fieldwork may seem to support this sort of analysis. Among reasons why respondents say they like living downtown, several mentioned the convenience of getting to work, and mostly all mentioned the proximity of such facilities as movie-houses and theatres, bookstores and restaurants. But on closer analysis, the logic of this line of thinking seriously weakens. At least three factors suggest that more complex processes are at work.

First, only a couple of respondents – both non-parents – indicated that they would be willing to move to a high-rise building in order to maintain their downtown location. The remainder of the sample was as vigorously hostile to modernist inner-city form as they were to suburbs and would rather depart for a smaller city or small town than be forced to live in a high-rise condominium or apartment in order to stay in downtown Toronto.

The second factor concerns several individuals in the sample who work at suburban locations – and one whose job is outside the Toronto region entirely, about an hour's drive distant – as well as two students attending a suburban university. They numbered sixteen in total, about one-quarter of the sample:

	Parents	Non-Parents	Total
Work downtown	24	21	45
Work in suburbs	7	6	13
Work outside the Toronto area	–	1	1
Attend downtown university	–	1	1
Attend suburban university	–	2	2
Not currently working	1	–	1

On the one hand, many of the respondents who worked downtown stressed that they would strongly dislike having to commute to their jobs. But, on the other, *none* of the respondents who travelled daily to out-of-city locations said that they would consider moving to a suburban residential setting to be closer to work (or classes). They are entirely happy to commute in order to maintain an inner-city residential location.

The third factor arises from response-patterns that occurred in a number of the interviews. Many respondents ticked off various conveniences of their location in a somewhat rote manner as though they anticipated that, in asking what they liked (and disliked) about living in their part of town, such a list was the sort of thing the fieldworker had in mind; they sought to be amenably cooperative. Frequently, though, this kind of recitation of specific locational advantages was an afterthought, sometimes offered in response to a probe ('Anything else?'), tagged onto an initial answer that had consisted of an animated discussion of various intangibles of inner-city life. Some respondents even apologized for their first foray at the question, saying they were sorry they had become so vague or insubstantial. (With impressions of the interview process shaped by positivist-oriented undergraduate courses, occasional encounters with market research, and years of reading newspaper articles about survey-style opinion polls, they needed reassurance that the fieldworker's concern was simply whatever came into their heads on a subject – not to be misled by preconceptions of what they thought he might want.) In other cases, an orderly, monotone catalogue of spatial 'conveniences' shifted ground to a more impressionistic discussion of intangibles as the fieldworker continued to probe; and here the respondents often began to become more interested – this was what *they* really wanted to talk about.

The argument is not that the convenience of jobs and amenities does not matter to the respondents. It clearly does figure into their levels of *satisfaction* with their housing location. But it does not account for their *choice* of this location in the first place – the more subterranean reasons why many of them were initially attracted to this locale and, over the years, have chosen to remain. Overall, questions of spatial 'convenience' seemed a highly inadequate mode of interpreting respondents' attitudes; deeper processes of preference were involved. To return to the example of the proximity of traditional retail-commercial strips, respondents do not value their presence simply because they are nearby (or dislike shopping malls simply because they are less easily accessible); rather, the central issue is a cluster of specific qualities of life that older urban places are perceived to engender – respondents' desire for spatial immersion within a distinct setting of everyday activity. They believe that walking is not just more convenient than driving but is qualitatively different, that the intensity of human activity bred by density and mixed land-use is a desirable feature of daily life, that inner-city retail districts have qualities of *place* in contrast to the functional *space* of facilities like shopping malls. A focal argument of this chapter again becomes salient: among most of the respondents interviewed, preference for inner-city residential locales represents not instrumental concerns but the choice for a lifeworld.

Parents and the Inner-City Spatial Field

To the limited degree that the simple 'convenience' of downtown living did emerge as a central factor in respondents' satisfaction with their housing location, this was particularly so among parents, who mentioned a number of reasons why they found the inner city more practical for child-rearing than they believed a suburban locale might be. For example, they find a wide range of activities available for children downtown, as well as lots of other kids close by for theirs to knock around with. And as children get older, inner-city location makes it easier for them to get around on their own:

> They can take their subway token and go wherever they want. They have a freedom of movement that they don't have to involve us in. They have mobility at a younger age and a sense of independence. (A1)

Parents see this mobility not only as good for the kids but as a significant benefit for themselves because they don't have to play 'chauffeur,' a word repeatedly echoed by respondents who believe that in a low-density, segregated-use suburb they would be required to spend constant hours ferrying their children hither and yon to give them access to the same range of friends and activities that are available downtown by bike, foot, and transit:

> I definitely don't want my two boys to be teenagers and ... have no place to go except the shopping centre. I also don't want to have to spend my time hauling them around in a station wagon. I don't want to have to drive them to their friends' houses when they're twelve years old; I want them to be able just to go. Now, the older boy – he's nine – he walks to school by himself; he's got a couple of friends he can visit. I think there'd be far fewer things for him to do easily in a suburb – go to the library, go to the park. (B11)

Another practical convenience parents report about living downtown concerns the availability of services like daycare for younger children:

> I work, and I need good daycare. Well, there's a hell of a lot more good daycare in the city. I've spoken to mothers in suburbs, and they have a much more difficult time finding daycare. (A2)

Several parents also mentioned the proximity of drop-in centres for parents with toddlers (in one case, organized by a respondent's wife), easily accessible on foot and offering opportunities for workaday socializing that parents with tots highly appreciate. Nearly every parent interviewed believes that caring for younger children downtown is a much less isolating activity than it would be in a suburb – for example, a mother with an infant:

> I was brought up in the city, downtown by Kensington Market ... I've always hated the suburbs. The idea of living there is just anathema to me – the houses in their little developments, just blocks of houses and nothing else, cut off from everything unless you get in your car and drive to the shopping mall – having to drive everywhere ... I have a friend out there, and I visited her last weekend. We took the kids out for a walk, up and down these empty streets. There was nobody there. She feels kind of isolated. (A14)

In this connection, some parents again mentioned the nearby commercial streets:

> When the kid starts to get on your nerves, you can just whack it in the stroller and head off a couple of blocks to where there's people and streetlife. (A9)

> One of the things with small kids is that you have to take them out for walks, and you want to be accessible to somewhere that you'd *like* to walk around in. I like to take them up to the Danforth; there's a lot to see there, lots going on. To have that convenience – I mean, it's a big hassle if you have to use the car, getting them in the car, driving them somewhere, getting them out of the car ... (B8)

The single most significant practical advantage respondents reported about raising children downtown is the convenience of the spatial triangle of home, work, and essential services (food stores, daycare, the doctor's office), a view expressed by both male and female parents but especially by mothers, nearly all of whom work. While many of the fathers interviewed take an active role in childcare, it remains the case in Canadian middle-class life generally that 'women are still primarily responsible for childcare and housework, even when they are also engaged in full-time employment outside the home' (Wekerle 1984: 12). Two mothers talked about the time-pressures of simultaneously working and parenting:

> We had our house and lived here before we had the kids, but then it subsequently became quite obvious that having children is a very time-consuming thing; and being in jobs that are also very time-consuming, we didn't want to waste any time with unnecessary travelling. (A12)

> It's awful, the lack of time there is to spend with the kids. If we added another hour or two hours commuting, forget it – we'd never see the kids. (A13)

The requirement for a convenient round of life is particularly critical for working mothers whose husbands' jobs involve travelling and for single parents. In the latter respect, the fieldwork and some ancillary evidence support the hypothesis that, from across the entire range of city-dwellers, the demographic group most likely to be attracted to the inner city primarily for reasons of practical spatial convenience are single parents.

Married fathers also appreciate being close to their jobs for reasons directly related to child-rearing – for example, a lawyer who sometimes works evenings and a writer whose office is only a few blocks from his home and his young daughter's school:

> I work hard, but I see them almost every night – because I'm so close, I see them. I'm committed to seeing them every day. I will come home and see them at lunch. I probably see more of my kids than a suburban father does during the work-week. (B6)

> Most days I go and pick her up at school and bring her back here and have lunch with her. (B14)

There is an irony here. The suburb was created to serve as the ideal locale for domestic life, a spatial ideology that has become so deeply entrenched in North American culture that – as noted earlier – it even has become embedded in the way social scientists sometimes perceive and theorize patterns of residential location. Yet among the parents sampled here (in whose households, conspicuously, nearly all the women have careers), the suburb is perceived as highly *in*compatible with family life.

Most respondents did not self-consciously decide to raise children downtown. Inner-city housing location was not initially chosen with family life in mind:

We decided to live in downtown Toronto long before we decided to have children. That came much later. But there wasn't any question about whether there would be a different place to live. We didn't ever think about moving anywhere else. (A10)

It's not so much a question of our choosing to raise kids in the city as of *our* choice to live in the city, which means that our kids live in the city too. (B3)

And they do have some misgivings about raising children downtown. For example, they are concerned that inner-city pollution is harmful for their kids, and they worry about cars that sometimes speed along city sidestreets with little regard for playing children. Most parents with daughters, clearly aware of an apparent increase in sexual assaults in Toronto, report they are fairly cautious with the girls – for example, meeting teenagers at the subway station when they are coming home alone after dark. On balance, however, they generally believe that they would find a suburban child-rearing locale highly unsatisfactory.

To my mind most suburban neighbourhoods are not friendly to family life ... Suburbs aren't very friendly for families with small children. (A6)

Conclusion

The four qualities of inner-city life perceived by respondents are only conceptually separable. For example, the sense of community that most respondents perceive in inner-city neighbourhoods is partly contingent on these neighbourhoods' spatial character and would be diminished in the absence of the population density and mix of activities that breed continuous streetlife. The tolerance of difference that often characterizes city life is (as Wirth theorized) partly contingent on urban demographic complexity. Thus, the inner city is to be conceived as a coherent system, not simply an aggregation of discrete features; and it is precisely this holistic character of the system, of which the four factors identified are really only outcroppings, that attracts middle-class resettlers of the kind interviewed in the fieldwork. Many respondents, however, were concerned that the traditional social fabric of the inner city is threatened in Toronto. These concerns are the focus of chapter 8.

8

Perceptions of Inner-City Change
Eclipse of a Lifeworld?

The crux of respondents' misgivings about the future of Toronto's old downtown neighbourhoods focused on the increasing cost of inner-city housing in recent decades. As was reported in chapter 3, this was a fitful process that was centred mainly in three periods of rapidly rising prices during the mid-1970s, early 1980s, and late 1980s, episodes characterized by widespread speculative activity coupled with growing middle-class anxiety about diminishing opportunities to secure downtown housing. The third of these periods was concurrent with interviewing – timing that clearly influenced the intensity of respondents' attitudes.

In the months that followed fieldwork, Toronto's housing market cooled, partly mirroring similar slumps that had also come hard on the heels of the two earlier rounds of spiraling prices, but also partly the consequence of wider economic forces that had bred a deep recession throughout Ontario. By the time this manuscript was in preparation, the market was dropping. During 1991, the average cost of a Metropolitan Toronto house fell nearly 7 per cent from about $255,000 to $238,000, a pattern reflected in declining prices in the inner city (McCarthy 1991). Such commercial properties as office space and shopping malls, meanwhile, were losing ground at an even more rapid pace.

Prospects for the immediate future are not clear. According to more optimistic forecasters, the metropolitan economy and real estate market are experiencing only short-term throes of adjustment to transnational economic restructuring. Another outlook, however, is that

Ontario's once-prosperous economy is in a condition of critical free-fall as a consequence of capital's increasing globalization and of the amplifying effects of the Canada-U.S. free trade treaty on processes of deindustrialization; this scenario envisions a period of traumatic economic dislocation of uncertain length accompanied by a severe shortfall of state revenue. The situation seems volatile and may have shifted significantly even by the time this book is in print.

What is clear, though, is that in the period since the mid-1960s, the nature of many of Toronto's inner neighbourhoods has altered radically and irrevocably as many working-class districts of the industrial urban era were shattered by the transition to 'postindustrial' urbanism. Marginal middle-class communities, meanwhile, were kept constantly on the run by property investors' relentless appropriation of new blocks of downtown space. Thus, while Toronto's immediate future is uncertain, the restructuring of its inner-city spatial fabric is already largely a *fait accompli*.*

Hence, the fieldwork reported in this chapter should be read in two intertwined but distinct contexts, that of the immediate circumstances of the overheated housing market of the late 1980s, when interviewing was carried out, and that of more enduring and fundamental patterns of inner-city transition often witnessed by respondents over the course of many years.

Housing Cost, Diversity, and Community

An immediate consequence of the rising cost of inner-city housing in Toronto has been a steady erosion of demographic complexity as working-class and immigrant communities and marginal and middle-income groups have been displaced or effectively blocked from living in inner-city neighbourhoods they formerly occupied. For most respondents who expressed concern about this process – the large majority of the sample – this issue had two aspects. First, they were disturbed by the effects of rising inner-city housing prices on the general character of downtown neighbourhoods; second, they perceived the cost of inner-city housing as a direct threat either to themselves, in the case of respondents who are tenants, or to people like them, in the case of respondents who became homeowners several

---

* A similar point is made in a recent article by Ley (1992).

years ago but would have been wholly unable to do so in the current market.

Many respondents were upset by the steady disappearance of their working-class neighbours:

> I worry that gentrifiers will take over the whole neighbourhood ... It's spreading like a blight. In the long haul it means the loss of affordable housing. There were boarding-houses on this street, there were multi-unit houses, just five years ago. There were working-class people here. There are still some at the end of the street, but they're living on borrowed time ... guys who work down at the Colgate plant or work for CN or for Eaton's. There are some people with very limited incomes down there who are tenants. And there are the older folks who are dying off – and what's gonna happen? Those houses are going to pass to people who can afford them, and it's not going to be working-class people at that end of the street any longer. (B2)

> When I first moved here, fifteen years ago, the neighbourhood was mainly ... lower-middle-class. Everything had a very different feel. It wasn't rich people – there were Greek families, Italian families, Chinese, people from the Maritimes. There's still some of that, but it's changed a lot. It's much wealthier than it used to be; these are *rich* people living around us now. (C5)

Respondents recognized that a number of working-class and immigrant homeowners are happy to sell off at top prices and move to the suburbs. But many other working-class residents would prefer to remain, and they depart only because the old communal base of their neighbourhood has lost its critical mass. Tenants, meanwhile, have no choice at all:

> The children of people living in this neighbourhood can't afford to buy a house on the very street where they grew up, and so there is a very direct sense of being pushed out. (A6)

Respondents often took a jaundiced view of their newer neighbours:

> So who buys houses that sell for $400,000? They're not Portuguese families, and they're not Italian families ... They're no particular kind of person. They have nothing in common except the money, which is not much of a thing to have in common. (B13)

A perceived consequence of this process is the disappearance of local communities. In some cases, this occurs because more affluent in-movers are short-term speculators. One respondent lived on a street of small houses that were originally constructed around the turn of the century as workers' cottages, buildings that now sometimes serve as starter-homes for gentrifiers:

> For the long-term people here, this is where they're connected, this is where they live. But the yuppies who come in are in a kind of transition stage. They're buying in, but they're not involved in the community, they're not interested in the people here. They turn over really fast – a year, two years. They're on their way up to some other neighbourhood. This is just an investment; it's a stop-off point. (C4)

But many respondents also believed that community diminishes in districts where affluent households settle more permanently:

> Property values in this area are going up on a pretty steep gradient at the moment ... [and] the people who are moving in are not very focused on the neighbourhood. They're very much fixed in their own little space ... The old integration of these neighbourhoods is breaking down, and there won't be the same sense of neighbourhood. (B4)

One respondent had moved from a rapidly gentrifying neighbourhood to a nearby working-class district because she disliked the trajectory she believed her former area was taking:

> The neighbourhood we lived in before was upper-middle-class. Everybody was a yuppie, like an up-and-coming professional, that kind of person, and it wasn't very neighbourly at all. It was like everybody had their own life separate and apart from the street ... [and] never paid attention to their neighbours. I never felt any affinity to the street. (A12)

In fact, this respondent's perception of the 'neighbourliness' of a rapidly gentrifying district may not be entirely accurate. There is evidence that community networks do arise in areas where, like Riverdale, families with children are a major component of the new, more affluent population; in the words of a respondent living there:

> There is a strong sense of community here. I don't feel our house fits

into it, but it's here ... You get a lot of stuff coming through the mail slot, community newspapers, stuff from neighbourhood groups concerned about different problems. (C14)

But unlike the communities of *in*clusion that respondents enjoy in more socially diverse downtown neighbourhoods, the new formations are communities of *ex*clusion, often hostile to the values and interests of people who are not like themselves. A prototype of this phenomenon occurred in the Donvale district in the 1970s, a case discussed in earlier chapters. A grouping of well-to-do newcomers battled a coalition of longer-term working-class and middle-class residents that was seeking to develop a local non-profit cooperative project meant to supplement the neighbourhood's stock of affordable housing and help sustain its social mix. A journalist who chronicled the issue, Janice Dineen, described the values in collision:

A good number of Don Vale's middle-class residents ... simply liked the area and found it a pleasant place to live, but had no desire to displace large numbers of low-income earners. There was a vocal element, however, which wanted in Don Vale only the people who would put as much money and effort into renovating the houses there that they did. They felt they had restored high property values to the area, and if one couldn't afford to live there any more, then he should go somewhere else. They looked forward to the day when the renovating trend led to Don Vale being a community of nothing but expensive townhouses with no residents other than those who could afford the fancy prices that came with the new look. They saw [the cooperative] plans as a serious roadblock to this end. They could not understand why the people involved in [the cooperative] would give so much time and effort to the project without any profits as the aim. (1974: 22)

Respondents in several neighbourhoods reported similar attitudes among newer, well-to-do residents. In one area, for example, an affluent group of newly arrived renovators wanted their Italian and Portuguese neighbours to maintain rather than 'mediterraneanize' the traditional façades of their houses. Their proposal was to petition city hall to legislate 'heritage preservation' for the area. One respondent characterized this kind of viewpoint:

They'll go into these areas that are filled with Italian and Portuguese and Chinese people, and it's like they can't accept what the neigh-

bourhood is like – they have to come and dictate their style onto it.
It's almost like a sense of we're not like you, we've got good taste.
(C12)

A respondent who was a long-term homeowner in the neighbourhood
vocally opposed 'heritage preservation' at a community meeting:

> I was very angry. And I just enraged these nice, well-meaning young
> architects by saying who are you to demand that they should have
> your taste. I don't like angel-brick, but I certainly don't think there
> should be a law that says no angel-brick. That's absolutely the oppo-
> site of what cities are, that some damned university architect can say
> to a neighbour that you can't do this or that with your house. (B13)

Another respondent observed that the fundamental character of
inner-city neighbourhoods partly arises from the serendipity of their
traditional processes of change:

> City living is a very egalitarian thing, because you usually have vir-
> tually no say about who your neighbours are. (A6)

Nor, she might have added, do people have much control over how
their neighbours decorate their houses or use their yards, a fact that
has traditionally distinguished downtown residential districts from
the kinds of new suburban subdivisions Relph has characterized as
the result of 'hyperplanning.' Here, 'planning is so thorough and all-
embracing' that it 'effectively determines the form and content of the
entire landscape.' Near Toronto, for example, are subdivisions where
clotheslines, vegetable gardens, and 'inappropriate' house and yard
decorations are prohibited:

> The only unauthorized alterations ... that are possible are trivial ones,
> some flowers around the front lawn perhaps, a change in the colour of
> the house paint (and even that is sometimes restricted to a pre-selected
> range of colours). With hyperplanning the responsibility for making and
> changing environments has effectively passed from the people who live
> in them and use them to experts and properly trained professionals who
> devise and implement the regulations and standards which are necessary
> to ensure that nothing untoward ever happens. (1981: 96–7)

The ambition of affluent gentrifiers to shape their neighbourhoods

Mediterraneanized house, the west end. Respondent B13: 'I was very angry. And I just enraged these nice, well-meaning young architects by saying who are you to demand that they should have your taste. I don't like angel-brick, but I certainly don't think there should be a law that says no angel-brick. That's absolutely the opposite of what cities are, that some damned university architect can say to a neighbour that you can't do this or that with your house.'

is not quite the same. Their claim to authority is not technocratic expertise but good taste; they are cultural 'experts.' But the outcome is similar – a canonization of appropriate appearance, an acceptable image. This goal cannot easily be achieved by civic fiat in Toronto. Irate neighbours (like the respondent above), reformist politicians, and progressive planners create too many stumbling blocks for widespread 'heritage preservation' or like-minded by-laws. But the same objective can be, and is, often accomplished by the sheer weight of economic clout. As happens often in urban study, Georg Simmel's voice echoes:

> Money, with all its colourlessness and indifference ... irreparably hollows out the core of things, their individuality, their specific value, and their incomparability. All things float with equal specific gravity in a constantly moving stream of money. (1988: 20)

As neighbourhoods are homogenized by the stolid and inexorable force of money – and irksome influences are weeded out – the new canons of good taste are as effectively promulgated as might occur by ordinance. What is lost in this transition for city-dwellers like the respondents is the inner city's egalitarianism; seeking to outlaw 'mediterraneanization' is only a small symptom of this deeper process.

In another neighbourhood, a group of well-to-do residents sought to diminish public use of a nearby commercial strip by asking city hall to reduce the number of bars and restaurants through its licensing procedures. Again, a respondent vocally opposed this attitude:

> They think the street and the clubs bring noise and rowdyism into the neighbourhood. But the people who come to the street and patronize these places really aren't a problem. They're not breaking any laws – there isn't a drug problem here. They're just people. People on the streets at different hours is part of city life, it's part of what you accept when you choose to live downtown. And if you don't want that, don't live here. Go to the suburbs. You shouldn't try to have a suburbs-in-the-city. (B15)

In a third district, affluent newcomers sought to eliminate some small industries that were long-term components of local social structure, places where a number of nearby working-class residents had traditionally found jobs. Here, too, a respondent had vocally defended the neighbourhood's old fabric:

These new people don't want any factories, they don't want any pollution. How convenient, too; their property values go up ... Hey, if you move into a place, that's part of the deal. You don't turn around and try to change it afterward. (D7)

These attitudes of the new whitepainters toward 'heritage preservation,' commercial strips, and local industries illustrate a more general political outlook that troubled many of the respondents – for example, a writer who was a veteran of community struggles in both the gay community and his local neighbourhood and who described the politics he sees emerging in a number of inner-city areas:

That's something I'm really concerned about in downtown neighbourhoods, that they're losing their compassion, that somehow neighbourhoods are starting to become the problem instead of the solution ... the obstacle to social change as opposed to the locus of social change, and I don't know what the answer is here ... If someone wanted to put any kind of low-income housing or group home into this neighbourhood, I'm sure there would be a huge uproar from the ritzier residents. The neighbourhood association has become pretty reactionary ... They're just waiting for the last rooming-house to go ... That certainly isn't the way things were ten or fifteen years ago. (D14)

Another respondent commented,

Neighbourhoods will change less because there will be pressures not to let them change ... so that there will be less assisted housing, there likely won't be halfway houses. There'll be a sense of turning neighbourhoods into protected zones for the people who can afford them. It'll be a real conservative force. (B9)

A third respondent talked about her impression of the new gentrifiers' attitude toward a housing cooperative that has been in her neighbourhood nearly twenty years:

I don't like the word yuppie much. I didn't believe in yuppies for a long time. I didn't think the way they were being described in the media could be accurate, that there could be people who were so self-centred and ruthless and materialistic ... But now I think it's probably pretty accurate. They're not pleasant people to be around. A lot of them are agitating politically on the right wing. They're all for prop-

erty values. They won't support any kind of public housing. And I
think the presence of the co-op really depresses them – that it's here
and that it's holding on ... They call it 'the project.' (C5)

One consequence of the inner city's emergent social structure that
disturbed many respondents is an increasingly visible economic bifurcation. Although working-class and less affluent middle-class
households have been steadily extirpated from downtown neighbourhoods, a substantial low-income population still remains, living
mainly in public-housing blocks like Regent Park and Alexandra Park.
Meanwhile, the growing number of the city's homeless is largely
centred downtown. In this circumstance, tension between class groupings is more and more evident to several respondents:

The problem is that there are some people who clearly are affluent.
And the kids from the public housing down the street see that, they
see a lot of things that you have and other people have, and they
don't have it. (D9)

It's getting to be very much a have-and-have-not town with attitudes
that are at times very bitter and very angry ... You have people
who've lived in poverty here for years, and they resent the proliferation of BMWs on the streets and will deface them. (D15)

[The gentrifiers'] money has changed the character of shopping
around here. We have beautiful stores now that most of the lower-
income people can't afford to shop in. We have our own health-food
store now, and it's a wonderful store, but it's the most expensive
health food in the city ... We have some of the most expensive children's clothing stores in the city – and a lot of them. They're wonderful to go window-shopping in, much more interesting than some of
the seedy places that used to be there. But the lower-income people
can't afford to buy clothes there ... Those shops are the source of
some resentment. (C5)

In this context, one respondent talked about the frequency of house
burglaries along a highly gentrified adjacent street:

They're not only hit because they're well-to-do but because I think
there's a kind of anti-wealthy feeling among some of the old residents, the not-so-wealthy families. The police come and say, oh yeah,
it's the kids from down the way – they sort of know who it is, but

Danforth Avenue, the Carrot Common. Respondent C5: 'Their money has changed the character of shopping around here. We have beautiful stores now that most of the lower-income people can't afford to shop in. We have our own health-food store now, and it's a wonderful store, but it's the most expensive health food in the city.'

> they can't prove it; they're kids from families who aren't so well off. I think there is a feeling with those kids – they see the difference between the new people and themselves, and I think there's a kind of class feeling at work – the poor are gonna get the rich. It's not just that this house is worth breaking into. (D3)

Another respondent talked about the rising incidence of street crime in the inner city:

> It's going to become very much an overclass/underclass kind of situation ... All of the really awful urban problems that Toronto has avoided are going to arrive here in a very accelerated fashion ... You're going to see things like muggings and murders disappear off the front page, because there's gonna be enough of them that it's no longer front-page news. I'm already seeing indications of that ... where people are starting to become inured to violent crimes. (D5)

It is partly in the framework of their perception of an increasing demographic division of the inner city that several respondents support development of a larger volume of non-profit and cooperative housing downtown, projects they believe might not only increase the stock of affordable accommodation but also, because they house mid-income as well as low-income households, help sustain greater social complexity. How is this attitude that social diversity is a partial antidote for growing class conflict to be assessed? A clear pattern that emerged in the interviews was that respondents east of downtown, where there is a much greater degree of conspicuous whitepainting, low-income public housing, and visible socio-economic difference, were more likely to raise the issues of class tension and crime then west-end respondents, who still live in more demographically varied neighbourhoods. Thus, at least at the level of perception, the limited data reported support the view that greater social diversity may breed a stronger sense of neighbourhood cohesion.

Respondents and 'Gentrification'

Another set of concerns voiced by respondents about the rapidly rising cost of inner-city housing relates to threats they feel to themselves and to people like them. A number of respondents reflected on their own position in Toronto's current housing market or the positions of people they know:

> If we were just starting out now, we simply wouldn't be able to do it, own a house, and probably not even rent ... I was talking to a friend of mine this morning who lives north of town but might be getting a job in the city. There's a house to rent across the street, and he was exclaiming about the price of it. And what is going to happen is that increasingly people like him – which is to say, friends of mine – won't be able to move in because they can't afford it. The only people who will be able to afford it are Bay Street lawyers and stockbrokers and businessmen. If I wanted to move here now – no, I couldn't do it ... It was literally blind luck that we bought this house when we did. (B14)

> The house across the street was just sold; it listed for $375,000. That kind of thing bothers me, because I'm in a position now where I couldn't come close to affording my own house. (D9)

> It's frightening. We benefited, because when we sold our first house to get another place, it had gone up in value a lot, so we could afford to stay in the city. But we couldn't do it now ... I don't like the idea

of the poor and the middle class getting forced out. That's why my
friend lives in the suburbs; she can't afford to live downtown ... The
kind of downtown neighbourhood that I grew up in, that my parents
moved to when they immigrated to Canada, won't exist any more.
(A14)

I have the real sense that I'm running out of time. When I lived in
my last place, I knew long before we got the eviction notice that I
was living on borrowed time there. Everywhere else around us people
were being thrown out. Every time you turned around, your neighbour was gone because the owner had sold the house overnight and
they got evicted. (C14)

Some respondents reflected on the effects of the cost of Toronto
housing on their daily lives:

I want to live downtown, but I can't necessarily afford it. So even
though making a lot of money isn't a real priority for me, it sort of
pushes itself up on the list. (C11)

An example of this re-prioritizing was a respondent who recently
closed his small, economically marginal law practice oriented to so-
cial-issue advocacy in order to take a well-paying civil service job, a
move he was forced to make in order to afford a larger house for his
family in the wake of the arrival of a third child. He said that he
believed this is the kind of choice more and more people seem to
have to make in Toronto as a direct consequence of housing costs.
In a similar context, another respondent talked about his perception
of the effect of housing costs on people's involvement in community
activities:

There are people who have to move away because they can't afford
to live here ... When the cost of living is as high as it is, people not
only don't come here but, if they're here, they have to spend all of
their energy making a living, and they have no energy left to do any
of the things that create a community ... The commercialization of
housing and real estate is so overwhelming that it influences everything else around it, so that people are constantly forced to think
about ways of coping. They don't have time for other things. (B10)

A woman who is seeking to establish herself as a writer talked about
finding time to write:

It used to be that you could live downtown and work part-time ...
When I first moved downtown, about ten years ago, I lived in a
shared house. It cost me about $70. I was twenty, I was working as a
part-time clerk, and [it felt like] I had lots of money. I never felt poor,
I had money to buy clothes, I had money to buy food and stuff. In
those days I could work for a couple of days or a week, then take a
few days off, and I always seemed to have money in my pocket ...
But now you can't live in a shared house for less than maybe $400.
You can't really get along on part-time work any more; you have to
work full-time. This is a crucial issue for me, because I want to have
time to write, and I don't know how I'm gonna be able to do it in
Toronto. (C7)

Respondents who are tenants and whose occupational lives are oriented to artistic or political work expect to be subjected indefinitely
to the vicissitudes of the rental market or to be forced out of Toronto.
Otherwise, their only alternatives are to abandon their artistic or political activities or to secure space in a housing cooperative – an option
they recognize is increasingly unlikely given the length of the waiting
lists for the scarce stock of the city's non-profit housing.

In the course of the interviews, respondents who identified heightening gentrification as a source of concern about inner-city neighbourhoods (the bulk of the sample) were asked whether they
considered themselves in some way connected to or complicit in this
process. A few replied that they believed they were – one, for example,
who was a film-maker and another who was a visual artist who had
temporarily curtailed his painting career in order to make a living by
creating designer-interiors for well-to-do gentrifiers:

Yeah, definitely. It's a vicious circle because people like my wife and I
are practising artists, and if you were gonna make money in real estate, well, you'd follow where the artists are living ... People like us
are trouble; we're the end of a neighbourhood. (B13)

Consider the number of neighbourhoods that artists have taken and
made into points of interest and that, the moment they became interesting, got boutiqued to death. Artists lead the way ... My own job
wouldn't exist unless there was gentrification going on. I deal in luxury products for people who are making it big in this city who want
to express themselves on the level of I-can-hire-an-artist-to-do-this. I
really haven't reconciled my own role in terms of what I'm aligning

with ... in terms of the blatant objectification and the wonderful acknowledgment – the dollars – I get for how well I can create a for-
gery. I'm aware that I will not necessarily come out of this clean.
(D15)

For the most part, however, respondents were reluctant to find connections between their housing activities and those of their newer,
more affluent neighbours:

I don't really see myself as a gentrifier. If the street all went that way,
I don't know whether I'd feel like I fit in. I'm not rich enough ... I'm
not upwardly mobile. I've worked at the library for thirteen years,
and I reached the top of my earning power in my job classification
years ago. I get the annual increment that the union manages – 4 per
cent or whatever – and that's it ... I picture them as lawyers and business types – people who take briefcases to work. (C1)

Am I a gentrifier? No, I wouldn't think of myself that way ... I mean,
statistically, maybe, but attitudinally, no. There's something obsessive
about gentrification, an obsession with appearances and with having
things just so, the right house with all the right features, the right furniture, the right car. I don't live like that; I wouldn't want to live like
that. (B4)

No, that isn't me. When I moved here, I needed affordability. I had to
scrape together everything I could to buy this house. Then I couldn't
afford to live here, so I rented it out and lived in a one-bedroom
apartment; that's how I afforded it. It's not like I came here with all
this money. It was a struggle. (D9)

I'm young, I live in the city, I'm a professional ... So I fit the mould.
But in terms of my beliefs, no, I don't fit the mould ... What it appears to be is people who are driven by the need to purchase commodities and fit into the world of the rich, and that's not me ... I'll
move back to Montreal before I'll let Toronto do that to me. (D13)

I have nothing to say to the gentrifiers. I don't want to know them,
although statistically I am probably in some ways like them ... But
somehow I imagine my life is very different. As more and more of
those people take over, I feel stranger and stranger here. (D11)

There may be some truth in that connection, but it strikes me as a
profoundly superficial observation. There are undoubtedly similarities,

but they're very superficial similarities. I didn't just come here to exploit the benefits of living in the middle of the city. The values I hold
are totally different. Consuming things is not my main reason for existence. My individual gratification is not the central reality of my
universe, and I believe it is for them ... There are far more fundamental differences between us than whether maybe we both like to live in
old houses or like the same kind of architecture. (B10)

Most other respondents with whom this issue was raised shared
the view that, whatever demographic similarities might exist between
themselves and the recent influx of well-to-do gentrifiers, these were
largely negligible, and that they had little in common with their newer
neighbours in terms of either cultural and political outlooks or rounds
of everyday life. They generally acknowledged that, yes, they had
often been among the earlier middle-class resettlers of their neighbourhoods – to that extent perhaps there was a kind of apparent
connection. But they did not find much similarity between the values
and interests bearing on their own housing choice and those they
associate with more affluent gentrifiers who may follow them.

In this context, many of them expressed a deep ambivalence about
the future of the inner city. They believe it is a good thing that Toronto's older downtown neighbourhoods have been saved from the
destruction threatened by postwar boosterism's project of transform-
ing the inner city to a grid of high-rise apartments, commercial towers,
public-housing blocks, and expressway right-of-ways. They like the
fact that old neighbourhoods have remained popular places to live
for a diversity of households that has included people like themselves,
and they believe that the regeneration of inner-city housing, commercial strips, and municipal services that has occurred over the last
couple of decades, as neo-modernist planning ideas have been abandoned, has generally been a benefit to the city and people living in
it.

But many of them are not optimistic about their neighbourhoods'
apparent ultimate fate. These respondents repeatedly stressed a key
difference they perceived between themselves and the well-to-do
whitepainters. They had sought to live within the kind of place and
kind of lifeworld that they believe has traditionally characterized the
inner city. But the newer wave of gentrifiers seems to want to change
downtown neighbourhoods to suit its own particular world-view and
material interests. While these respondents were militantly out of
sympathy with this process and the values in which they believe it

is rooted, they felt they had few resources to fight back. Many of
them are active in municipal politics, working to elect progressive
city councillors from their wards, but they recognize that a minority
of such politicians can simply not be effective in redirecting the inner
city's apparent current course. And so they find themselves increasingly but impotently surrounded by attitudes they believe are hostile
to their own vision of urbanism and destructive to their streets and
neighbourhoods – attitudes many of them directly trace to the city's
larger process of structural change. It is in this framework that it was
observed in chapter 6 that the inner city of their preference seems
more and more to have become an imaginary, an absent locale of
their nostalgia:

> I do have to say that I like Toronto less and less all the time. I am
> getting inclined to move away. (B10)

As was noted at the outset of this chapter, interviewing took place
at a time when prices in Toronto's inner-city real estate market were
rising sharply. The market's subsequent slump has at least temporarily forestalled some of the changes respondents most feared for
their neighbourhoods; at the same time, it has exacerbated others.
More affluent households continue to infiltrate these districts but at
a slower, less conspicuous pace; the counterpoint of privilege and
poverty, meanwhile, daily becomes more vivid.

The cusp of metropolitan transition – if that is what the present
situation does portend for urban Ontario – is a difficult vantage point
from which to grasp directions and meanings of change. For the moment, one can say only that it appears that Toronto's younger cohort
of well-to-do corporate and professional elites – still a group in abun-
dant supply who, while currently often apartment or condominium
residents, will aspire to homeownership in their turn – appear to
constitute a continuing market for inner-city houses; that those most
victimized by the current economic crisis are working-class and underclass city-dwellers, including many who are still the neighbours
of downtown's middle-class residents; and that the attitudes and values expressed by the respondents are a good picture of their views
at a particular and provocative moment in time.

Conclusion

It would be inaccurate to give the impression that the picture sketched
in these chapters uniformly represents the sample. Two respondents,

for example, expressed support for 'heritage preservation'; perhaps not coincidently, the same two respondents also said they did not perceive widespread gentrification by more affluent households as a problem and, as well, reported no particular sense of affinity with their working-class and immigrant neighbours. A third respondent raised the topic of cooperative housing in a negative context, indicating that he thought non-profit projects neither benefit neighbourhoods where they are built nor are required to help counter the inner city's shortage of affordable housing; rather, he believed that the repeal of rent controls and letting the market take its course would solve the problem. In these and other ways, fragments of the sample illustrated outlooks that are certainly prevalent in Toronto's downtown neighbourhoods; but they were also attitudes inconsistent with those voiced by most respondents.

In this context, it may be well to stress again that the purpose of fieldwork was not to examine attitudes among middle-class resettlers of older inner-city neighbourhoods in general or to gather data purported to represent the population of middle-class old-neighbourhood resettlers at large. To be sure, fieldwork of this kind would be worthwhile, but it was not the objective of the work reported here. Rather, the interviews were an attempt to contact individuals who were mainly earlier middle-class in-movers to downtown neighbourhoods and whose housing activities might be explored as a form of critical social practice; fieldwork sought to document their views toward their residential preferences and living environments. Hence, these sixty-three respondents are in no sense illustrative of middle-class resettlement of older inner-city neighbourhoods in Toronto overall. Nevertheless, they clearly do represent a larger universe than themselves – many other people also living in Toronto's older downtown neighbourhoods who share similar outlooks and values.

This is the third and final chapter that reports on the fieldwork. In summary, respondents generally had a sense of a kind of ideal living locale that they seek in the inner city, one they believe has qualities of life that cannot be found in suburban or modernist residential settings. In particular, these qualities are a closely grained mix of private and public urban realms; a high degree of demographic, cultural, and political diversity and tolerance; and the nature and sociospatial effects of inner-city land-use and architecture. While the inner city was a convenient housing locale for many respondents, the fieldwork did not bear out the central importance ascribed to downtown locational convenience by 'lifestyle' theories of residential choice; more holistic processes of preference appear to be at work. Nor did the fieldwork confirm the hypothesis that inner-city living and 'familism' are inconsistent. Finally, the fieldwork indicated that middle-class inner-city resettlers are in no sense a coherent aggregation to be theorized in juxtaposition to the largely working-class inner-city population of the industrial urban period.* On the contrary, a significant component of them express a desire to live within the traditional lifeworld of older inner-city neighbourhoods and a strong antipathy for 'gentrifiers' whom they perceive as a threat to this lifeworld and to themselves.

---

* This perspective contrasts with the viewpoint of a recent article that focuses on 'an accentuation of class disparities' created by the arrival and political activities of 'gentrifiers' in Toronto (Filion 1991: 570). The article's strength is its consideration (consistent with Smith [1987], Jager [1986], and Williams [1986]) of 'gentrification' in the context of 'postindustrial' class relations. But it overlooks the polyphony of middle-class inner-city resettlement, arguing that 'gentrifiers share from the outset similar ... attitudes' (Filion 1991: 563) and reducing the pattern as a whole to monologic processes of class formation and conflict.

Conclusion

Postmodern urban forms, like those of modernism, are often paradoxical, embodying both dominant and resistant social forces. The paradox of modernist urbanism derives from the appropriation and evisceration of its utopian spirit by property capital and the technocratic local state. While there are clear similarities between such modernist visions as Le Corbusier's sketches for the Contemporary City and the Plan Voisin and such features of current-day urban space as St Jamestown's apartment towers or Regent Park's public-housing blocks (or the clusters of high-rises often adjacent to suburban expressway corridors), it does violence to modernist thinking to ascribe construction of these places mainly to modernism's influence. To be sure, the visions of modernists like Le Corbusier and Giedion were grounded in an autocratic subtext. But the forms they imagined were also rooted in a comprehensive critique of the city of industrial capital and of bourgeois urban architecture of their period.

In like manner, the attack against modernism and defence of traditional urban form initiated by such writers as Jacobs, Mumford, and Venturi is distinct from the wholesale commercialization of postmodernist style by property capital and the codification of postmodern cityscape as the orthodoxy of 'postindustrial' civic boosterism. Harvey's characterization of postmodernism as 'the cultural clothing' of contemporary capital (1987: 279) is not inaccurate – no more than it would be to characterize modernism as the appropriated cultural clothing of capital in an earlier urban era. In regard to the production of urban space, however, Harvey's indictment overlooks a crucial point by conflating the two faces of postmodernist urbanism to its commodified form. In correctly identifying capital's deployment of postmodern fashion as an accumulation strategy and ideological device, he has lost sight of a key germinator of anti-modernism: its holistic critique of the city forms of modernist urbanism – or, more accurately, of the distorted version of modernist city-building that occurred under the aegis of capital and the bureaucratic state. As well, he loses sight of the *dialogical* nature of social life.

A writer like Jacobs had little to say about capital; political economy was not part of her project. But she had an instinctual grasp of the economic role of the city in history and of the economic and social functions of traditional urban fabric. She did not naturalize this fabric according to an evolutionary or mechanical metaphor but rather viewed it as a historical and practical set of forms that emerged and developed in almost organic concert with specific human interests. It was here that she rooted her attack against urban space made in modernism's image that discarded the historical city: 'This is not the rebuilding of cities. This is the sacking of cities ... the entire concoction is irrelevant to the working of cities' (1961: 4, 25).

To be sure, it was not only modernism's forms that attracted anti-modernist dismay but also its spirit. Modernist urbanism had declared an end to urban spatial history, spatial culture, and spatial politics. Henceforth, city-dwellers might abandon their ill-advised attachments to vernacular city fabrics and urban forms of the past and place faith in the salutary workings of the new 'science' of city-building – a serenely totalitarian ideology whose renunciation has not been especially surprising. Again, Jacobs was caustic. Fabricated urban utopias were very nice kinds of places 'if you were docile and had no plans of your own and did not mind spending your life among others with no plans of their own. As in all Utopias, the right to have plans of any significance belonged only to the planners in charge' (1961: 17). Relph's view is more measured, finding a bitter paradox in the forms of urban modernist 'hyperplanning' (with particular reference to typical suburban designs) – 'products of rational human intelligence [that] are dehumanising because they are excessively humanised,' painstakingly engineered to fulfil bland technocratic perceptions of human needs and desires (1981: 104). But either way, the outcome is the same: 'freedom to participate in making one's own place and community has been quietly and unwittingly sacrificed to social and environmental manageability' (Relph 1981: 100).

Still, the anti-modernist critique is not to be read as a rejection of the idea of an urban vision in itself. Mumford's attack against modernism's city was rooted in his belief in the civilizing and redemptive character of urbanism in history; Jacobs celebrated the pragmatism of human inventiveness to have created such useful artefacts as cities. Rather, it was the specific vision of a closed and universalist utopia devised by an ahistorical and assertedly apolitical *technique* – the erasure of locality and *place* for the production of functionalized *space* – that anti-modernism condemned. In contrast, postmodernist urbanism's vision stresses the play of history, difference, combination, and locality that unfolds toward a future whose features are not theoretically apprehensible – a vision in which human life is understood as a polyphonic cluster of possibilities. As Laclau observes (1988), this in no sense constitutes a repudiation of Enlightenment reason but rather its orientation away from a monologic metatext toward a more democratic and contingent discourse of *phronesis* – a very different process than the incapacitating moral relativism ascribed by Harvey to postmodernist vision (1989: 117, 351).

Structural and hegemonic forces, to be sure, are clearly evident in the production of 'gentrified' city neighbourhoods: the logic of capital pursuing its commodity lifeblood in the situated form of postmodern urban design; the interactive demographies of a growing corporate workforce and a recent bulge in the younger, more educated (and sometimes more affluent) social cohort that has composed a key market for varied forms of inner-city placement; processes of class formation contingent on and constitutive of 'postindustrial' urbanism; the efforts of civic boosters to adapt to a global economy of hypermobile capital amid the ruins of the industrial city; an apparent historical affinity of the bourgeois for the heart of the city that was rudely interrupted by industrial urbanism.

But also immanent in these landscapes are critical social practices of actors engaged in constructing their lives in resistance to dominating institutions and structures. In a more general context, these practices arise from the deep disaffection some city-dwellers feel toward the suburban and neo-modernist forms whose production has characterized recent decades of city-building, forms perceived to have cleaved a 'disconnection ... between people's lives and urban meaning,' engendering an impulse 'to siphon off a small part of the city ... that it should be a real neighbourhood, with intense urban life and historical tradition' (Castells 1983: 314, 318). In a more specific framework, these practices also arise as part of feminism's rejoinder to the urban geography of patriarchy. In both respects, the fieldwork is very clear. It is partly because of the paradoxical nature of middle-class resettlement of old inner-city neighbourhoods – an urban form in which both resistant and dominant forces are immanent – that it was suggested in the Introduction that the word *gentrification* may obscure as much as it clarifies.

'Gentrification' as it has occurred in Toronto has, in part, constituted an urban social movement. The housing preferences of at least one segment of the inner-city middle-class population may be concep-tualized within the general framework of desires Castells describes as the basis of such movements – impulses toward urban placement organized around use value, toward cultural identity and existential meaning in everyday life, and toward an effective role in managing one's daily activities and local circumstances. These objectives directly collide with the interests and agendas of corporate property capital and the technocratic state.

The initial phases of defence and retrenchment of older inner-city neighbourhoods in Toronto were closely interwoven with the emer-gence of two movements of civic political reformism. One was more conservative in character, rooted in the city's more affluent com-munities, and mainly oriented to more cautious and urbane planning policies and to conservation of the city's traditional architectural fab-ric. The other was a left-populist movement drawing support from a range of socio-economic strata and particularly concerned with prac-tices of property capital and of growth-booster civic officials that were systematically destroying the social and physical fabric of inner-city neighbourhoods, especially low- and moderate-income neighbour-hoods. Both reformisms were partly linked to the growing pattern of middle-class movement into downtown housing. The more conser-vative grouping found support among well-to-do whitepainters in various parts of town; and there was a crucial connection between the emergence of the left-populist grouping and the increasing pop-ulation of more socially marginal and politically disaffected middle-class subcultures that was settling in inner-city housing.

Among shortcomings of the interview fieldwork was that it failed to explore sufficiently linkages between the respondents and reformist civic politics; hence, the data in this respect is somewhat anecdotal and fragmentary.* But it is also persuasive. A preponderance of re-spondents explicitly indicated an affiliation with some variety of 'pro-gressive' or left politics (in some cases, including past or present participation at an organizational level in civic reformism) or attitudes consistent with the left-populist municipal program – for example, support for non-profit housing. The tone of segments of many in-terviews was, at least implicitly, strongly political, focusing on a range of social, economic, and environmental dilemmas that confront the city, and framed in the context of respondents' feelings about their everyday lives. In other words, they generally understood that settling in an older inner-city neighbourhood was not just a personal housing choice but was linked to a wider socio-political context; in this respect, these respondents clearly sensed the *social* nature of their residential activities – their 'collective' and 'conscious' character, terms central to Castells's model of urban movements.

This account is not meant to imply that political activism oriented to the institutionalized state is necessarily an essential element of urban social movements. On the contrary, critical movements that privilege state structures as the focus of resistance may, as Magnusson and Walker suggest (1988), become trapped on the terrain of the very forces of dominance they seek to transcend. Michael Goldrick, a po-litical scientist and city councillor during the heyday of Toronto re-formism, has argued that this is precisely what happened to Toronto's more radical reform grouping (1978). But the machinery of the local state is certainly one legitimate focus for urban movements, and it was among the early objectives of many participants in the movement that contested the forms, functions, and meanings of Toronto's older inner-city neighbourhoods, individuals who viewed municipal insti-tutions as a locus to pursue such goals as policies to defend older neighbourhoods against demolition for modernist megaprojects or

---

* One effort that has been made to identify connections between middle-class settle-ment in downtown neighbourhoods and municipal reformism – and is consistent with the view taken here – is Ley and Mills's analysis of local demography and voting patterns in the 1982 Montreal civic election. They report that 'the core area of support for the social democratic party [i.e., Montreal's left-populist grouping] coincided with the districts where gentrification, or an upward movement in social status, had been most pronounced in the 1971–1981 period' (1986: 426). Similar fieldwork was not undertaken for this book because methodological issues raised by Toronto's municipal electoral records compromise their usefulness for this pur-pose.

commercial specialization and to promote the construction of self-managed, mixed-income cooperatives.

As well, many participants in this movement contested the roles and meanings of older inner-city neighbourhoods in the course of their daily lives by choosing, together with neighbours who were often not highly politically oriented, to occupy housing in these locales. In its initial phases, this choice frequently predated individuals' municipal political involvement; this often occurred only after their neighbourhoods had come under attack. Thus, their residential activity was, in many cases, critical practice wholly unrelated to municipal political or institutional goals but rather was oriented to seeking to constitute the social and spatial conditions of their own and their households' everyday lives. Civic political awareness and activity frequently arose only in tandem with this housing choice.

The urban social movement oriented to the roles and meanings of Toronto's older inner-city neighbourhoods does not fit easily into various taxonomies of such movements. Magnusson and Walker typologize critical social movements (as distinct from 'reactionary' movements) as 'struggles of specificity' oriented to particular local issues, 'struggles of connection' oriented to identifying linkages among different kinds of issues or different realms of social life, and 'struggles of imagination' oriented to instituting new modes of social life and social organization (1988: 60–2). Castells, using terms coined by Charles Tilly, distinguishes between 'reactive' and 'proactive' urban movements – on the one hand, those that seek to secure limited cocoons of critical practice within the context of a wider urban field over which the dominance of hegemonic forces remains uncontested; on the other hand, those that actively challenge this dominance and 'propos[e] ... new relationships between space and society' within the broader arena of the metropolis (1983: 311–31). Habermas makes a distinction between 'defensive' and 'offensive' social movements (1981a).

It is problematic to characterize the urban movement oriented to Toronto's older inner-city neighbourhoods according to these categories. Often, participants in the movement did seek to articulate connections between immediate issues and larger forces – for example, the efforts of reformist political activists to frame local housing issues in the wider context of the workings of multinational property capital or to situate such local economic issues as deindustrialization in the broader context of Toronto's emerging role in the global economy. Critical imagination has also been an aspect of the movement; Toronto's cooperative housing activists, for example, have been engaged in 'proactive' (or 'offensive') practice insofar as they have sought to create and, with some success, proselytize new forms of tenure, antithetical to property capital, through which city-dwellers may relate to their neighbours and living space.

Arguably, the whole foundation of left-populist reform was 'proactive' inasmuch as – in a fragile alliance with 'urban conservatism' – it forced the local state and the property industry to jettison their program for the eradication of a number of older neighbourhoods and thus helped sustain traditional spaces of inner-city life that might otherwise have been largely obliterated. Kensington Market, Chinatown, the Queen Street West bohemian district of the 1970s, large swathes of Donvale and the Annex, for example, would simply have vanished. Though the movement was initially closely grounded in people's own immediate neighbourhoods, it came to seek a broader transformation of the city-building process that was not oriented solely to local turf. In this context, it may be important to interpret the concept 'struggles of imagination' to refer not only to incubation and production of 'emergent' social forms but also defence and consolidation of 'residual' forms that hold possibilities for critical social practice (Williams 1977: 121–7); for many of the respondents, downtown neighbourhoods clearly do have such possibilities.

Two decades after its inception, left-populist municipal reformism in Toronto has ceased to be an especially effective political movement. The most recent illustration of this denouement was in the 1991 civic election when left-populist activists and politicians were unable to reach agreement on the strategic issue of whether to run a mayoral candidate – to be sure, a prestigious post and arguably worth winning, yet only one of seventeen votes at city council. Subsequently, some local ward campaigns supported the candidate selected to run, but others did not. The outcome was a squandering of substantial campaign resources on a quixotic mayoral race while, at the local ward level, progressives lost control by one or two seats of a city council on which they might easily have managed a majority. In the election's wake, reformist incumbents were summarily shuttled out of key positions they had formerly occupied in the city's planning and budgetary processes.

This lack of consensus about the mayoral candidate was not surprising. Municipal politicians who are (or claim to be) direct descendants of left-populist reformism have not formed a cohesive unit in

Kensington Market, 1993. Left-populist reform – in a fragile alliance with urban conservatism – forced the local state and the property industry to jettison their program for the eradication of a number of older neighbourhoods and helped sustain traditional spaces of inner-city life that might otherwise have been largely obliterated. Kensington Market, for example, would simply have vanished.

recent years, frequently opposing one another on key development and social issues. At a grassroots level, meanwhile, the co-op housing movement does endure, and occasional efforts in the tradition of 'urban radicalism,' to resist specific aspects of corporate dominance in city-building, do spring up – for example, a group named Bread Not Circuses that arose in opposition to a late-1980s proposal framed by city hall and a cluster of entrepreneurial interests to host the 1996 Olympics. But as a popular political movement, left-populist reformism has been largely unable to maintain its momentum.

Is this because it was the political expression of an inherently 'reactive' social movement? Was the movement oriented to the roles and meanings of Toronto's older inner-city neighbourhoods mainly engaged in only a defensive 'struggle of specificity'? These are moot questions. On the one hand, there is no dearth of current issues to sustain progressive political activism. Toronto has become a city many of whose poor depend for their meals on volunteer food-banks, where homelessness has become endemic and the children of disadvantaged communities appear to have little future apart from marginal employment in the service sector or a lifetime on welfare, and where city hall's most recent ideas of bold economic initiative have been seeking to host an Olympics and World's Fair and build a $500-million trade centre *cum* commodity showplace. But in spite of these and other issues, it appears that the conditions for a sustained and 'proactive' popular urban movement do not presently exist – a hypothesis for which the principal evidence may be that there is no such movement. (This reasoning is not entirely tautological; if the necessary and sufficient political circumstances to germinate such a movement were present, it would arise.) In this context, the spirit of left-populist reform has become mainly a seed with nowhere to grow except in small patches, still occasionally a lively force but not widely subscribed to and no immediate hazard to corporate urbanism.

A further complexity in assessing the nature of the social movement that arose in relation to Toronto's older inner-city neighbourhoods concerns the processes of change that the city experienced during the 1970s and 1980s as its momentum propelled it rapidly toward its new status in the global corporate economy – processes with such consequences as Toronto's emergence by 1990 as the most expensive North American city in which to live *exclusive* of housing costs (a status the city has maintained in spite of the onset of a deep recession). The social movement associated with left-populist reformism arose before these processes were fully or obviously under way – before their implications were even imagined, much less understood.

Hence, in many important ways, the Toronto that was familiar to its citizens in 1969, when the first clutch of municipal 'reformists' was elected to city council, has vanished. Many of the social and spatial issues confronting the city today are of a very different kind and order of magnitude than those that animated its politics two decades ago; the politics are still catching up. What has occurred recalls the 1921 observation of Toronto writer Barker Fairley in a commentary on the cityscape paintings of Lawren Harris. In just a few decades, Toronto had experienced an explosive transition to industrial urbanism, a shift accompanied by rapid population growth, the construction of massive factories and the city's first downtown skyscrapers and middle-class streetcar-suburbs, and the sudden appearance of inner-city working-class slums. Toronto seemed to Fairley to have abruptly crossed 'a vast gulf between [its] present and its immediate but somehow almost mysterious past' (1921: 276). He might have been writing in 1990.

It is precisely the sense of political powerlessness bred by such patterns of overarching change that Castells has argued engenders 'reactive' rather than 'proactive' social movements (1983: 330). Today, the remaining inner-city communities of the marginal middle class and of individuals like the respondents interviewed for this book do appear to have become largely 'defensive' locales, places of refuge rather than springboards of wider resistance to the corporate city – a fact reflected in some respondents' descriptions of their small corners of the city as an 'island' or 'lifeboat' amid the wider metropolitan reality. In this context, it may be relevant to cite again Zukin's prognosis of the central dilemma of middle-class resettlement of the inner city:

> The basic problem ... is not ... that capitalism eventually transmutes all ideas into commodity fetishes. Rather, the danger is that the realization of ideas in urban space re-creates an unequal distribution of the benefits these ideas represent. (1982a: 190)

As the fieldwork sought to illustrate, housing in old inner-city neighbourhoods fulfils not simply certain practical needs but also specific desires in respect to everyday life for a segment of contemporary city-dwellers. This is not just an illusion of use value; traditional downtown neighbourhoods are not simply capital's spectacular packaging for a range of postmodernist amenity bundles and commodity fetishes. But even as the possibilities of traditional urban space are realized by more materially privileged city-dwellers who have the resources to constitute their lives according to their aspirations, the working-class and underclass communities that sustained inner-city neighbourhoods through the decades of industrial urbanism, and the marginal communities that characteristically sought niches among them – people for whom these places were home – become strangers in their own city.

The argument that middle-class reoccupation of older inner-city neighbourhoods in Toronto has partly constituted an urban social movement has been grounded in the more general proposition that desires arising in the context of the culture of everyday life exercise

Theatre doorway, Sunday morning. 'The basic problem ... is not ... that capitalism eventually transmutes all ideas into commodity fetishes. Rather, the danger is that the realization of ideas in urban space re-creates an unequal distribution of the benefits these ideas represent.' – *Sharon Zukin*

a discrete force on processes of city-building irreducible to the workings of the economic realm. Hence, the book invoked the perspective of Walter Firey, whose critique of 'economic ecology' argued that local urban meanings and social practices were a basic well-spring of the production of urban space. In this vein, the book demurred from the logic of economic structuralism and from a key fixture in structuralist analysis of 'gentrification,' the rent-gap theory.

To reiterate a central idea at the basis of the book's perspective, the genius of capital is not an ability to fabricate from whole cloth a coherent social totality of thesis and antithesis but rather a relentlessly parasitic capacity to appropriate and saturate social life – a skill that it requires for its livelihood and in which it displays chameleonlike adaptability. But this capacity is not ineluctable; it is not a structurally forgone conclusion. Rather, it is the dialogical tension between capital's rapacity and cultural resistances that is often central to the construction of urban forms. The outcome of this tension are paradoxical

230 City Form and Everyday Life

forms, of which the main examples the book has raised have been modernism, suburbanism, and the recent pattern of middle-class re-settlement of older inner-city neighbourhoods. (The latter process is sometimes termed 'gentrification' but is, in fact, the inner city's re-gentrification: the bourgeois – a word that *means* city-dweller – is returning to the city of its heritage.) In particular, the book explored the interactive way in which entrepreneurial efforts to commodify the inner city as a spectacular form and the resistance of a segment of city-dwellers to this process reflects a basic dynamic in the rela-tionship of capital and culture.

The terms used by Firey to denote the influence of culture on urban form were 'sentiment' and 'symbolism,' words that may not seem to suggest matters of significant concern in a society dominated by ra-tionalism. 'Sentiment' connotes emotionalism; 'symbolism' implies an attitude akin to illogical religiosity. In the patriarchal and ethnocentric climate of Western society, it is women who are 'sentimental' and 'backward' cultures that trade in 'symbolism' – baser outlooks best expunged from one's world-view. A sounder attitude toward reality is one couched in self-conscious, instrumental logic.

Needless to say, this is a view with which this book is out of sympathy. In place of 'sentiment' and 'symbolism,' however, it has used the word *desire* to refer to impulses toward resistance arising in the context of everyday life. Consistent with Mumford's account of the origins of cities (1961: 5–10), the book has treated desire as a crucial building block in the construction of urban spatial form. For modernist urbanism, the city was foremost a machine. An alternative view, evident in the outlook of many of the respondents, stresses urban meanings of community and carnival – cities as the domicile of free citizens and *homo ludens*. Whether the inner zones of cities like Toronto will continue to play this role in the era of corporate urbanism, commodified postmodernism, and increasing socio-economic bifurcation may be an open question.

References

Allaby, I. 1987. 'Blockbusted.' *Toronto Life* 21 (4)

Allen, I. 1984. 'The ideology of dense neighbourhood redevelopment.' In J. Palen and B. London, eds, *Gentrification, Displacement and Neighbourhood Revitalization*, 27–42. Albany: University of New York Press

Andras, M. 1971. 'Lionstar prowling Bloor-Dufferin.' *Toronto Citizen* 2 (15): 6–7

Appleby, T. 1990. 'Residents organize vigilante group.' *Globe and Mail*, 9 July, A1

Armstrong, F. 1988. *A City in the Making: Progress, People and Perils in Victorian Toronto*. Toronto: Dundurn Press

Aronowitz, S. 1988. 'Postmodernism and politics.' In A. Ross, ed., *Universal Abandon: The Politics of Postmodernism*, 46–62. Minneapolis: University of Minnesota Press

Arthur, E. 1974. *Toronto: No Mean City*. Toronto: University of Toronto Press

Ayanoglu, B. 1989. 'Sunday meal scene rescued by Jerry's.' *Now*, 30 March–6 April, 65

Badcock, B. 1989. 'An Australian view of the rent gap hypothesis.' *Annals of the Association of American Geographers* 79 (1): 125–45

Bakhtin, M. 1984. *Problems of Dostoevsky's Poetics*. Minneapolis: University of Minnesota Press

Barker, G., J. Penny, and W. Seccombe. 1973. *Highrise and Super-profits*. Toronto: Dumont Press Graphix

Barthes, R. 1973. *Mythologies*. London: Paladin

– 1986. 'Semiology and the urban.' In M. Gottdiener and A. Lagopoulos,

eds, *The City and the Sign: An Introduction to Urban Semiotics,* 87–98.
New York: Columbia University Press

Baudrillard, J. 1981. *For a Critique of the Political Economy of the Sign.*
St Louis: Telos Press

– 1983. *Simulations.* New York: Semiotext(e)

Bauman, Z. 1976. *Towards a Critical Sociology: An Essay on Commonsense
and Emancipation.* London: Routledge & Kegan Paul

Beauregard, R. 1986. 'The chaos and complexity of gentrification.' In
N. Smith and P. Williams, eds, *Gentrification of the City,* 35–55. Boston:
Allen and Unwin

Bebout, R. 1972. 'Progress and history: The future of Union Station.' In
R. Bebout, ed., *The Open Gate: Toronto Union Station,* 97–107. Toronto:
Peter Martin Associates

Bell, W. 1968. 'The city, the suburb and a theory of residential choice.' In
S. Greer, D. McElrath, D. Minar, and P. Orleans, eds, *The New Urbanization,* 132–68. New York: St Martins Press

Berger, P. 1977. 'In praise of New York: A semi-secular homily.' *Commentary* 63(2): 59–62

Berry, B. 1980. 'Inner city futures: An American dilemma revisited.' *Trans-
actions of the Institute of British Geographers* 5 (1): 1–28

Bess, P. 1989. 'City baseball magic: Plain talk and uncommon sense about
cities and baseball parks.' *Minneapolis Review of Baseball* 8 (4): 1–48

Bondi, L. 1990. 'Landscapes of change: Masculinity and femininity in the
city.' Paper presented at the annual meeting of the Association of American Geographers, Sheraton Centre, Toronto

Bonnett, A. 1989. 'Situationism, geography and poststructuralism.' *Environment and Planning D: Society and Space* 7: 131–46

Boyer, M. 1988. 'The return of aesthetics to city planning.' *Society,* May/
June, 49–56

Brolin, B. 1976. *The Failure of Modern Architecture.* New York: Van Nos-
trand Reinhold

Buck-Morss, S. 1981. 'Walter Benjamin – Revolutionary Writer.' *New Left
Review* 128: 50–75

Burgess, E. 1925. 'The growth of the city.' In R. Park, E. Burgess, and
R. McKenzie, eds, *The City,* 47–62. Chicago: University of Chicago Press

Burton, L., and D. Morley. 1979. 'Neighbourhood survival in Toronto.'
Landscape 23 (3): 33–40

Campbell, N. 1990. 'Orioles will play in ballpark linked to past.' *Globe and
Mail,* 21 May, C3

Careless, J. 1984. *Toronto to 1918: An Illustrated History.* Toronto: Lorimer

Caro, R. 1975. *The Power Broker: Robert Moses and the Fall of New York.*
New York: Vintage

Carss, B. 1989. 'Food, class and the world-class city.' *Kick It Over* 23: 1–2, 4–5

Castells, M. 1983. *The City and the Grassroots*. Berkeley: University of California Press

CATF – Core Area Task Force. 1974. *Core Area Task Force Technical Appendix*. Toronto: City of Toronto Planning Board

Caulfield, J. 1972a. 'An alternative to the razing of downtown Toronto.' *Toronto Citizen* 3 (17): 8–9

– 1972b. 'Decision at city hall.' *Toronto Citizen* 3 (6): 8–9

– 1974. *The Tiny Perfect Mayor: David Crombie and Toronto's Reform Aldermen*. Toronto: Lorimer

– 1988a. 'Canadian urban reform and local conditions.' *International Journal of Urban and Regional Research* 12 (3): 477–84

– 1988b. '"Reform" as a chaotic concept.' *Urban History Review* 17 (2): 107–11

– 1989. '"Gentrification" and desire' *Canadian Review of Sociology and Anthropology* 26 (4): 617–32

– 1992a. 'Augurs of "gentrification": City houses of four Canadian painters.' In G. Norcliffe and P. Simpson-Housley, eds, *A Few Acres of Snow: Literary and Artistic Images of Canada*, 189–202. Toronto: Dundurn Press

– 1992b. 'Gentification and familism.' *City and Society* 6(1): 72–86

Chorney, H. 1987. 'Walter Benjamin: The culture of technical reproduction and the modern metropolis.' Paper presented at the annual meeting of the Canadian Political Science Association, McMaster University, Hamilton

– 1990. *City of Dreams: Social Theory and the Urban Experience*. Toronto: Nelson

Clark, S. 1966. *The Suburban Society*. Toronto: University of Toronto Press

Clark, T. 1984. *The Painting of Modern Life: Paris in the Art of Manet and His Followers*. Princeton: Princeton University Press

Colton, T. 1980. *Big Daddy: Frederick Gardiner and the Building of Metropolitan Toronto*. Toronto: University of Toronto Press

Cox, H. 1968. 'The restoration of a sense of place: A theological reflection on the visual environment.' *Ekistics* 25: 422–4

Crow, T. 1983. 'Modernism and mass culture in the visual arts.' In B. Buchloh, S. Guilbaut, and D. Solkin, eds, *Modernism and Modernity: The Vancouver Conference Papers*, 215–64. Halifax: Nova Scotia College of Art and Design

CTA – City of Toronto Archives. 1987. *Art in Architecture: Toronto Landmarks 1920–1940*

CTHD – City of Toronto Housing Department. 1987. *Living Room II: A City Housing Policy Review*.

– 1988. *St. Lawrence Square*

CTHWG – City of Toronto Housing Work Group. 1973. *Living Room: An Approach to Home Banking and Land Banking for the City of Toronto*

CTLUC – City of Toronto Land Use Committee. 1990. *Land Use Committee Report No. 2, [Item] 25: 1991 Office Space Limits in the Central Core: Options for Action*. Toronto: City of Toronto Department of the City Clerk

CTPB – City of Toronto Planning Board. 1963. *Plan For Downtown Toronto*

– 1967. *Proposed Plan for Toronto*

– 1972a. *Bloor-Dufferin Study, Report Two: Tentative Planning Proposals*

– 1972b. *Toward A Part II Plan for Southeast Spadina*

– 1972c. *The Trefann Court Urban Renewal Scheme*

– 1973. *Toronto's Island Park Neighbourhoods*

– 1974. *Housing in King-Parliament (King Parliament Site Office: Report Four)*

– 1976. *Trends and Planning Goals: South Parkdale*

– 1978. *Official Plan Proposals: Kensington*

CTPDD – City of Toronto Planning and Development Department. 1986a. *1986 Quinquennial Review: Overview Report*

– 1986b. *1986 Quinquennial Review: Summary Report*

Dantas, A. 1988. 'Overspill as an alternative style of gentrification: The case of Riverdale, Toronto.' In T. Bunting and P. Filion, eds, *Essays on Canadian Urban Process and Form IV: The Changing Canadian Inner City*, 73–86. Waterloo: University of Waterloo Department of Geography

Debord, G. 1983. *Society of the Spectacle*. Detroit: Black and Red.

DeGiovanni, F. 1983. 'Patterns of change in housing market activity in revitalizing neighbourhoods.' *Journal of the American Planning Association* 49 (1): 22–39

DeGiovanni, F., and N. Paulson. 1984. 'Household diversity in revitalizing neighbourhoods.' *Urban Affairs Quarterly* 20 (2): 211–32

Dendy, W. 1978. *Lost Toronto*. Toronto: Oxford University Press

Dendy, W., and W. Kilbourn. 1986. *Toronto Observed: Its Architecture, Patrons and History*. Toronto: Oxford University Press

Desfor, G., M. Goldrick, and R. Merrens. 1988. 'Redevelopment on the North American water-frontier: The case of Toronto.' In B. Hoyle, D. Pinder, and M. Husain, eds, *Revitalising the Waterfront*, 92–113. London: Belhaven Press

Deutsche, R., and C. Ryan. 1984. 'The fine art of gentrification.' *October* 31 (Winter): 91–111

Dineen, J. 1974. *The Trouble with Co-ops*. Toronto: Green Tree

Drainie, B. 1989. 'Painted into a corner: The fine art of finding artists' housing.' *Globe and Mail*, 2 Dec. C3

Duffy, A. 1990. 'Hemisphere's costliest city? Why it's ours.' *Toronto Star*, 9 May, E1

Fairley, B. 1921. 'Some Canadian painters: Lawren Harris.' *Canadian Forum*, June, 275–8

Filion, P. 1987. 'Concepts of the inner city and recent trends in Canada.' *Canadian Geographer* 31 (3): 222–32

– 1991. 'The gentrification-social structure dialectic: A Toronto case study.' *International Journal of Urban and Regional Research* 15 (4): 553–74

Firey, W. 1945. 'Sentiment and symbolism as ecological variables.' *American Sociological Review* 10: 140–8

Fishman, R. 1982. *Urban Utopias in the Twentieth Century: Ebenezer Howard, Frank Lloyd Wright, Le Corbusier*. Cambridge: MIT Press

– 1987. *Bourgeois Utopias: The Rise and Fall of Suburbia*. New York: Basic Books

Foster, H. 1985. *Recodings: Art, Spectacle, Cultural Politics*. Seattle: Bay Press

Fraser, G. 1972. *Fighting Back*. Toronto: Hakkert

Freedman, M. 1991. 'Doesn't apologize.' *Globe and Mail*, 26 Nov., A18

Freeman, B. 1982. 'John Sewell and the new urban reformers come to power.' In D. Roussopoulos, ed., *The City and Radical Social Change*, 283–300. Montreal: Black Rose

Frisken, F. 1988. *City-Policy Making in Theory and Practice: The Case of Toronto's Downtown Plan*. London: University of Western Ontario

Garreau, J. 1991. *Edge City: Life on the New Frontier*. New York: Doubleday

Gestrin, B. 1990. 'World cla$$.' *Globe and Mail Report on Business*, 2 Feb., B2

Gibson, S. 1984. *More Than an Island*. Toronto: Irwin

Giedion, S. 1967. *Space, Time and Architecture: The Growth of a New Tradition*. Cambridge: Harvard University Press

Gill, B. 1990. 'The sky line: Homage to Mumford.' *New Yorker*, 2 April, 90–3

G&M – Globe and Mail. 1990. 'TSE ranks third in N. America with $83.5-billion in transactions.' 24 March, B7

Goheen, P. 1977. 'Currents of change in Toronto, 1850–1900.' In G. Stelter and A. Artibise, eds, *The Canadian City: Essays in Urban History*, 54–92. Toronto: McClelland and Stewart

Goldberg, M., and J. Mercer. 1986. *The Myth of the North American City: Continentalism Challenged*. Vancouver: University of British Columbia Press

Goldberger, P. 1989. 'Architecture view: A radical idea – baseball as it used to be.' *New York Times*, 19 Nov., H39

Goldrick, M. 1978. 'The anatomy of urban reform in Toronto.' *City Magazine* 3 (4/5): 29–39. Reprinted in D. Roussopoulos, ed., *The City and Radical Social Change*, 260–82. Montreal: Black Rose 1982

Gottdiener, M. 1985. *The Social Production of Urban Space*. Austin: University of Texas Press
– 1986. 'Recapturing the centre: A semiotic analysis of shopping malls.' In M. Gottdiener and A. Lagopoulos, eds, *The City and the Sign: An Introduction to Urban Semiotics*, 288–302. New York: Columbia University Press
Gutstein, D. 1983. 'Vancouver.' In W. Magnusson and A. Sanction, eds, *City Politics in Canada*, 189–221. Toronto: University of Toronto Press
Habermas, J. 1981a. 'New social movements.' *Telos* 49: 33–7
– 1981b. *The Theory of Communicative Action, Volume 1: Reason and the Rationalization of Society*. Boston: Beacon Press
– 1983. 'Modernity – an incomplete project.' In H. Foster, ed., *The Anti-Aesthetic: Essays on Postmodern Culture*, 3–35. Seattle: Bay Press
Hamnett, C. 1984. 'Gentrification and residential location theory: A review and assessment.' In D. Herbert and R. Johnston, eds, *Geography and the Urban Environment: Progress in Research and Applications, Volume VI*, 283–319. New York: Wiley
Hansen, P., and A. Muszynski. 1990. 'Crisis in rural life and crisis in thinking: Directions for critical research.' *Canadian Review of Sociology and Anthropology* 27(1): 1–22
Harris, I. 1976. 'How to run and win.' In J. Lorimer and E. Ross, eds, *The City Book: The Politics and Planning of Canada's Cities*, 148–59. Toronto: Lorimer
Harris, R. 1987. 'A social movement in urban politics: A reinterpretation of urban reform in Canada.' *International Journal of Urban and Regional Research* 11: 363–81
Harvey, D. 1973. *Social Justice and the City*. Baltimore: Johns Hopkins University Press
– 1985. *The Urbanization of Capital*. Oxford: Basil Blackwell
– 1987. 'Flexible accumulation through urbanization: Reflections on "postmodernism" in the American city.' *Antipode* 19 (3): 260–86
– 1989. *The Condition of Postmodernity: An Inquiry into the Origins of Cultural Change*. London: Basil Blackwell
Hodge, G. 1986. *Planning Canadian Communities: An Introduction to the Principles, Practice and Participants*. Toronto: Methuen
Hoffman, J. 1980. 'Problems of access in the study of social elites and boards of directors.' In W. Shaffir, R. Stebbins, and A. Turowetz, eds, *Fieldwork Experience: Qualitative Approaches to Social Research*, 45–67. New York: St Martin's Press
Holcomb, B., and R. Beauregard. 1981. *Revitalizing Cities*. Washington: Association of American Geographers

Holden, A. 1988. 'Skyrocketing costs of downtown life make city artists endangered species.' *Toronto Star*, 30 Oct., A1, 12

Howell, L. 1987. 'The affordable housing crisis in Toronto.' *City Magazine* 9 (1): 12–19

Hoyt, H. 1939. *The Structure and Growth of Residential Neighbourhoods in American Cities*. Washington: Federal Housing Administration

Hutcheon, L. 1989. *The Politics of Postmodernism*. London: Routledge

Jacobs, A. 1985. *Looking at Cities*. Cambridge: Harvard University Press

Jacobs, J. 1961. *The Death and Life of Great American Cities*. New York: Random House

Jager, M. 1986. 'Class definition and the esthetics of gentrification: Victoriana in Melbourne.' In N. Smith and P. Williams, eds, *Gentrification of the City*, 78–91. Boston: Allen and Unwin

James, B. 1984. *The Bill James Baseball Abstract, 1984*. New York: Ballantine Books

Jameson, F. 1984a. 'The politics of theory: Ideological positions in the postmodernism debate.' *New German Critique* 33: 53–65

– 1984b. 'Postmodernism, or the cultural logic of late capitalism.' *New Left Review* 146: 53–92

Jeffrey, I. 1978. 'Concerning images of the metropolis.' In I. Jeffrey and D. Mellor, eds, *Cityscape, 1910–1930: Urban Themes in American, German and British Art*. Sheffield: Arts Council of Great Britain

Jencks, C. 1977. *The Language of Post-Modern Architecture*. New York: Rizzoli

Kahn, B. 1987. *Cosmopolitan Culture: The Gilt-Edged Dream of a Tolerant City*. New York: Atheneum

Kalman, H. 1985. 'Crisis on Main Street.' In D. Holdsworth, ed., *Reviving Main Street*, 31–53. Toronto: University of Toronto Press

Kary, K. 1988. 'The gentrification of Toronto and the rent gap theory.' In T. Bunting and P. Filion, eds, *Essays on Canadian Urban Process and Form IV: The Changing Canadian Inner City*, 53–72. Waterloo: University of Waterloo Department of Geography

Kealey, G. 1982. 'Toronto's industrial revolution, 1850–1892.' In M. Cross and G. Kealey, eds, *Readings in Canadian Social History, Volume 3: Canada's Age of Industry, 1849–1896*, 17–61. Toronto: McClelland and Stewart

Kerr, D. 1973. 'The economic structure of Toronto.' In J. Spelt, *Toronto*, 54–81. Toronto: Collier-MacMillan

Kilbourn, W. 1972. 'Conclusion.' In R. Bebout, ed., *The Open Gate: Toronto Union Station*, 109–11. Toronto: Peter Martin Associates

Kirkup, D. c. 1972. *Boomtown Metropolitan Toronto: A Photographic Record of Two Decades of Growth*. Toronto: D. Kirkup/Lockwood Survey Corporation

Knoop, L. 1987. 'Social theory, social movements and public policy: Recent accomplishments of the gay and lesbian movements in Minneapolis, Minnesota.' *International Journal of Urban and Regional Research* 11 (2)

Krupat, E. 1985. *People in Cities: The Urban Environment and Its Effects*. Cambridge: Cambridge University Press

Kuhn, T. 1970. *The Structure of Scientific Revolutions*. Chicago: University of Chicago Press

Laclau, E. 1988. 'Politics and the limits of modernity.' In A. Ross, ed., *Universal Abandon: The Politics of Postmodernism*, 63–82. Minneapolis: University of Minnesota Press

Layton, J. 1987. 'To people concerned with gentrification in Toronto.' Memorandum prepared by Alderman Jack Layton, Councillor, Ward 6, City of Toronto

Lefebvre, H. 1971. *Everyday Life in The Modern World*. London: Allen Lane

Lemon, J. 1985. *Toronto since 1918: An Illustrated History*. Toronto: Lorimer

Levin, C. 1981. 'Introduction.' In J. Baudrillard, *For a Critique of the Political Economy of the Sign*. Telos Press: St Louis

Ley, D. 1980. 'Liberal ideology and the postindustrial city.' *Annals of the Association of American Geographers* 70 (2): 238–58

– 1984. 'Inner-city revitalization: A Vancouver case study.' In J. Palen and B. London, eds, *Gentrification, Displacement and Neighborhood Revitalization*, 186–204. Albany: University of New York Press

– 1985. *Gentrification in Canadian Inner Cities: Patterns, Analysis, Impacts and Policy*. Ottawa: Central Mortgage and Housing Corporation

– 1986. 'Alternative explanations for inner-city gentrification: A Canadian assessment.' *Annals of the Association of American Geographers* 76 (4): 521–35

– 1987a. 'Reply: The rent gap revisited.' *Annals of the Association of American Geographers* 77 (3): 465–8

– 1987b. 'Gentrification: A ten-year review.' *City Magazine* 9 (1): 12–19

– 1987c. 'Styles of the times: Liberal and neo-conservative landscapes in inner Vancouver, 1968–1986.' *Journal of Historical Geography* 13 (1): 40–56

– 1992. 'Gentrification in recession: Social change in six Canadian inner cities, 1981–1986.' *Urban Geography* 13 (3): 230–56

Ley, D., and C. Mills. 1986. 'Gentrification and reform politics in Montreal, 1982.' *Cahiers de géographie du Québec* 30 (81): 419–27

Lipton, S. 1980. 'Evidence of central city revival.' In. S. Laska and D. Spain, eds, *Back to the City*, 42–60. New York: Permagon Press

Lithwick, N. 1970. *Urban Canada: Problems and Prospects.* Ottawa: Central Mortgage and Housing Corporation

Lofland, L. 1973. *A World of Strangers: Order and Action in Urban Public Space.* New York: Basic Books

London, B., and J. Palen. 1984. 'Issues and perspectives in neighbourhood renovation.' In J. Palen and B. London, eds, *Gentrification, Displacement and Neighbourhood Revitalization,* 1–26. Albany: University of New York Press

London, B., B. Lee, and S. Lipton. 1986. 'The determinants of gentrification in the United States: A city-level analysis.' *Urban Affairs Quarterly* 21 (3): 369–87

Lorimer, J. 1970. *The Real World of City Politics.* Toronto: James Lewis & Samuel

– 1978. *The Developers.* Toronto: Lorimer

Lorimer, J., and M. Phillips. 1971. *Working People: Life in a Downtown City Neighbourhood.* Toronto: James Lorimer

McCarthy, S. 1991. 'More Metro renters can afford homes.' *Toronto Star,* 29 Oct., D1

McCarthy, T. 1981. 'Translator's introduction.' In J. Habermas, *The Theory of Communicative Action, Volume 1: Reason and the Rationalization of Society,* v–xxxvii. Boston: Beacon Press

McDonnell, K. 1972. 'Lionstar's last stand.' *Toronto Citizen* 3 (7): 5–6

McHugh, P. 1985. *Toronto Architecture: A City Guide.* Toronto: Mercury Books

MacKenzie, S., and D. Rose. 1983. 'Industrial change, the domestic economy and home life.' In J. Anderson, S. Duncan, and R. Hudson, eds, *Redundant Spaces in Cities and Regions: Studies in Industrial Decline and Social Change,* 155–201. London: Academic Press

Magnusson, W. 1983. 'Toronto.' In W. Magnusson and A. Sancton, eds, *City Politics in Canada,* 94–139. Toronto: University of Toronto Press

Magnusson, W., and R. Walker. 1987. 'De-centring the state: Political theory and Canadian political economy.' Paper presented at the annual meeting of the Canadian Political Science Association, McMaster University, Hamilton

– 1988. 'De-centring the state: Political theory and Canadian political economy.' *Studies in Political Economy* 26: 37–71

Marcuse, P. 1986. 'Abandonment, gentrification, and displacement: The linkages in New York City.' In N. Smith and P. Williams, eds, *Gentrification of the City,* 153–77. Boston: Allen and Unwin

Martins, M. 1982. 'The theory of social space in the work of Henri Lefebvre.' In R. Forrest, J. Henderson, and P. Williams, eds, *Urban Political Economy and Social Theory*, 160–85. Gower: Aldershot

Michelson, W. 1977. *Environmental Choice, Human Behavior and Residential Satisfaction*. New York: Oxford University Press

Mills, C. 1988. '"Life on the upslope": The postmodern landscape of gentrification.' *Environment and Planning D: Society and Space* 6: 169–89

Moorhouse, E. 1973. 'The St. Jamestown bonanza: The gold-rush began in the 50s.' *Toronto Citizen* 4 (12): 5–6

Mouffe, C. 1988. 'Radical democracy: Modern or postmodern.' In A. Ross, ed., *Universal Abandon: The Politics of Postmodernism*, 31–45. Minneapolis: University of Minnesota Press

MTPB – Metropolitan Toronto Planning Board. 1964. *Report on the Metropolitan Toronto Transportation Plan*

MTPD – Metropolitan Toronto Planning Department. 1986. *Metropolitan Plan Review, Report No. 2: The Changing Metropolitan Economy*

MTTPR – Metropolitan Toronto Transportation Plan Review. 1975. *Choices for the Future: Summary Report (Report No. 64)*

Mumford, L. 1961. *The City in History*. New York: Brace and World

– 1963. *The Highway and the City*. New York: Harcourt, Brace and World

Muszynski, L. 1985. *The Deindustrialization of Metropolitan Toronto: A Study of Plant Closures, Layoffs and Unemployment*. Toronto: Social Planning Council of Metropolitan Toronto

Nader, G. 1975. *Cities of Canada, Volume One: Theoretical, Historical and Planning Perspectives*. Toronto: Macmillan

Nowlan, D., and N. Nowlan. 1970. *The Bad Trip: The Untold Story of the Spadina Expressway*. Toronto: New Press/Anansi

Nunes, J. 1990. 'Consultant's report predicts Toronto will lose more artists if affordable space isn't found.' *Globe and Mail*, 13 April, C6

Oziewicz, S., P. Moon, J. Kates, D. Wilson, and J. Mays. 1986. 'Toronto the rich: Life in a material world.' *Globe and Mail*, 8–13 Nov.

Palen, J., and B. London. 1984. 'Through the glass darkly: Gentrification, revitalization and the neighbourhood.' In J. Palen and B. London, eds, *Gentrification, Displacement and Neighborhood Revitalization*, 256–66. Albany: University of New York Press

Podro, M. 1982. *The Critical Historians of Art*. New Haven: Yale University Press

Raban, J. 1974. *Soft City*. London: Hamish Hamilton

Reid, B. 1988. 'The story of a new middle class.' *City Magazine* 10 (1): 31–40

Relph, E. 1976. *Place and Placelessness*. London: Pion

– 1981. *Rational Landscapes and Humanist Geography*. London: Croom Helm

– 1987. *The Modern Urban Landscape*. Baltimore: Johns Hopkins University Press

Rioux, M. 1984. 'Remarks on emancipatory practices and industrial societies in crisis.' *Canadian Review of Sociology and Anthropology* 21 (1): 1–20

Rose, D. 1984. 'Rethinking gentrification: Beyond the uneven development of Marxist urban theory.' *Environment and Planning D: Society and Space* 1: 47–74

– 1989. 'A feminist perspective of employment restructuring and gentrification.' In J. Wolch and M. Dear, eds, *The Power of Geography: How Territory Shapes Social Life*, 118–38. Boston: Unwin Hyman

RVA – Read, Voorhees and Associates. 1968. *Central Area Transportation Study: Metropolitan Toronto*. Toronto

Rybczynski, W. 1986. *Home: A Short History of an Idea*. New York: Viking

Sabourin, J. 1988. 'The process of gentrification: The example of private housing renovation in Don Vale, Toronto.' PHD diss., Department of Geography, York University, Toronto

Salsberg, L. 1970, 'Public places: Manifesto.' *Toronto Citizen* 1 (4): 4

Salter, M. 1988. 'Hot, hot houses.' *Report on Business Magazine* 5 (2): 38–44

Samuel, D. 1971. 'On the trail of Lionstar.' In J. Sewell, D. Crombie, W. Kilbourn, and K. Jaffary, eds, *Inside City Hall: The Year of the Opposition*, 90–1. Toronto: Hakkert

Sancton, A. 1983a. 'Montreal.' In W. Magnusson and A. Sancton, eds, *City Politics in Canada*, 58–93. Toronto: University of Toronto Press

– 1983b. 'Conclusion.' In W. Magnusson and A. Sancton, eds, *City Politics in Canada*, 291–317. Toronto: University of Toronto Press

Saunders, P. 1986. *Social Theory and the Urban Question*. London: Hutchinson

Sayer, A. 1982. 'Explanation in economic geography.' *Progress in Human Geography* 6: 68–88

Seamon, D. 1979. *A Geography of the Lifeworld*. London: Croom Helm

Sellgren, T. 1971. 'The community that wouldn't be transformed: Province shuts off hydro in Grange Park.' *Toronto Citizen* 2 (17): 5

Sewell, J. 1971. 'Objections to Lionstar proposals.' In J. Sewell, D. Crombie, W. Kilbourn, and K. Jaffary, *Inside City Hall: The Year of the Opposition*, 89–90. Toronto: Hakkert

– 1972. *Up against City Hall*. Toronto: James Lewis & Samuel

Sewell, J., D. Crombie, W. Kilbourn, and K. Jaffary. 1971. *Inside City Hall: The Year of the Opposition*. Toronto: Hakkert

Shein, B. 1987. 'Regent Park: The untold story.' *Toronto Life* 21 (10)

Simmel, G. 1988. 'The metropolis and mental life.' In R. Warren and L. Lyon, eds, *New Perspectives on the American Community*, 17–25. Chicago: Dorsey Press

Simpson, C. 1981. *Soho: The Artist in the City.* Chicago: University of Chicago Press

Sjoberg, G. 1955. 'The preindustrial city.' *American Journal of Sociology* 60: 438–45

Smith, N. 1979. 'Toward a theory of gentrification: A back to the city movement by capital not people.' *Journal of the American Planners Association* 45 (4): 538–48

– 1986. 'Gentrification, the frontier, and the restructuring of urban space.' In N. Smith and P. Williams, eds, *Gentrification of the City*, 15–34. Boston: Allen and Unwin

– 1987a. 'Of yuppies and housing: Gentrification, social structuring and the urban dream.' *Environment and Planning D: Society and Space* 5: 151–72

– 1987b. 'Commentary: 'Gentrification and the rent gap.' *Annals of the Association of American Geographers* 77 (3): 462–5

Smith, N., and M. LeFaivre. 1984. 'A class analysis of gentrification.' In J. Palen and B. London, eds, *Gentrification, Displacement and Neighborhood Revitalization*, 43–63. Albany: University of New York Press

Smith, N., and P. Williams. 1986a. *Gentrification of the City.* Boston: Allen and Unwin

– 1986b. 'Alternatives to orthodoxy: Invitation to a debate.' In N. Smith and P. Williams, eds, *Gentrification of the City*, 1–12. Boston: Allen and Unwin

Smith, V. 1972a. 'Southeast Spadina.' *Toronto Citizen* 3 (8): 7–8

– 1972b. 'Wrecking Toronto: The beginning of the end for Darcy Street.' *Toronto Citizen* 3 (14): 1

Spatafora, R. 1988. 'Gentrification in the countryside: A case study of the community of Stouffville.' Paper prepared for Social Science 3760.06, York University, Toronto

SPCMT – Social Planning Council of Metropolitan Toronto. 1979. *Metro's Suburbs in Transition, Part I: Evolution and Overview*

– 1984. *Metropolitan Social Profile: A Guide to Social Planning Facts in Metropolitan Toronto*

Spurr, P. 1976. *Land and Urban Development: A Preliminary Study.* Toronto: Lorimer

Stelter, G. 1982. 'The city-building process in Canada.' In G. Stelter and A. Artibise, eds, *Shaping the Urban Landscape: Aspects of the Canadian City-Building Process*, 1–29. Ottawa: Carleton University Press

– 1986. 'Power and place in urban history.' In G. Stelter and A. Artibise, eds, *Power and Place: Canadian Urban Development in the North American Context*, 1–11. Vancouver: University of British Columbia Press

Stieren, C. 1973. 'East-end espressway fight dead ahead.' *Toronto Citizen* 4 (13): 1

Swadron, B. 1981. *Pressure Island: The Report of the Commission of Inquiry into the Toronto Islands.* Toronto: Commission of Inquiry into the Toronto Islands

TAC – Toronto Arts Council. 1988. *No Vacancy: A Cultural Facilities Policy for the City of Toronto*

Thompson, R. 1979. 'Ethnicity versus class: An analysis of conflict in a North American Chinese community.' *Ethnicity* 6: 306–26

Tuan, Y. 1974. *Topophilia: A Study of Environmental Perception, Attitudes and Values.* Englewood Cliffs, NJ: Prentice-Hall

Venturi, R. 1966. *Complexity and Contradiction in Architecture.* New York: Museum of Modern Art

Walker, R. 1981. 'A theory of suburbanization: Capitalism and the construction of urban space in the United States.' In M. Dear and R. Scott, eds, *Urbanization and Urban Planning in Capitalist Society.* 383–429. New York: Methuen

Warde, A. 1991. 'Gentrification as consumption: Issues of class and gender.' *Environment and Planning D: Society and Space* 9: 223–32

Wekerle, G. 1984. 'A woman's place is in the city.' *Antipode* 16 (3): 11–19

Welch, T., and E. Ellmen. 1988. 'Flipping houses out of reach.' *Now*, 19–25 May, 9–10

Whitford, F. 1985. 'The city in painting.' In E. Timms and D. Kelley, eds, *Unreal City: Urban Experience in Modern European Literature and Art*, 45–64. Manchester: Manchester University Press

Williams, P. 1986. 'Class constitution through spatial reconstruction: A re-evaluation of gentrification in Australia, Britain and the United States.' In N. Smith and P. Williams, eds, *Gentrification of the City*, 56–77. Boston: Allen and Unwin

Williams, R. 1977. *Marxism and Literature.* Oxford: Oxford University Press

– 1980. *Problems of Materialism and Culture.* London: Verso

Wirth, L. 1938. 'Urbanism as a way of life.' *American Journal of Sociology* 44 (July): 1–24

Zarocostas, J. 1990. 'Toronto ranked as most expensive city in Western Hemisphere, 28th in world.' *Globe and Mail*, 9 May, A1–2

Zukin, S. 1982a. *Loft Living: Culture and Capital in Urban Change.* Baltimore: Johns Hopkins University Press

– 1982b. 'Loft living as a "historic compromise" in the urban core.' *International Journal of Urban and Regional Research* 6: 256–67

Index

The following abbreviations are suffixed to page references: c – citation;*
f – figure; i – illustration; n – footnote.

---

* Citations are indexed for authors named in the running text; authors named solely
in citations are not indexed.